All day, every day

Sallie Westwood

All day, every day

Factory and family in the making of women's lives

with a foreword by Louise Lamphere

University of Illinois Press

Urbana and Chicago

Published in the USA by arrangement with Pluto Press
Limited of London, England.

The song on pages v-vi, "Working-class Woman," written by
Peter Boyd and Barbara Dane, from the album *I Hate the
Capitalist System* (Barbara Dane, Paredon Records, Brooklyn,
N.Y.). The publishers and author wish to thank Peter Boyd
and Barbara Dane for permission to reproduce their song in
this volume.

Manufactured in the United States of America

This book is printed on acid-free paper.

Library of Congress Cataloging in Publication Data

Westwood, Sallie.
   All day, every day.

   Reprint. Originally published: London: Pluto Press,
1984.
   Includes index.
   1. Women—Employment—Great Britain. 2. Sex
discrimination in employment—Great Britain. 3. Equal
pay for equal work—Great Britain. 4. Wages—
Women—Great Britain. 5. Women—Great Britain—
Social conditions. I. Title.
HD6135.W47 1985   331.4′0941   84-23989
ISBN 0-252-01191-0 (cloth; alk. paper)
ISBN 0-252-01192-9 (paper; alk. paper)
ISBN 0-86104-760-5 (UK edition, Pluto Press)

Joe Workingman's wife, that's how I was defined.
As if that was my life, my hope and my mind.
But I worked in a bakeshop, did the housework at night,
There was no time to stop for a young bird in flight.

And in time there were babies, had to make us a home.
Joe was working two jobs, I was always alone.
I needed some time, and just a little control,
Just to keep my right mind, just to try to stay whole.

I wanted a partner, to be his friend, not just his wife.
I'll work hard for my children, but they're my love, not my life.

Went to work in a factory, and it's rough in this world.
My kids are in high school, and the boss calls me 'girl'.
But the woman beside me, as we sweat out the line,
Says, 'Tomorrow is payday, and the next day is mine!'

It's a race for the strong, 'cause it'll grind up the meek
When your money runs short, at the end of a week.
And your car needs some tyre, and your kid needs some shoes,
For a working-class woman that's an old kind of blues.

This system buys hands, but you must not use your head.
It'll shake you and break you, 'til all your senses are dead.

But I know there are answers, I gotta get to the source.
I think me and this system gotta get a divorce.
I can't make enough money, I can't find enough time.
But I'm a hard-working woman, and the future is mine.

Well there's more where I come from, and we got anger to burn.
And we're talkin' and movin', gonna study and learn.

Build a unity train, on a straight-arrow line.
If today is the bosses', I know tomorrow is mine.

And I know it takes lovin', and I know it takes time,
But I'm a working-class woman, and the future is mine.
I'm a working-class woman, and the future is mine!

Contents

Foreword

Sallie Westwood's vivid description of the lives of working women who are employed as stitchers in a British factory provides us with a number of insights into the complex relationship between work and family and between capitalism and patriarchy. Her research adds to the growing literature on women in blue collar jobs both in the United States and abroad. It helps us see the similarities and differences in women's work in apparel, textile, and electronics factories in such seemingly different locations as Britain, New England, California's Silicon Valley, the U.S.–Mexican border, the Philippines, and Taiwan. (Two recent collections of articles, one edited by Karen Brodkin Sacks and Dorothy Remy and the other edited by June Nash and María Patricia Fernández-Kelly, provide an overview of this research, while important case studies have been written by Janet Salaff, Lydia Kung, and Fernández-Kelly.) Westwood's book makes important contributions to the study of the labor process, to the analysis of women's work culture, and to the debate about the relationship between Marxism and feminism—all topics that have been of interest to American researchers and feminists.

Westwood's aim is to analyze the intersection of capitalism and patriarchy in a particular historical period. Borrowing from the work of Heidi Hartmann, she views patriarchal relations to be those social relations between men which enable them to control women's labor power and women's sexuality. Most analysts have viewed this control primarily in terms of the capitalist wage labor system as it combines with marriage and the nuclear family. This in turn creates a situation where men earn higher wages than women, and where women as either housewives or secondary workers become dependent on men and do the reproductive labor (housework and child care) for the family. Westwood takes this analysis further and examines the way in which the work place itself helps to ratify and sustain notions of the family, marriage and femininity. She argues that waged work is as much about becoming a woman as it is about becoming a worker. Shopfloor culture is a creative attempt to overcome the alienating aspects of work, but involves embracing an oppressive version of womanhood.

In the first chapters, Westwood describes the women of "StitchCo" at work in an atmosphere which is cozy and homelike but which defines women as subordinates. The women are not just docile workers, however, and Westwood describes conversations that show that women clearly see their interests as opposed to those of management. The two themes of consent and resistance run throughout the analysis and are comparable to Nina Shapiro-Perl's research on women in the costume jewelry industry in Rhode Island.

Westwood's chapter "Up against the minutes" is a detailed ethnography of the work which sewers do and the measured day work (MDW) system through which their wages are calculated. Each worker is assigned a grade with target numbers that define her daily production quota. If a sticher produces at the next higher level for a month, she could be upgraded; if her production level drops, so will her grade. Despite superficial differences, there are a number of similarities to the piecework system used in some large apparel plants in the United States. Here workers are paid by the piece (with the minimum wage as a "floor") but are still pushing themselves against a clock and working to keep their production from falling, despite potential difficulties with the machine, shortages of work, and unfair rates. American women have developed strategies of resistance in coping with piece-rate systems that are remarkably similar to those described by Westwood in the factory she studied. The details of pay systems may seem trivial or overly complex to those who have never worked in a factory, but for most women blue-collar workers, these points define the nature of work itself as well as the size of a weekly paycheck. With detailed observations like those in Westwood's account we are able to assess the nature of this kind of control.

The richness of Westwood's descriptions and her ear for recording conversations are part of the best chapters in the book on women's shopfloor culture. Here Westwood's work adds to the significant amount of American research on women's work culture, particularly that of Susan Porter Benson, Barbara Melosh, and Karen Sacks. Her point is, like Benson's, that work culture is oppositional and embodies a number of subtle forms of resistance. However, she is also careful to point out that it is "collusive," mainly because it emphasizes women's traditional roles in the home and family. Westwood describes work-place friendships, the sharing of food, and the giving of birthday parties at work. But for Americans perhaps the most interesting descriptions are those which revolve around marriage: the bride's ritual and the hen party. These events do not seem to have an American counterpart and thus are fascinating in and of themselves. Westwood describes the bride's ritual—in which the brides wear raunchy home-made outfits and spend a good part of the workday partying with their colleagues—and the hen's party, a night on the town where the bride and her friends make the rounds of several pubs, including those who cater to such groups. The hen's party, like the bride's ritual, if full of jokes, sexual innuendo and ribaldry. But, as Westwood is careful to point out, the male world is the ever-present context through which women's behavior is interpreted. Her exploration points to the double-edged nature of women's work culture, the resistance to hierarchical relations on the shopfloor, yet the acceptance of women's roles as girl friends, brides, and wives, and of culturally defined notions of femininity.

It is against this background of the enthusiasm that surrounds engagements and weddings that Westwood describes the realities of married life, the tediousness of housework, the absence of a husband or his lack of involvement in chores, and the struggles over money. The reality is particularly brought home in Westwood's account of a woman's relationship with a husband who beat her and of a co-worker's difficult decision to have an abortion. These chapters indicate that some women are developing a critique of their situation, that "they are not interested in simply reproducing the same privations and limitation on their lives and handing these on to the next generation" (p. 229). How far this critique will go and whether shopfloor culture will continue to ratify women's domestic roles and emphasize a mixture of resistance and consent is a question for the future.

Since the factory described in this book is multi-ethnic, the comparative analysis of English "girls" with their hen parties and brides' rituals and the Gujarati women's arranged marriages is particularly important and adds a final dimension to the book:

the intersection of class, gender, and race. Westwood's description of a Gujarati wedding and her discussions with women trying to break away from tradition give a sense of the changes going on in the lives to immigrant women. Throughout the book Westwood is sensitive to the differences between white and minority women, and in her concluding chapters she discusses the complexities of racism in women's lives, showing how women "worked with and against racism and at the same time, reproducing it and undermining it through their lives on the shopfloor" (p. 234). Although in the United States the research of Remy, Sacks, Bonnie Dill Thornton, and others has touched on the lives of Black women workers, and several researchers are studying Hispanic women in the work force, we need more attention to this issue. Thus Westwood's analysis can point us in new directions in terms of both research and theory.

Westwood's study has much to recommend it. She is a keen observer and her account of conversations and events draws us into the lives of working women. Parts of the book read like a novel, yet give us a vivid sense of the reality of women's lives. Westwood is always careful to point out the theoretical implications of her data, however, to show how the details of daily existence illuminate the relationship between capitalism and patriarchy. Many American researchers are interested in a more careful analysis of the interconnections between work and family life. Here is a book that makes these connections in a new way. For example, several of us have been interested in potlucks and wedding showers as a component of women's work culture: Westwood has taken the analysis of these informal rituals one step further showing us how they fit traditional definitions of womanhood and ultimately support what she calls patriarchal social relations. We have much to learn from this study that will take our analysis of women's lives in new directions.

Louise Lamphere
Department of Anthropology
Brown University

REFERENCES

Benson, Susan Porter. *Counter Cultures: Saleswomen, Managers, and Customers in American Department Stores, 1890-1940.* Urbana: University of Illinois Press (in press).

Fernández-Kelly, María Patricia. *For We Are Sold, I and My People.* Albany: State University of New York Press, 1983.

Hartmann, Heidi. "The Unhappy Marriage of Marxism and Feminism," in Lydia Sargent, ed., *Women and Revolution: A Discussion of the Unhappy Marriage of Marxism and Feminism.* London: Pluto Press, 1981, pp. 1-42.

Kung, Lydia. *Factory Women in Taiwan.* Ann Arbor: UMI Research Press, 1983.

Melosh, Barbara. *"The Physician's Hand": Work Culture and Conflict in American Nursing.* Philadelphia: Temple University Press, 1982.

Nash, June, and María Patricia Fernández-Kelly. *Women, Men, and the International Division of Labor.* Albany: State University of New York Press, 1983.

Sacks, Karen Brodkin, and Dorothy Remy. *My Troubles Are Going to Have Trouble with Me: Everyday Trials and Triumphs of Women Workers.* New Brunswick, N.J.: Rutgers University Press, 1984.

Acknowledgments

This book would not have been possible without the generosity of the women whose lives are presented here. I am grateful to them all for sharing so much with me, with such tolerance and goodwill. This book is for them. In addition, I am indebted to both management and union officials in the factory who facilitated the research in so many ways, especially 'Annie' and 'Clare'. I am grateful to John Cunningham for securing my entry into the factory and to friends who have helped my work in so many ways. I would like to thank Jyoti Chotai, Peter Loman, Ros Morpeth, Maggie Pearson, Parin Rattansi, Taruna Tanwar, Wynne Westwood, and the Bose family. In addition, I am indebted to Irene Bruegel for comments on the earlier chapters; to Cynthia Cockburn, whose enthusiasm for the study, and perceptive comments on the book overall, greatly enhanced the final product; and to Tracy Cullis for her help in compiling the glossary. To Dorothy Brydges I owe special thanks for transforming my tatty pages into a manuscript and for being a valuable critic. Thanks also to Richard Kuper for providing sympathetic editorial skills and, much more, patience. I also owe a debt to all the women who have supported the women's studies courses with which I am involved — their enthusiasm for feminism has kept me going in arid times. Finally, I owe an enormous debt to Ali Rattansi, whose support has sustained me throughout this project.

Any errors, omissions, or misunderstandings are all mine.

S.W.

1
Introduction

This book is about sisterhood and strength, weakness and division, the inherent contradictions of women's lives under conditions set by patriarchal capitalism. In order to understand these contradictions better I spent over a year, from March 1980 to May 1981, on the shopfloor with women who worked for a company I have called StitchCo, a reputable and paternalistic firm which recruits workers in a way which is often mediated by the family, rather than the job centres or careers officers in schools. Management saw in this a continuity between the present and a past when whole families moved out of the home and into the factory together. The intervention of familial ties in the labour market illustrates clearly the case upon which this study is founded: that home and work are part of one world.

StitchCo and its workers are part of the hosiery industry which is based on mechanised knitting. A wide variety of machines produce socks and tights, sweaters and cardigans for a range of consumer markets – from school uniforms to high fashion – in wools and a range of synthetic yarns. But the industry also makes cloth which is knitted on vast circular machines to produce tubes of jerseyknit fabric which becomes vests and tee-shirts, as well as dresses, skirts, pyjamas and other clothes. Unlike the textile industry, the cloth is not woven on looms and fabric-making does not take place in factories that are separated from the other processes. A large company like StitchCo houses all the processes connected to hosiery and knitting: making, stretching, rolling, bleaching and dyeing knitted fabric alongside the production of sweaters and socks. The role of women in transforming knitted fabric into clothes is described in the next chapter where I discuss the labour process.

Throughout this book the names of people, places and organisations have been changed in order to protect the identities of those involved. Consequently, the setting for this story is a city I have called Needletown which has a population of over a quarter of a million and which is ethnically and racially diverse. Since the Second World War the city has become home to refugees and migrants from Poland and other Eastern European states that were absorbed into the USSR. It has a thriving Irish community and since the 1950s it has had a black population which has grown in the last decade with the arrival of many Asians from East Africa. The city has a long history as a centre for the hosiery industry, and many of the more recent immigrants have come to work in this sector.

My entry into the factory was facilitated by a local contact. Once management realised that I did not want to take women away from the production process to conduct lengthy interviews, they were surprisingly open to my suggestion that I be allowed to immerse myself in the life of the shopfloor. For some reason, the idea of an anthropologist studying the culture of the shopfloor by hanging around the coffee bar, lurking in the lunch canteen and sharing a few 'risqué' jokes, appealed to management who saw my immersion as a baptism of fire. I was a participant observer in one department (described in detail in the next chapter) where I watched and listened, talked and worked, and generally joined in the life of the shopfloor. The problems associated with this methodology are well known: subjective intrusions by the researcher, lack of a foundation for generalisations, unreliability, for example. I am conscious of these criticisms, but unimpressed, because the attempt to inhabit and record a cultural space requires this method of working. This does not mean that the methodology did not raise practical problems. I had to find a way of keeping copious notes, but in ways that did not intrude upon my relations with the women. I took notes during the day which formed the basis for field notes which I wrote up at the end of every day, and it was not long before the writing-up period was longer than the hours I spent in the factory. It became more complicated once I started to move beyond the factory and into the women's homes, or when I started to go out with groups of women in the evenings or on day trips. I did conduct more formal interviews with management and union officials, but these were set within the context of already developed relations in the factory.

I hoped that my year on the shopfloor would enable me to illuminate the lived experiences of women workers who come together to generate and sustain a culture, a world of symbols and meanings which has to be unravelled. But there is an important caution: lived experience, everyday life, the 'real' world, are not simple unambiguous phenomena which can be easily caught and reproduced in the pages of books. Life does not lie around like leaves in autumn waiting to be swept up, ordered and put into boxes. The drama of everyday life is richly textured, multifaceted and dense and we cannot hope to make sense of our world and, more, interpret it, without a coherent theoretical understanding. We need theories to explain the world in which we struggle, to inform our practice and our politics, but this does not mean that we necessarily need a spectacular set of mental acrobatics, or a fencing match with all that has gone before. In this book theoretical issues arise at every turn and they inform the under-standing that I have brought to the world of the factory, but it is not my purpose to fetishise theories. My hope is that the world presented here will contribute to the development of feminist theory because it draws attention to the complexities of women's subordination, but in a way that is rooted in the experiences of women's lives, just as our politics has been and must remain.

It is the capitalist mode of production that concerns us and this is a system in which formally free labourers sell their labour power to employers for wages and thereby enter the world of social production and relations of exploitation in the workplace which give them a class position. But women are also workers in the home and within this setting they are exploited through the gift of unpaid labour to the men who are their husbands and fathers. Both these situations are oppressive and conceptually we might want to distinguish two systems, to analyse two modes of oppression. But it is becoming increasingly clear that patriarchy and capitalism are not so easily divided between the home and the workplace. I have always been uneasy with the division and in an effort to look at it anew I went first to the workplace to seek out patriarchy, rather than start from the home. I am not alone in sensing that the terrain in which women's subordination is generated and reproduced cannot be so easily divided. Cynthia Cockburn has pointed out that the sex-gender system and the class structure are two interlocking systems, but without a perspective from both we cannot hope to make sense of our world.[1] Moreover Lucy Bland and her co-writers have argued convincingly that:

> It is incorrect to see the nature of women's subordination as either determined solely by the economic and political needs of capitalism or the results of class struggle; women's subordination under capitalism lies in the articulation between patriarchal relations and capitalist development.[2]

The study presented in this book endorses this view and the position expressed by Carol Smart when she writes, succinctly: 'Patriarchy is as much a feature of the political economy as of the domestic economy or women's consciousness.'[3] In order to understand more fully the implications of this conception, it is necessary to draw out more clearly the meaning attached to patriarchy.

Veronica Beechey has usefully reviewed the history of the concept of patriarchy as it has been used in feminist debates and the problems that surround it.[4] I support her call for a more historically specific understanding of patriarchy and endorse her conclusion that we have to find a way of bringing together the worlds of production and reproduction in a feminist account of women's oppression. I do not think that the concept of patriarchy should be abandoned, not least because it allows us to think our way through 'the woman question' in ways other than those offered to us by sociology, for example, or marxism which has so enriched the study of capitalist formations. To seek out and analyse the articulation between patriarchy and capitalism is to move on to political questions about the nature of the relationship between feminism and marxism. Heidi Hartmann has pointed out that this relationship is an unequal one with a deep tension because class relations and the forms of exploitation on which they are premised are given pre-eminence by marxists.[5]

The concept of patriarchy has been criticised, for example, by Sheila Rowbotham, for its lack of explanatory power because it concentrates attention upon biology and the universal condition of female subordination.[6] But this view ignores the important attempts that have been made to provide an historicised and contextual understanding of patriarchy by feminists like Roisin McDonough and Rachel Harrison, who argue for an understanding of patriarchy that is rooted in the specific conditions of its existence.[7] Consequently, they argue for a materialist understanding of patriarchy grounded in both sexual and economic exploitation which does not alter the power of patriarchy to 'infest' other aspects of the social formation. They concentrate upon the workplace and the family as the crucial sites for patriarchal relations, an emphasis shared by this study and reproduced in Heidi Hartmann's work. The latter provides a definition of patriarchy that I have used to guide my own analysis because it includes a materialist understanding of male power:

> We can usefully define patriarchy as a set of social relations
> between men, which have a material base, and which,
> though hierarchical, establish or create interdependence
> and solidarity among men that enable them to dominate
> women . . .
> The material base upon which patriarchy rests lies most
> fundamentally in men's control over women's labour power.
> Men maintain this control by excluding women from access
> to some essential productive resources (in capitalist
> societies, for example, jobs that pay living wages) and by
> restricting women's sexuality. Monogamous heterosexual
> marriage is one relatively recent and efficient form that
> seems to allow men to control both these areas.[8]

By basing an analysis on this understanding of patriarchy it is quite clear that the lives of the women I studied were encompassed by patriarchal relations, which are one part of 'patriarchal capitalism'. Consequently, neither capitalism nor patriarchy are wholly autonomous in their actions and effects, nor are they reducible one to the other. Rather, patriarchy and mode of production are simultaneously one world and two, relatively autonomous parts of a whole which has to be fought on both fronts. This is also a view expressed by Heidi Hartmann.

'As feminist socialists, we must organise a practice which addresses both the struggle against patriarchy and the struggle against capitalism.'[9] If we accept this, as I do, we are bound to return to the problems posed by the attempt to build a feminist marxism out of an already fractured movement which has at its base what Brian Easlea has called 'marxist viriculture'.[10] He characterises marxism as 'a movement of strong men who disdained softness and sentimentalism, rejected airy fairy discussions about a future communist society, and who were convinced of the correctness of their analysis, tactics and strategies – Marxism was a science.'[11] Such an edifice as this is not easily contested.

One of the most important recent developments in marxism

has been the reassessment of the role of ideologies in the social formation. My analysis takes seriously the claim that the economic level is also affected by the ideological and the political and that because of this patriarchy has a material base not only in the way in which men control and exploit women's labour power, but in the way in which patriarchal ideologies intervene at the economic level. Ideologies are both outside and within individual subject-ivities, and they play a vital part in calling forth a sense of self linked to class and gender as well as race. Thus, a patriarchal ideology intervenes on the shopfloor and subverts the creative potential of shopfloor culture to make anew the conditions of work under capitalism.

This is a complex notion and one which, I am acutely aware, is more easily illuminated in relation to the actual practices of shopfloor culture which are explored later in this book. What I am suggesting is that, within the setting of capitalist production, we have not only the reproduction of capitalist exploitation through the way that women are positioned in the production process as workers, but through patriarchal ideologies we have the repro-duction of gendered subjects and the social construction of masculinity and femininity on the shopfloor. Consequently, this book examines the way in which women who enter into waged employment become workers and, therefore, classed subjects. But working outside the home is not only about becoming a worker; it is most crucially about becoming a woman. Shopfloor culture offers to women at work a version of woman and they take upon themselves elements of this in ways which tie them more firmly to a 'feminine' destiny and the culture of femininity. However, it is a deeply contradictory culture which the women fashion: it reveals a resistant and creative attempt to overcome the stultifying aspects of the capitalist labour process – only to find that this creativity has bound itself securely to an oppressive version of womanhood. This book provides glimpses of shopfloor life and culture as both oppositional and resistant in form and as a site in which patriarchal ideologies and therefore the materiality of patriarchy is reproduced. The contradiction is in creativity and sisterhood and its subversion by the common-sense world which makes of all women wives and mothers.

This book is suggesting that gender identities are not produced and reproduced simply in the home or through schooling and the mass media (although they all play a part), but centrally through the workplace – both the capitalist labour process, which enshrines the subordination of women, and the culture that is produced in opposition to it by the women. The move from the home into the factory simultaneously opens and closes doors. The liberating potential moves women together to take on a collective struggle, but it is also in the workplace that young women are encouraged to embrace domesticity, become brides and have children. When Paul Willis studied 'lads' in school they showed just how much they wanted to leave school and rush in through the factory gates, viewing this as a moment of choice and freedom; young women rush out of the factory in the opposite direction, into domesticity, with the same sense of a decision freely made, a choice exercised.[12]

Before I embark upon the world of the factory more has to be said about the post-colonial setting for the interaction of patriarchy and capitalism. We live in Britain in a society which, as a colonial power, exploited the riches and the labour power of women and men in Africa, Asia and the Caribbean and which then brought this labour power to Britain to work in unskilled, poorly paid jobs. And if their economic privations were not enough, the British state and society confounded the pain of black workers by racism, institutionalised in the laws and practices of Britain and internalised within the cultures of all sections of British society. As Amrit Wilson writes:

> Having indirectly and inadvertently brought Asian women to Britain, the racism of the state and racism of British society now defines the wider position of Asian women in this country – as the lowest paid and most exploited workers, or as the wives and daughters of such workers – an unstable and unacceptable situation full of conflicts and contradictions. Inside their families, too, their roles are in a state of flux, with the past, the peasant past, the tribal past and the colonial past each with its own particular prescriptions for the woman's role constantly intruding on the present. Out of these multiple fields of conflict the future of Asian women in Britain is being resolved.[13]

Immigrants, from what the statistics call the New Commonwealth countries, have been arriving in Britain since the 1950s. Asian women are the most recent arrivals, often coming after male family members, or as brides, following the expulsion of the Asians from East Africa. They are faced with a multiplicity of contradictory demands upon them; some part of this will be discussed in the chapters that follow. Initially, however, it is important to reflect upon the issue of racism in relation to both the class structure and patriarchal relations. The women in this study all share the same relationship to the means of production: they are all 'free' labourers selling their labour power for wages. But because they are women their position in the labour market is always affected by their domestic lives; being a woman counts. Nevertheless, not all women are white: women of colour are faced with an additional ideological hurdle – racism – and this affects the class position of black workers generally and black women in particular, giving them a specific place in the working class. They are, in the view of Annie Phizacklea and Robert Miles, a class fraction because the position they occupy is 'determined by both economic and politico-ideological relations'.[14] They adopt this position as a way of understanding both the links between race and class and the specific situation of black workers and other migrant workers. Racism is an ideology which, when reconstructed and analysed, exhibits an internal coherence. This does not mean that in the common-sense world of racism individuals will demonstrate such coherence.[15] The internal complexity of ideologies means that a definition of racism is not easy to provide but Annie Phizacklea and Robert Miles do offer a useful suggestion in this respect:

> We use racism to refer to those negative beliefs held by one group which identify and set apart another by attributing significance to some biological or other 'inherent' characteristic(s) which it is said to possess, and which deterministically associate that characteristic(s) with some other (negatively evaluated) feature(s) or action(s). The possession of these supposed characteristic(s) is then used as justification for denying that group equal access to material and other resources and/or political rights.[16]

This definition can include, or not, the issue of skin colour because, as the writers point out, this allows for the racism of the British towards the Irish. This does not mean that being black or brown is not an issue; it is so often the centrepiece of the politics of race relations in present-day Britain.

My purpose in this study was not to take a detailed predetermined position on the crucial question of what black and white women share beyond their membership of an already stratified working class. Of course, I set out with the view that patriarchal relations oppress all women, but I was conscious of the need to be sensitive to the specificities surrounding the position of black women.

In so far as this study concentrates attention upon the generation and reproduction of shopfloor culture by women and sees this as both oppositional and collusive and, moreover, as contributing to the processes whereby gender identities are formed, what are the implications for black women of a culture formed in a specific cultural and historical setting? This raises important and complex questions because shopfloor culture promotes sisterhood and makes appeals to the universal woman through the symbols of the bride, and the mother and yet we must recognise that the idea of universal woman is a problem. I think it important to be aware that the abstracted woman is an inadequate beginning for our analysis. We cannot use a simple unity 'woman' as the basis of our understanding; instead, we have to posit real women, human beings formed and sustained materially in a specific social formation who may, nevertheless, have come from other cultures and another part of the global economic system. To find out what unites these women, who come together as workers on the shopfloor, and what divides them is part of the reason for undertaking a study such as this.

So far, I have written of black women, of Asian women and of women of colour, but these are more than designations because language is political. The idea of black women suggests a unity, perhaps, which ignores the very different historical and cultural backgrounds of both immigrant women and those born black British, but as Valerie Amos and Pratibha Parmar have written:

> We are aware that many differences exist in the cultures, languages and religions not only between Afro-Caribbean and Asian communities but between these two groups. We do not see our cultural differences as operating antagonistically because we recognise the autonomy of our separate cultures. By working together, we have developed a common understanding of our oppression and from this basis we build our solidarity. The black struggle is a political one and it is important that we fight our oppression together.[17]

Valerie Amos and Pratibha Parmar speak for a growing number of women in the black communities who find in the force of racism a common cause around which to unite. In this, they recognise their own potential to become a collective expression of the resistance of black people in Britain. At the same time, they recognise that 'a black woman . . . is also oppressed in class terms, as part of the working class, and in gender terms, because she is a woman.' Thus, 'as black women we also need to organise separately around the issues that are particular to our experiences as black women, experiences that come out of the triple oppression we face.'[18]

The triple oppressions were amplified in Amrit Wilson's painful evocation of the lives of Asian women in Britain. She uses the term Asian, a term which is part of the colonial heritage (and which is used by the British state) and has become commonplace. In this book I rarely use the term Asian because the women I knew consistently referred to themselves as Indian. In so far as it is their voices that we hear in this book, I have tried to be faithful to their account of themselves and it is this latter designation I have followed throughout. Perhaps, in the future more of them will come to refer to themselves as black women.

Before I set the scene in a substantive sense, it is useful to sum up. This book gives a central role to patriarchal relations in defining and elaborating the lives of both black and white women while acknowledging that they share a class position within contemporary capitalism. This is, however, a post-colonial capitalism and in its institutions and its populace it is deeply racist; thus I recognise that black women share a triple, not just a double, burden of oppression through class, gender and race. But as white women struggle against class and gender oppressions so black women fight to overcome the constraints upon their own lives. Yet in their very struggles these constraints are made anew, through the family and the workplace. Relations in both areas are deeply contradictory: they offer the possibilities of free spaces within the lives of women whereby they can enact their own cultural creations, but cultures are not simply lived experiences. They are shot through with ideological components, or manifest ideological consequences. There is a deep tension born of this contradiction and the women of the factory live this out with consummate skill. Given these material circumstances, how and in what ways are the individuals that come to understand themselves as women produced? I am suggesting that it is not just class identities that are forged at work, but gender identities. Girls arrive in the factory and they become women on the shopfloor. This process encompasses the same contradictions as those that are found in the culture of the shopfloor itself. The family and school have a major part to play, but it is at work that adulthood is acknowledged and made through the wage that itself generates a class identity and through the way that women workers are always subordinated in the capitalist labour process and the labour market.

The women in the factory were workers in a declining industry and many of the jobs that were lost in the hosiery industry during 1980 and 1981 were women's jobs. Of the women who work in manufacturing, half of them work in only four areas: food and drink, clothing and footwear, textiles, and electrical engineering and they do so in the low paid sectors of these industries.[19] Black women are over-represented in all low-paid sectors, including low-paid manual work in the state sector.[20] Of the 10.4 million women (over 40 per cent of the workforce) who were working in 1980, an estimated 45 per cent worked in totally segregated jobs.[21] This book provides a case study of this situation of low-paid, segregated work, commonly known as 'women's work'.

Workplace studies are not new and I have drawn upon the insights offered by the earlier work of Tom Lupton, Theo Nichols, Huw Benyon and Peter Armstrong who have all contributed to our understanding of the world of waged work. These writers, however, have been predominantly concerned with class issues and the lives of male workers.[22] Anna Pollert's work, which used the inspiration of these earlier studies, offers a major corrective to the concentration upon men in her study of women workers at Churchmans, a major tobacco company.[23]

This book begins with some of the concerns of these studies, concentrating initially upon the world of the factory and the labour process as it has been formed within capitalist and patriarchal constraints. The organisation of work has major implications for sisterhood and worker resistance; we move into these areas through a discussion of wages and the bonus scheme, and this, in turn, introduces the trade union and its relations with the shopfloor. The women resist both management imperatives and union manipulations, turning their energies instead to the generation of an elaborate shopfloor culture which celebrates everything from birthdays to babies. It is the ritual and the celebration which surrounds the life-cycle events of women's lives – such as marriage and motherhood – which are elaborated in the latter part of the book. The penultimate chapter, on motherhood, is a long chapter because I could not find a shorter way to deal with the complex issues that surround the politics of reproduction. I hope the reader will bear with me on this. In the conclusion to the book I return again to the issues we have confronted here – class, patriarchy and race.

2

The domestication of work

You know, you used to be somebody if you worked at
StitchCo. Then, all the buses had big signs: The Best
People Work at StitchCo.

Welcome to StitchCo

Like other large companies, StitchCo offers to each new employee
an ideological package in the form of a small blue booklet which
codifies the intentions of the company towards the individual and
the community. This package emphasises the responsibilities of
the worker and the company in maintaining the high-quality
products for which it is famous. The company, it says, believes in
high quality, including high-quality profits. Welfare facilities and
sporting and social clubs are all part of the world of StitchCo. It is
the image of the family firm which is displayed, with all its
attendant paternalism. StitchCo *cares* about the people who work
for the company and the community to which owners have
traditionally belonged. As a prominent local trade unionist put it:
'StitchCo is a good company. They try to keep up the old family
tradition. They give money away to all these local charities.' The
company is, in fact, very successful in maintaining its image with
local people and in the city generally. At the same time this 'old
family firm' is busy investing in new technology and new production
methods, on a model borrowed from the German industry.

StitchCo is a large national company and the factory I studied is
the centre of operations in the UK at Needletown, in the heart of
the hosiery world. It was here, and in the surrounding districts,
that in the nineteenth century, before the development of factory
production, the early owners of StitchCo organised the putting
out, collection and marketing of goods produced by the stockingers.
The family-based system of production was one in which men
worked the knitting frames, supported by women and children. It
was a system in which men controlled the labour power of women

and children and in which men monopolised the skill and technology of knitting, as they still do today. It was, therefore, a very clearly patriarchal system, heavily dependent upon female and child labour.[1] The move into the factories was slower than in other comparable industries, due partly to problems in the application of power to knitting-frames and partly to the resistance among stockingers to the factory system. Men are reported to have valued their independence and also their control over their wives and daughters.[2]

StitchCo brought the outworkers into the factory and the company continued as a family firm based upon a dynasty of Cammillas, who still have a major interest in the company. In the 1920s the Cammillas joined forces with the beginnings of what was to become a major distribution chain. After the Second World War, the company became a public company and now produces for the High Street chain stores and exports when it can.

While the company has a reputation for providing good working conditions and security of employment, it is well known that it does not pay the highest rates for the job. High rates are traded against security and good working conditions by a management which prides itself upon its open approach to managing the workforce.

The company's internal structure reflects the division of labour in the industry overall which includes, for example, knitting, dyeing and the make-up process. The heads of these divisions are the senior executives in the company and they, like the managing director, are white and male. The departments within the divisional structure offer a high degree of autonomy to the individual manager and for those on the shopfloor he appears much more like 'the boss' than the more distant figures of the boardroom.

The Needletown factory is a large one, employing over 2,000 workers; women make up nearly two-thirds of these workers – typical of the hosiery industry generally. Currently, nearly half of the StitchCo workers are Afro-Caribbean and Asian men and women who have settled in Needletown during the last decade. The gender division of labour in the factory is typical of that in the industry as a whole: the men are knitters, mechanics, dyers and top managers; the women work in the finishing processes as they have traditionally done, and in personnel and white-collar jobs.

This forms the background to the study: a company which

prides itself on its welfare provisions for its employees, from sports clubs to Christmas gifts; an outwardly benign organisation concerned with the individual workers and the community in which it operates. StitchCo's cosy picture of the world leaves out the tedium of the job, the level of exploitation and the nature of control. The company emphasises its good labour relations, its family-like atmosphere and the long periods that workers have stayed with the firm. Clearly, this company is not operating a sweatshop, nor is it anti-union (it employs two full-time officials). But of course it still operates to make a profit and profits emanate from the shopfloor where workers sell their labour power to StitchCo. The women I worked with were no less clear about this than were the owners of the company:

Rosie You see how hard we work. You see all those tee-shirts.
 Well, now you know where all the profits come from.
 Us . . . , that's right.
Jenny Well, I'm exploited aren't I, that's how the company makes its profits.

The cosy bubble that surrounded StitchCo was punctured by the way in which the women workers read their situation and then proceeded to reinterpret it, to make anew the world of the shopfloor. It was this creative activity which provided the basis for living through each day. In the department where the women worked it was, as they will show, both a marvel and a displacement.

John's department

Through the factory gate, past the flag-pole and up the stairs rushed a stream of women, huddled against the dank morning, clutching large bags just in case there was time to catch the shops on the way home. Otherwise, the bags carried flasks and lunch-packs or some clothes that needed mending or pressing. The women always talked to each other and somehow managed to find the wit to crack jokes at eight in the morning: my presence provided the standard morning jibe, 'not again, teacher, run away from school . . .'

The floor which housed the department was a large L-shaped space with rows of industrial sewing machines and presses: the machinery of production enveloped in a riot of pastel colours, pale pinks and greens, apricot and mauve, ice-cream colours that were fashionable in the summer of 1980. The place was warm, bright and cheerful, bathed in light from the strip-lighting overhead. This was the fashion make-up department where the production process was finalised and where finished garments left in dozens for the shops. Throughout the factory the department was known as 'A' department (from an earlier time when all the departments had letters) or, more simply, as John's department. John, as the manager, claimed proprietorial rights over the space and the workers in this area. It was his domain.

Statistics in relation to the department are problematic because the size and composition of the workforce was constantly changing (labour turnover ran at 40 per cent during my year on the shopfloor). But, of an average 285 women working in the department 43 per cent were under twenty-five and 35 per cent were over forty. Only 11 per cent were in their thirties. This was partly accounted for by the lack of part-time work in the department, and factory generally. Sixty per cent of the women were married and most had children – 20 per cent had three or more. The women in the department were, like the city, racially and ethnically diverse and they included a tiny handful of Polish and Irish women alongside Asian and Afro-Caribbean women, who together made up 43 per cent of the workforce. Most of these women were Indian women, but 5 per cent were black women of Caribbean origins and there were also 4 young black women who had been born in Britain. Although there was a small number of women (4 per cent) who had worked for the company for over twenty years, 82 per cent had been at StitchCo for less than ten years, 53 per cent for less than five years and, significantly, in terms of eligibility for benefits, 25 per cent had worked for less than two years.

This was a women's world in which the shopfloor workers, the production managers, the time-and-motion officers and the personnel manager were all women. It was also a woman's world looked down upon from a great height by the male manager, John. This was a world of sewing machines and irons, presses and menders, a world of skills that were also located in the home and were historically based there before they transferred to the factory. (For some women – homeworkers – these skills remain securely tied to the home, transferred back to the domestic sphere.) This is women's work and the link between what counts as women's work and domestically based skills was understood very clearly by the women in the department. Anya, a post-war refugee from Poland, told me: 'Well, I used to sew at home and my friends said I was really good at sewing, so why not get paid for it. So, I came to StitchCo. But, it's not the same at all doing sewing here and sewing at home.'

Women come into social production as wage labourers selling their labour power in the market. While at the most abstract level labour power is not differentiated by gender, in the concrete historical case it is.[3] Women workers are to be found throughout industry in jobs similar to those done by the women in this book: low-paid, repetitive work based upon skills or dexterity which is conceived to be part of a woman's make-up, a natural attribute, not a skill.[4] The woman worker is locked out of highly skilled capital-intensive work and thereby high wages. The hosiery industry is a model of this situation. The women work largely separated from the men in labour-intensive departments such as John's. The women of StitchCo are a case study of both job segregation, and the social construction of skills as male attributes.[5]

The women rushing through the factory gate did not clock in and it was only the older women, and those who have worked for the company for a long time, who could remember when they did have a clocking-in system. They laughed as they recounted the strict control that was exercised over time-keeping by the man at the factory gate:

> In those days you was fined for five minutes late, one penny
> and for ten minutes, tuppence and then at 8.15 they shut
> the gate and locked us out so we lost our money. But do
> you know what happened? The man who took the money at
> the gate ran away with it. He hadn't given it to the
> company but kept it and he took it. They caught him and
> he went to prison I think. The real laugh was he was
> supposed to be an ex-CID man. We stopped clocking in in
> 1960 I think, it was a long time ago.

Today, time-keeping is no less important. It is recorded and filed by the supervisors: the freedom from the clock is more apparent than real. The bonus system itself ensures this, and the buzzer that punctuates the working day sounding the lunch-breaks and finally its close, is a constant reminder of the way in which capitalist production fragments time, bending it in the service of profit.

The labour process

The labour process in John's department was organised on the basis of units which were made up of 20 to 40 women who were under a female supervisor and her assistant, or two supervisors on the larger units. The organisation was similar to being 'on the line', but units sounded more friendly and were familiarised by the use of the supervisor's name. So a woman was not 'on the line', but on Gracie's unit. Supervisors were distinguished by grey overalls, assistants wore red or blue.

Each unit was organised for the production of one or more garments. Alternatively, they produced stylistic variations on a particular article of clothing. Some units worked on large orders for the same garment over a period of time. This meant that the women on the unit could increase their speed over time and earn a bonus. Other units were constantly switched from one type of work to another and did not have long runs on any style. This encouraged competitiveness between the units and worked against solidarity between the women as workers.

Each unit was made up of a variety of machines and women skilled in different processes. There were those who were involved in joining fabric together, the lockstitchers and overlockers and others who bar-tacked the hems and operated the button-sewing machines. Machines and workers were moved in relation to the production process necessary for different styles and different garments; tee-shirts, for example, rarely needed a button-holding or button-sewing machine. The material that came onto the units marked the end of the earlier production processes of knitting fabric, dyeing, stretching and rolling the fabric and cutting out pattern pieces to designs created earlier in the design department. These other processes were hidden from the women workers who may have known where the dyehouse was but had not, themselves, been there.

The job of the women of John's department was to turn pattern pieces into finished clothes, but they were at the end of the production process and the co-ordination of the other processes was not always as streamlined as it might have been. A blouse, for example, would come into the department ready-cut for only half the sizes required by the customer, in the wrong colours and with parts missing. Delays and frustrations seemed to be an ever-present part of the production process.

The supervisors had a major role in organising the technical division of labour on their units. It was they who set the work onto the units and they who judged how many different tasks were necessary and in what proportion to the number of workers. In order to maintain a steady flow of production the supervisors had to ensure that the women in the middle of the work process could co-ordinate their production with those in the later stages. The supervisors' responsibility to the women on the units was to provide a continuous flow of work so that no one was idle. They, and their assistants, spent their time fetching and carrying large boxes of pattern pieces on wheeling shelves. The boxes with the incoming work were placed on the track which ran between the machines. This meant, in effect, that unlike the case of car workers (say), the flow of work was mediated by human hand and interactions between the supervisor and the process worker. But the mediation was marked by the unequal relation which surrounded it: the machinist could not move from her machine, she was dependent upon the supervisor to bring the work to her. This, as others have shown, could be an endless source of frustration and aggravation.[6]

Women sat at individual machines and unless they were moved to make up another unit or the machines changed (both of which called forth a protest) they always worked at the same machine. In an attempt to impose something of themselves on the production process, the women always referred to their machines individually as 'my machine' and their chairs as 'my chair'. Any encroachment upon 'my chair' was likely to cause a major row. Production was marked in a work-book with the code from the ticket the worker received with each new bundle of work. The book, which was marked with the woman's name, contained her production record and it was checked by the supervisor with the help of a calculator.

The women in such a system were, therefore, both part of a unit and individuated. They had responsibilities to other members of the unit to maintain the flow of production, but they did not control this. Production levels were dependent upon the flow of work onto the units and the complicated measured day-working scheme in operation in the factory, which will be discussed in detail in the next chapter. Each woman was responsible for making up part of a garment – no one made a whole dress, or a whole blouse. Instead, a woman might sew side-seams all day, every day, week in and week out. The work was highly repetitive and, as the women attested, very boring. Changes of style and seasonal variations rang a superficial change in the nature of the work, but whether the cloth was cotton or wool, sewing pieces together was the same. The individual worker had no control over what she would do, but she tried to boost her speed on each operation in order to secure the highest rate for the job. This is one reason the women protested at being moved around; management, on the other hand, were looking for flexibility in the use of labour power and the opportunity to use skills wherever they decided they fitted into the production process.

The work that the women did was physically tiring and monotonous. The noise in the department was itself exhausting, backs ached, arms were tired, fingers were sore and damaged by the needles on the machines. Like the women described by Marianne Herzog in different industries in Germany, the machinists seemed sometimes to be swallowed up by the mountains of material that surrounded them.[7] The women sat in line with their backs to one another and at some distance across the track, separated by baskets and quantities of polythene bags full of cut pieces of clothes. The centre of a unit looked more like a rubbish heap than anything else. This physical distance did not stop the steady flow of conversation and jokes which went on throughout the day. The talk, the jokes, the smiles and the laughs promoted the solidarity of the women; the emphasis placed upon individuation by the production process cut across this solidarity and helped to reinforce control from above.

Once the pattern pieces were machined into clothes they left the machinists for the women who worked at the presses and on the irons. These women stood all day at a press or an ironing-board with a heavy steam iron. Again, these pieces of machinery were referred to as 'my press' or 'my iron' by the women who used them. The nature of the work in this section was physically more arduous than that at the sewing machines, and it was interesting that over half the women doing this work were Indian and Afro-Caribbean women. The press area was noisy and hot with even greater distances between the machines. Nevertheless, the women kept the flow of conversation going, passed sweets around and managed to instigate and maintain some fierce and lively quarrels.

The pressed clothes were passed on to the examiners and those who did the final sorting and packing. The examiners worked alongside one another under bright lights where they stood all day detecting faults and rejecting the products of the machinists, which made them less than popular with some of the other women. Those in the final section, 'the racks', who counted the clothes and packed them ready for the waiting vans, had more freedom to move around than the women in the other sections, and I worked largely in this area, the least skilled in the department. Women who had not succeeded as machinists, but whom the company chose to keep on, were employed here.

The clothes were taken to the waiting vans by three young men – 'the lads', as they were called by both management and workers. Just as the lads in Paul Willis's study of school counter-cultures spent their time resisting the organisation of the school, so Gary, Russell and Mick resisted the organisation of their time by management.[8] Each of their designated tasks was stretched to ensure maximum time away from supervision. They, of course, could bend the rules in this way because they were mobile, unlike most of the women who were tied to their machines.

Domesticating production

Throughout the floor, which also had an area designated as a training unit for young women coming into the company and for additional cleaners and menders, the women attempted to reinsert their lives, as women and as workers, into the production process. They did this in a variety of ways: first of all by the notion of possession, expressed through the phrase 'my machine' which suggested some control over machinery. Possession was reinforced by the women through the use of decorations. The machines would be adorned with pictures of family members, a favourite dog, a current heart-throb or a picture from a card or magazine which was usually a sweet and sentimental study of children. The pictures the women chose presented the world of the home, of domesticity and dependent creatures – dogs and kids – quite unlike the pin-ups and motorbikes of the dyehouse male workers. These signs of domesticity were further reinforced by the habit, common among the women, of wearing slippers at work. Slippers were, they said, practical, comfortable and cheap. But there were women who objected to this – Jessie, for example: 'I go straight for my slippers when I get home, but it's not right wearing them to work. Slopping about in slippers looks terrible, but they all do it; it's dilatory, that's what it is.' For her, slippers crossed the divide between home and work, bringing them together in a way that she found unacceptable. It was precisely why other women liked them. Slippers added a touch of comfort amid the discomfort and they reinforced the way in which women inserted themselves, as women, into the production process. Paradoxically, they were also a way of switching off, of being elsewhere (at home) when in reality the women were tied to the factory chairs. Slippers were a reassertion of a domestic and feminine presence on the shop-floor.

The world of work was further familiarised through the use of first names for supervisors, the production managers and, at times, for the male manager. For management it encouraged the belief in the cosy world of StitchCo where everyone was getting on with the job in a friendly way. But just as the cosy world of the home is undercut by forms of domination and the subordination of women, so, too, is the cosy world of StitchCo.

The domestication of John's department, with its slippers and first names, was further reinforced by the way in which the women used spare oddments of material to make aprons for themselves. These were often individual works of considerable creativity with embroidered names, pockets in different materials and edgings in different colours. The aprons, made in company time from company fabrics, were countenanced by management who were aware that the women had to work with fabrics that left fluff on ordinary clothing. Aprons, then, might be said to be useful. But they were much more than a practical accessory to work-clothes; they were one way in which women workers insisted upon their 'womanhood' and, thereby, their selfhood as they saw it, in an environment which they conceived to be alien and masculine. Aprons brought the world of the home and of domestic labour right into the middle of the factory – by so doing, they extracted from the company something much more than fabric pieces and the labour time involved in their production.

The problem with the insertion of the culture of femininity was that it was collusive.[9] It reinforced a definition of woman that was securely tied to domesticity and, more than that, to domestic labour in the home. The women, like the women workers of Anna Pollert's study, insisted upon bringing the world of the home into the factory.[10]

Beware: men at work overhead

This penetration by the gender division of labour into the heart of the labour process was shown again by the fact that technical control over the production process was in the hands of men. The machinery in the department was serviced, repaired and moved by male mechanics under the authority of a senior male mechanic – all of them white. The latter was also in charge of setting the machines so that the tension, size of stitch, etc., were correct. Women are locked out of these skills. As machinists, the women were expected to clean their machines and to replace the needles should they become blunt or broken – but no more than this. If a machine broke down, a woman had to wait for a male mechanic to arrive. This, of course, was a situation in which women were made dependent upon male skills and expertise and they were, as a consequence, subordinated to men. This was not missed by the women who too often suffered the frustration of lost production and thus lost earnings whilst they waited for a mechanic. Men in the department were, quite simply, in a position where they could exercise great power over the earning capacities of women. The power relations involved here were based upon the enforced dependence of women at work; in this, they mirror the wider situation where women, because they earn low wages, may unwillingly become dependent upon the greater power of male earnings.

The relations between the women and this group of half-a-dozen men were, from the men's point of view, based on having 'a laff' and some harmless mild flirtations. Generally, such relations reinforced the power of the men through the way in which they trivialised the female members of the workforce. More seriously, there were clear cases of sexual harassment at work. But the women retaliated in quite uncompromising ways by capturing and attempting to strip the men as part of the Christmas celebrations. On a day-to-day basis the women produced a steady stream of taunts and jibes on the sexual prowess (or lack of it) of the men. None of this, however, altered the unequal relations between the men and the women and male control over the production process. One of the young supervisors, Carol, was keenly aware of the male monopoly on skill: 'They never train the girls for that kind of work. *The men keep it to themselves*. I would really like to know all about the technical side of things. If I could have done it,

I would have much rather been a mechanic.' Management and unions, however, are both agreed that training girls through an apprenticeship is a waste of time. But the issue is not time, this is used to obscure the real issue: male control over skilled work.

It would be untrue to suggest that it is only women workers who are excluded from technical knowledge of the production process. Generally, both men and women on the shopfloor lack knowledge and thereby control over production within the capitalist enterprise. There are degrees of ignorance, however, and it is the case that men claim and protect far more knowledge and competence in relation to production processes than women. That they should do this is part of the pattern whereby skills have been constructed in relation to the power of men. The construction of skills and knowledge as male attributes has in turn bolstered the power of men to define who knows what, when, where and how. It provides a basis for the patriarchal power of men described by Heidi Hartmann as social relations with a material base which allow men to join together to dominate women in relation both to their labour power and their sexuality.[11] The mechanics of John's department were but one representation of this power.

Patriarchy in process: managing the girls

By my emphasis upon patriarchal relations, I'm suggesting that authority relations located in the social division of labour in the factory not only subordinate the shopfloor in general, but specifically promote the subordination of women as gendered subjects in the workplace. John's department basically had a very simple chain of command with John at the top, followed by the production and personnel managers, the mechanics and supervisory staff. The relations between management and the shopfloor were mediated by the use of first names which promoted a spurious equality in an unequal situation and which also reinforced the subordination of women. But the patriarchal nature of authority relations on the shopfloor went further than this and was most transparent in the use of the term 'the girls' for the women workers. Management constantly used this term and it was echoed by the shopfloor. (The term 'girls' is such a taken-for-granted part of the language of the shopfloor that in a study by Peter Armstrong and others on shopfloor ideologies its significance was completely by-passed.)[12] The term 'girls' is a diminution; it signals dependence and it undermines women which, of course, makes control easier. But the shopfloor also used the term 'the girls' and this was a reappropriation of the term by the women themselves. They used the words to underline the shared nature of their lives on the shopfloor, to emphasise solidarity and strength. Nevertheless, the term was still the same, and even though it was reclaimed by the women of the shopfloor, the connotations of school and of compliance remained.

Management at StitchCo, like elsewhere, sought ways to manage by consent, thereby consolidating the control that they exercised over the lives of their employees. The appeal to a common purpose shared by both workers and management in 'getting the job done' was one that was often made within the context of a company that was proud of its industrial relations record. Management's vision of the harmonious relations between themselves and the shopfloor was tied to the progressive image of the company and its appeal to its past, the old family firm with the interests of the workers at heart. All of this allowed management to believe in their own rhetoric. Most of the managers, as in John's department, had themselves come from the shopfloor. But, again, this cosy vision of the world of StitchCo was confronted by the clear understanding from the women that there were sides in industry and that these sides maintained an uneasy truce which was easily broken.

There was no suggestion from the women in John's department that management had either the right or the ability to manage. Instead, the women were constantly critical of management. They asked, 'When are they going to manage? After all, it's what they get paid for and it's a darn sight more than we get.' The supervisors, especially, were very critical of management:

Gracie The trouble with this place is we never know what's happening and it's my bet that management don't know either. I tell you it's Fred Karno in charge in this place.*
Jessie Either we've got no work or there's a bloody panic on here. I ask you, what do management do with their time? I

---

* Fred Karno led a concert party before the First World War and troops during the war used to sing a song 'We Are Fred Karno's Army', which was a critique of the chaos of the army high command. It has passed into oral culture with Fred Karno becoming synonymous with chaos.[13]

reckon I could do better myself than this lot. This place
never runs smoothly.

Vi I tell you Fred Karno is organising this place. Management
don't know what they're doing.

Edna I agree, they tell you one thing, you get ready to do it
and then it doesn't arrive. We could do better ourselves, I
don't know what this lot get paid for.

When she was faced with management's complaint about poor-
quality work, Eve responded:

Well, I said the machine had broken. Well, you've got to
say something otherwise they make your life a misery.
You've got to confront them and face up to the problem. I
told them, it's the cutting, what am I supposed to do about
that? You've got to, they always want double production,
well blow that they can't have what we haven't got.

The women knew that, behind the smiles and first names, the
appeal to a common purpose, there was a deep divide which
separated the world of management from the world of the
shopfloor. This divide was not one which intimidated the women
in relation to judging management performance. Their judgement
was basically that management was not keeping their part of the
bargain and managing efficiently or effectively. Indeed, they went
further than this in suggesting that they could do the job better
themselves.

More generally, there was the sense that management belonged
to the other side. They didn't eat lunch in the canteen with the
workers, nor did they take home the pay packets that the women
did. The clear differences between the working lives of management
and the shopfloor, described here by Frankie, were expressed
often over chips in the canteen:

It's too blooming much to pay for this rubbish. They sack
all the staff down 'ere so we can't get a decent cup of coffee
any more,* put the prices up and then the managers are all
having new office equipment. Good, innit! I bet those
managers haven't had their luncheon club stopped. They
have waitress service over there. It's all part of it. They get

---

* The company had replaced the women who served drinks with two
machines bearing their names, DOL and LIL, in large letters!

new cars. John has a new car every two years and the others
like Dorothy get a car allowance. You know Sylvia, well,
she doesn't drive so the company pays for taxis to take her
everywhere. She gets a bleeding taxi and we get the bus.
They earn so much money these top managers, over £100 a
week, anyway. You think they could afford their own cars.
Here we are with chips and the bus. I bet we're the most
miserable workers 'ere. I am any rate. Be happy at work,
they say. I ain't in this place, it stinks.

Even this understanding of the differences was partial in relation
to the real differences between wages and salaries. The lack of a
true estimate of the earning power of top managers was a measure
of the distance between the higher echelons of the management
hierarchy and the women of the shopfloor.

Despite the women's misgivings about management, John was,
on the whole, a popular manager. He was 'a character' and the
women responded to his jokes and welcomed the interest he
showed in them. John used joking relations as a way of managing
tension on the shopfloor; being 'a character' gave him the freedom
to behave in unpredictable ways. It was he who so often broke the
truce between management and workers by simply flying off the
handle. At a safe distance from these outbursts the women would
shrug their shoulders, but those who were nearer the event, or
who were called to account, were usually the supervisors and were
less sanguine about his outbursts. Following one such tantrum,
Jessie told me, wearily:

This morning John came flying on to the unit saying, 'It
looks terrible, messy. It's too spread out, move it together,
get these machines closer together.' I told him *he* had
arranged the unit like that because we have two things
going on, the budget dress and the tee-shirt, and we have a
larger unit because of that. Now we have lost a few but he's
shouting at me and it was his decision. I told him to make
up his mind. He doesn't know which side his arse is
hanging!

John made quite sure that everyone knew he had 'worked his
way up in nearly 30 years with the firm'. He had started as a
knitter, moved into work-study and then into management.
Jessie, who had been an examiner in the knitting department, was

very fond of telling everyone what a 'lousy knitter' John had been. The fact that he had worked his way up was respected by the women and it helped his relations with them. John was very proud of his relations with the shopfloor. From behind his large executive desk he would point towards the open door and say: 'You see, no closed doors in this department. I don't believe in it. If the girls or anyone wants to see me then here I am and they can come along and tell me whatever it is that bothers them.' It was from this ever-open door, of course, that John made his forays onto the floor, arms flying, voice trumpeting. As these usually happened at the start of the day, I took to calling them his 'dawn raids'.

I talked to John about working with women:

John I can tell you right away that I prefer to work with women, and the differences are very simple; women are less reliable; they are more illogical and they work a lot harder.
Sallie Less reliable, what do you mean?
John Well, they do have time off for their children and to have babies and all the rest. But they make up for it by working so damned hard when they are here, that's the main reason I like working with women. Of course, you get the odd one who doesn't want to bother, same way you get men who aren't really conscientious, but overall, *it's the women who give good value to the company*. Our targets keep going up since we've had the new bonus scheme, but the women not only meet the targets they surpass them.

I've worked with men before I came to this department and you can talk straight to a man, tell him off, or whatever. You can't do that to women. You've got to be more roundabout and you have to have more different approaches. There's some like Jessie and Eve I can talk to like men, swear, all of that, but I wouldn't do that to Amita or Gillian and then with Clare, of course, I am always a gentleman talking to a lady. So, you have to vary it much more with women.

While you can't talk straight to women they are much better at understanding the wider situation, the national situation and the situation of the firm. They won't get shirty and all high and mighty, but will accept what is happening and do their best, not like the men who will start the rumblings, each individual worrying about himself.

John's views of women workers expressed an all too familiar stereotype which is itself internally contradictory. Women, he told me, are both illogical and more reasonable than men. They are compliant and work hard, yet they are unreliable. From management's point of view women gave good value to the company and it was this which most impressed John's view of women workers. As he said, 'women' are not a simple unity, but divided by class and by age. The women he could 'talk to like men' were older working-class women who had worked for the company for a long time. Clare, a middle-class woman, was the personnel manager, whom he felt required a different response. Yet the differences were all part of the pattern of sexism which pervaded the shopfloor. Women either counted as men or they were 'girls' or 'ladies'. John used this classification as a background to his strategies (a word he was fond of) with the women of the department. His words were a telling comment on the way in which management at StitchCo (like that at other companies) were clearly aware of gender as a factor in the control of the workforce.

Although the women did not dislike John they were quite clear about the responsibilities that he owed to them and the interests that he supported as a manager. John might be good for a few jokes, or interested in a wedding or the birth of a child – but he ultimately belonged to StitchCo in a way that they did not. He also belonged to the world of men. Some of the women even used the term 'father' to refer to him.

The female production managers – with less power and less charisma to invoke – faced the day-to-day routine enforcement of authority on the shopfloor and were subject to much greater levels of overt hostility than the senior manager. Dorothy, Sylvia and Ilse had all been recruited from within the company and some of the women in the department had known them in earlier days as supervisors, junior managers and quality controllers. Between themselves they demonstrated great affection and warmth, which they all agreed helped them through the more difficult days. As women in positions of authority they were often faced with contradictory demands from the other women. Some of the women, especially the younger ones, disliked them all for being 'bossy'; others maintained they were 'too soft', demanding instead a more authoritarian style. These women were more accessible to the women workers than was the male manager, and they were less of a threat – which accounted for the sometimes abusive responses they invoked from the shopfloor.

For most of the women, though, it was a question of management, not of the individuals who occupied these positions. The women rather generously acknowledged that the managers were people who made errors or had fits of anger like everybody else; behind this peopled world, however, was another where the interests of management and workers did not coincide. This showed very clearly in the communications meeting which was held in the department at irregular intervals (about every six to eight weeks). The meeting was officially a forum for complaints from the shopfloor direct to management and each unit sent a representative. This apparently democratic forum, in fact, provided management with an opportunity to offer a pep-talk to workers and to steer the discussion away from contentious issues. The format for the meeting was such that John controlled over three-quarters of the 'talk time' and issues raised centred on the lavatories and their cleanliness, or otherwise, and the pros and cons of Radio 1. The situation was carefully stage-managed to keep issues and discussion to trivial matters. But, as sometimes happens, even the most carefully prepared agendas can go off course. At one meeting, John decided to emphasise the issue of wastage in the department.

John We have to do better than we are doing, especially in the difficult times that the company is facing. We must be more conscious of the cost of wastage.

One woman faced John and, in a quiet voice, said:

Rene Well, I've been told there are 92 company cars. What about them, they must cost a lot.

John Well, um, I think it's only 50 for the whole company, and you could say it's expensive, but if you want the right people you have to offer such things. My Capri, for example, well, I've been working here for 29 years and I go home with all the problems of the department. I think I've earned the car. It's not like you. I don't put my coat on and that's that. I'm responsible for my job and yours. So, um, it's a perk, I agree, but one I think I earn. Well, what do you think?

The women from the shopfloor were silent, but one of the production managers commented:

Dorothy The cars might be better used. For example, why
  does everyone going to London on the same day use
  different cars? Why can't they all go together?
John Yes, we should look at that, note it down Lilian.

The meeting concluded on this note. Later, Rene told me that she
had expected John's response: 'I knew he'd say that, "29 years
with the firm", and all that, but it's important to ask them about it
when you think our jobs might be at risk for the sake of a few
company cars.'

Management's response had been couched within the language
of responsibility and commitment to the firm. The women were
wary of such claims in the same way as they were wary of meetings
that claimed to involve them in a free flow of information. They
understood, as workers, how workers might be invited to the table
but have no part in decision-making; they are powerless. To the
women of the shopfloor, the company car was the symbol of
power and privilege. In fact, there was also some disquiet among
lower management, who suggested that the company car was not
awarded on a fair basis, but in relation to favouritism by senior
management. It was used, in effect, as a carrot and as a means of
paying lower salaries to the more junior managers. It was part of
the overall paternalism of StitchCo which was often as mystifying
to younger managers as to the women on the shopfloor. When I
asked the personnel manager in the department, Clare, about the
management structure and the salaries paid to managers, her reply
was:

> I don't know what all of them earn. We don't have salary
> bands so one manager doesn't know what another earns. It's
> the source of some disgruntled comments and it's likely to
> change with the new man. Each person has to negotiate
> separately so you can't really gauge your worth and there's
> no real incentive because you don't know what's above you.
> Some people are clearly paid more than they are worth and,
> equally, some are paid less. It really should be changed.

It was, in effect, a way of operating which allowed StitchCo to
make private deals with individual managers. It was always the
company that had the initiative. As Clare said: 'Lower down
everyone knows what they are earning, but higher up, no. The big
divide is the company car.' Clare did not have a company car, and

she intimated that the company car was used as a means of paying lower salaries to managers: 'Officially managers are divided into three grades and I'm grade two, but I have no idea how I get to grade one.'

The structure was both cumbersome and hierarchical, but it allowed the company to operate with individuals, which was consistent with its overall paternalism. Individual careers were promoted within the company, which sustained the individualism of management and encouraged an individual commitment to the company. Younger and more junior managers found themselves in a position of powerlessness *vis-à-vis* the management hierarchy. Overall this hierarchy was constructed in such a way that older men exercised power over younger men and over the women in the management system. It was very clearly a patriarchal system.

For us and against us: the supervisors

For the women working at the machines, the power of management was mediated by the person of the supervisor. It was the female supervisor who organised the day-to-day running of her unit, disciplined her workers and judged their skills. She sat uncomfortably at the interface of management and workers, occupying a deeply contradictory position – not only because of her position in the authority structure but also because, as a woman, she shared in the celebrations of the shopfloor. She had been a machinist and knew what it was like to be on the line.[14] Equally, she was called upon to be a counsellor, to offer guidance and sympathy while, at the same time, she was in direct authority over the women workers.

Management were not unaware of the problems faced by the supervisors. Clare, herself a manager:

It is very difficult to get women to apply for supervision. We don't recruit from outside and often the ones we want just won't do it. They don't want the responsibility, nor do they want to leave the girls on the line. Let's face it, it is a very difficult job and it can be unpleasant. They really are stuck in the middle between the girls and management. Because they have always come from the line they feel for the girls, but they are always told quite clearly that their responsibility is towards management. It is quite clear.

Management were categorical about the position of the supervisors and this contributed towards the unpopularity of the job among the women on the shopfloor. The situation was summed up by Sadie: 'A supervisor, no. I've never wanted to do that. It's not my style. I like to muck in with the girls. I'm not the type to boss others about. I'd rather be with the girls and part of what is going on.'

This response was a very common one. For the women of the shopfloor supervision was about controlling other women, and they preferred to remain at a distance from it. The supervisors themselves were keenly aware of their position and the fact that few women envied them their job. When I asked Eve, one of the experienced supervisors, why supervision was so unpopular, she said:

> A lot of women don't want the responsibility, nor the aggro. You know John can be so bloody awful and they see us getting shouted at, blamed when anything goes wrong. It makes you sick. I suppose the girls see you and think, 'I don't want to do that job'. It's not worth the hassle for the money because you are stuck in between the girls and management and you can't please either most of the time.

The supervisors were a very diverse group of women, including women like Jessie who had worked for the company for 44 years and who was due to retire in the summer of 1981. Gracie and Edna were the other older women, while Eve, in her thirties, was also the union representative for the staff grade. There were three younger white women – Gina, Gillian and Carol, who worked with Jessie – and three Indian women – Savitri, who had come from Guyana in the 1960s, and Amita and Satwant, who were younger and who had grown up in Britain. The assistant supervisors were considered to be 'run arounds' and not necessarily in training for a supervisor's job; because of this, they were mainly young women of whom only two were Indian.

The supervisors had no specific training, as Savitri pointed out:

> No, I didn't have any training to speak of. I just had to jump in and swim. Later they sent me to a course, but it wasn't much help; it was just a couple of days. You really have to do the job to find out what to do. When I started I didn't know any of the women on the unit and what they

do, what they like to do, what they don't like to do. But I
got to know, so now it's easier. They are good workers on
this line, but, it's like now, we have no work here so we try
to send the girls to other places. Who do I say should go?
Some of them want to go, some of them hate to go. What
am I to do?

The supervisors were often worried by the demands of the job
they had to do and would seek support from one another in the
coffee bar. On one such occasion, Eve was talking to Jessie and
Gracie about a rash she had developed and the fact that she wasn't
sleeping:

Eve I never thought of myself as a nervous person before, but
the doctor says it's nerves. It's this bloody job that's doin'
it. I keep worrying that we won't get our bikinis out in
time and we'll lose the order.
Gracie You can't go worrying about losing orders, that's not
our job. You've got to look after what you've got to do,
that's for the manager to worry about.
Jessie Quite right Gracie, we're not responsible for StitchCo,
they are. There's no point in making yourself ill with worry
about these things. Look at the whole way the place is, up
and down, and it's not our fault it's like that.

Illness was, in fact, a common response to the pressures of the job
as Anna Pollert found among the women of Churchmans.[15]
Gillian, one of the younger supervisors, suffered from a succession
of minor ailments – headaches, colds, bad period pains – which she
felt were generated by the tensions of the job.

The major technical task for the supervisors was to set the work
onto their units, and this was described by Carol:

Well, Ilse and us [Carol worked with Jessie] decide in line
with how it's been set out in the design centre. That is the
way it will be cut out. We have to work out who we need
on each operation and how many girls at each to keep the
line flowing. Say, with this dress here there are 14
operations. A couple are very simple – the gathers, for
example – so we would try to put a C grade on that and,
perhaps, one girl would be enough. But attaching the yoke
is difficult and has to be done properly not to ruin the
dress. So, we would put a Star or an A grade on that,

especially one who is skilled rather than just fast. In order
to keep the line running smoothly we may need two on that
job. But you have to try it out.

As can be appreciated from Carol's description, the technical
demands of the job were considerable. Carol and Jessie were both
very competent and experienced supervisors, which meant that
special jobs – such as the make-up of sample or model dresses – fell
to them. On one occasion, they were presented with a trial dress
which had been made up in the design centre. Management wanted
four copies in one-and-a-half hours to send to the London office of
their major distributor. There were no instructions for the make-
up of the dress. Carol and Jessie agreed that the request was
ridiculous, but proceeded through a process of trial and error to
work the pattern pieces into a dress. The process was an infuriating
one: pieces were sewn together and unpicked to be sewn together
again. At the end of an hour, without any assistance from
management, they produced one dress which was dispatched with
an executive to London. Incidents like this added power to the
view held by the supervisors that it was really they, rather than
management, who were organising production. As Gracie said: 'I
don't know what management manages these days. StitchCo is
chaotic.'

Technical competence was one part of the supervisor's role, the
other was the ability to control the women on the units. The
younger supervisors, especially, felt very uneasy about their
authority. This showed when management at one point decided to
reassert their authority in relation to the time the women spent in
the coffee bar. Short breaks had been introduced in the last 12
months and the women used them to chat to friends on other
units (and to me), and generally to break up the working day.
Management decided that the breaks were becoming too frequent
and, in a display of naked authority, insisted that no breaks were
to be available to those who had not completed their targets. The
supervisors, designated to police this new system, were called in by
management and told that they must enforce the company rules
on the breaks. Women were allowed three to five minutes if they
were on target. This information was relayed to the assembled
women by the supervisors.

Eve told the women on her unit: 'Management say that the
breaks have to stop. Only women who have completed their

targets and who are in a C grade and above can go for a short break.'

The women looked sullen in response and a number of them made the point: 'Well, if we had plenty of work to do we wouldn't be going for breaks. It's not our fault there's no work to do. What are we supposed to do?'

Eve was sympathetic to this point of view: 'I don't blame the girls really because the problem is lack of work. How are we supposed to find work from out of the air. It's management's responsibility and then they want us to keep the girls in line.'

On the whole, the attempt to provide more control over the women was unpopular with the supervisors. Amita, the youngest supervisor, said:

> I hate all this fuss about breaks. I'm no good at ordering people around and then I'll get all the stick when my girls are in the canteen. Being a supervisor is a really difficult job because you are in the middle. The girls want you to be for them and management insist you are part of them. It gives me a real headache. I go home some days so worried because I haven't done my job right. I'm not kidding.

Amita lived out the contradictions of her position in the hierarchy – anxious to do her job well, but unhappy with a situation which placed her alongside management as an agent of control. It was not surprising that this should be the case: she had to face the women on her unit on a day-to-day basis and they were quick to respond to a supervisor who was overtly authoritarian.

At one point, women on Amita's unit were completing a garment for Eve's unit. It was a girl's skirt onto which the women were attaching braces. Eve came over to the unit with a bundle of skirts in her arm to complain about the work, and a heated interchange followed:

Eve You lot should have a look at these. The braces are all in the wrong place.

Jean We only did what we were told to do. Christine told us to do it like that and she should know.

Eve Well it's not what you are supposed to have done is all I can say.

Jean We do as we're told. If you don't like it go and see Christine.

Eve It's not Christine I'm after, it's you lot, you got it all
wrong.
Jean Ah, bugger off can't you [*pokes tongue out at Eve*].

Other women watching the interchange nodded in support and
June said to me: 'It's about time someone told Eve to fuck off.
She's more like a manager than a supervisor, always shouting at
people. It really gets on my tits.' The rest of the unit agreed and
murmured assent while Eve, still carrying her bundle of skirts,
tossed her head and walked away from the unit.

Eve was not alone in generating such a vitriolic response. Jessie
was often considered to be a bully. She seemed to have few
anxieties about exercising her authority and would rush into the
canteen and call the women from her unit back to the line.
Sometimes she would pull us bodily off the seats and march us
back to the machines. Needless to say, this was much resented by
the women. The younger women, especially, objected to the
control that the supervisors attempted to exercise over their
movements to and from the canteen, and over their working
lives in general. Julie and Kim discussed the problem over
coffee:

Julie Cor, Gracie is really getting up my nose. She's been on
at me since I arrived late this morning; she had me roarin'
[crying] and I can't do these fucking long johns we're
s'posed to be makin'. You want to see them. I have to go
all round 'em and I've just got my minutes, one dozen in
ten minutes. I can't do it. And Gracie just keeps nagging
me.
Kim Yeah, Jessie is just the same. They really get up my nose.
You're doing your work but they won't leave you alone.
The number of times Jessie has had me in tears. They don't
have to be like the army. We work hard enough without
that aggravation. This place is such a dump. You wait,
she'll be in here in a minute to *order* us back to work.

For some women the tensions of the supervisor's job were too
great. Laura, for example, had been a supervisor for a period of six
months before she left the company. Now back at a machine on
Eve's unit, she reflected upon the problems she had found with the
job:

I didn't like it at all. I was very young and at that time all
the supervisors were older, like Jessie. I really felt that I
wasn't doing a good job, that was the problem. It used to
really worry me. I'm not cut out for it. Some of the girls
need a lot of pushing to work, especially the younger ones
because they are not used to it. But I didn't like being on
their backs the whole time. I am much happier as an Indian
than one of the chiefs. I like to be with the girls, not over
them. I like being at the machine, same as the others.

Given this view by a woman who had been a successful
supervisor, well liked by her unit and by management for her
competence, and bearing in mind the earlier comments of some of
the supervisors, it was surprising that StitchCo managed to
recruit women to these positions. Certainly, there was very little
financial incentive; supervisors earned little more than the top-
grade machinist with a bonus. There was the security of being a
member of the staff grade rather than an operative, but this was
bought at a high price. For most of the supervisors the compensation was that the job was 'much more interesting', and the older
women seemed to enjoy the extra responsibility. But for many, the
job was marked by the tensions of being both a woman on the
shopfloor and the vital outpost of the management structure.
These contradictions are highlighted in the struggles over productivity which are discussed in the next chapter.

3
Up against the minutes

> The minutes, you know what that means? It just means that they break everything down more to speed it up so that we work more. We know that is what they are doing.

Eve was right. She had cracked the minutes code and she was not the only woman to have done so. In this chapter I try to show the way in which the women demystified the measured day-work scheme imposed on them. Although production targets, graded times and bonus rates may not seem riveting reading, they were all vitally important to the women of John's department. It was these rates for the job that promoted the resistance generated and sustained on the shopfloor and which called forth a response from the union reps when the women, in a final act of defiance, walked off the job and away from their machines. The struggle was fierce because there was so much at stake: a worker's attempt to control her own production, her skill and effort and, ultimately, how these were to be exchanged for wages in the unequal bargain between worker and employer.

'The minutes' was common parlance for the measured day-work (MDW) system in operation in the factory. With its pseudo-scientific job evaluations and mystificatory measurements, it might have confused or conned the likes of me – but it fooled no one on the shopfloor.[1] Quite simply, 'an MDW system is one in which pay is fixed against a *specified* level of performance. The system depends on some form of work measurement to set the perform-ance level required and to monitor the actual level achieved.'[2]

The workers of StitchCo were graded on the basis of production performance through seven bands, star grade followed by A, B, C, D, E and F. The last two grades were used for trainees; experienced workers whose production fell to that of an E or F grade would not keep their jobs. Each grade had a specific production level which guaranteed a certain wage packet; bonuses could be earned by producing more in less time. Workers were subject to monthly assessments at a meeting of management, supervisors and trade union representatives. There, a woman's production record would be considered, along with her time-keeping and any discipline problems that had arisen during the previous month. If the woman had maintained her production levels, she stayed in the same grade; if she had produced a consistently higher level of production over the whole month, she would be upgraded; and if she had consistently fallen below the specified level of production for her grade, she would be downgraded. Clearly, a woman's ability to maintain a steady level of production depended upon management's ability to keep a steady flow of work coming into the department. This was taken into account at the assessment meeting.

The introduction of MDW in the mid-1970s was not fortuitous. Like other employers, StitchCo had had to find a way to deal with both falling profits and labour unrest: MDW allows management to assess labour costs more accurately and thus increases their control over the labour process and the shopfloor.[3] As Tony Cliff has pointed out, the system undermines the shop steward and strengthens the supervisor; at the same time, it removes issues from the shopfloor and centralises disputes procedures.[4] StitchCo was typical of the system in operation: it had a unionised workforce whose dues were collected by a central check-off system and two union officials on site who were paid by the company.

It is worth considering, very briefly, the way in which MDW at StitchCo fits into the wider pattern of management control discussed in recent writings on the labour process. Clearly, MDW allows management to generate a better fit between its two main functions – the technical co-ordination of production and control of labour. As Harry Braverman has so cogently argued, capital's control over the labour process is essential. In this respect, Taylor's scientific management becomes crucial.[5] It is in such a system that labour is deskilled and degraded. However, as later writers have pointed out, scientific management has not had it all its own way. Worker resistance to the imposition of stopwatches, speed-ups and other such devices for cheapening and controlling labour power has been important in modifying management strategies.[6] Although Braverman acknowledged 'the hostility of workers to the degenerated forms of work', he did not explore this.[7] Andrew Friedman suggests that management in fact operates within two broad strategies – one, a direct-control strategy which operates by 'coercive threats, close supervisions and minimising individual worker responsibility'; and, the other, a responsible-autonomy strategy, which 'attempts to harness the adaptability of labour power by giving workers leeway and encouraging them to adapt to changing situations in a manner beneficial to the firm.'[8] These two strategies are not mutually exclusive; still, it is possible that, because the latter relates to the traditions of craftworkers, there will be differences in their application within a workforce.[9]

StitchCo was an example of this: the direct-control strategy was clearly in evidence in John's department among women who were classified as semi-skilled workers (much to their constant annoyance), whereas the responsible-autonomy strategy was in evidence with the skilled male workers, the knitters. They worked in a capital-intensive area and, although they were subject to the minutes and gradings, they were not subject to direct supervision and they did not work on units. In addition, they were graded on a three-monthly basis. Their gradings were also different. Once a knitter was trained, it was unlikely that he would not be a star-grade worker whereas the women in the department were spread throughout the grades. As Anna Pollert has argued, job evaluations and grading systems allow unequal wages and occupational segregation between men and women to be legitimised and the lines of demarcation to take on a fixed quality over and above the differences between skilled and semi-skilled workers.[10]

In John's department the ideal breakdown of grades was: star grade 10 per cent; A grade 15 per cent; B grade 30 per cent; C grade 25 per cent; D grade 15 per cent; E grade 5 per cent. This was not achieved during my year in the department. In week 50, for example, the breakdown, according to the company, was: star grade 25.78 per cent; A grade 17.42 per cent; B grade 17.07 per cent; C grade 19.51 per cent; D grade 14.63 per cent; E grade 4.81 per cent. The figures show that despite management's problems in maintaining a steady flow of work into the department, over a quarter of the women were in the highest grade. The profiles for black and white women were very similar. For instance, in the same week 26.66 per cent of the black women were classified as star-grade workers.

The grading system was, of course, an important part of the control strategy. It divided the workforce: women doing the same job but in different grades would be earning different wages on the basis of different targets for production. But all women were 'up against the minutes' and were clearly aware of this, despite the complexities of the MDW scheme which superficially mystified the contract between worker and employer. None of them believed there was a fair bargain to be struck between management and workers in a system that fragmented their effort and their time in the pursuit of profits. As Lata put it: 'I hope you don't think StitchCo is all nice, it's not nice. They try to cheat us and we complain. I would like another job, but what can I do? All the factories are the same.'

Like Lata, other women on the shopfloor believed they were cheated by a system which fractionalised time and disassembled operations for the purposes of reconstructing both in line with efficiency. Efficiency was to be achieved by the setting and monitoring of work processes which were analysed both on and off the shopfloor. The work-study team would come out to the worker with a chart broken down by seconds and would plot the actions in any operation against the time they take to perform. This was only part of the operation: as Christine (the minutes woman) explained the observed sequence of actions would be set against predetermined, synthetic time standards:

> You have to learn the values by heart. There is an overall value for different movements and once you know this you can calculate any job from this. You have to note each movement on this sheet and these are set against a category of 15–45 seconds. When I've done that I then write out the sheet for the woman and she can read it. If she doesn't accept it we do it again, or we can call the union rep. The jobs do vary a lot and no one is perfect, so we can get it wrong But it is very important because the cost of the garment will vary with the production time. It's broken down now more than it used to be. We have 495 minutes in every day and allow a 25 per cent relaxation time over every dozen.

This then, was the minutes as it was conveyed to women working at machines, presses, and examining clothes. As Christine went on to say: 'I'm not surprised the women question it. It's not easy making a living out there and we depend on them.'

Christine was right on all counts. Women on the shopfloor resisted the minutes as a set of relations which sought to control them, to deskill them and to cheapen their labour power. They battled against all these on a daily basis but it was an uphill struggle against a system that at once united and divided them. They understood its divisive potential and tried to support one another in protest because they were all bound to the same production process and depended upon one another – just as management depended upon them to deliver the goods. Like all workers, they understood the point made by Jim Powell in his book on work study: 'Think of rules and management techniques as the left hand and the right hand of management. With the rules they are able to hold you in a firm grip – and with the techniques they can clobber you.'[11]

As with other workers, the ultimate protest was to withdraw their labour – to walk off the job, call the union rep and wait. Resistance of this kind emerged at the point of production and was also a part of the lives of male workers who, in fact, resisted the introduction of the scheme more militantly than the women. But the scheme operated differently for men at StitchCo, and this was consistent with the way that patriarchal forms intervened in the labour process. Rules and management techniques had a special force for women workers who were more closely monitored, more highly supervised and, finally, paid less. This provides yet another example of the point made by Angela Coyle in her analysis of the clothing industry: 'Whilst the material fact of women's dependency is undermined by participation in paid work, it is ideologically reproduced within the organisation of the labour process itself.'[12]

By the piece

The older women who had known the piecework system were very clear in their understanding that 'the minutes' were not simply about increased production, but were essentially about control. They resented the loss of control over their time and their production: 'We used to have piecework here like the other firms, I loved that because if there was no work, like it is now here, you went home and you could see your children more. Since we've had the guaranteed week – 1973, I think it was – we have to stay, work or no work.' For Savitri, and many of the women, the freedom to exchange work for home, money for time, had been taken away. In this, it represented a real imposition and control over her life that had not previously been the case.

Savitri's views were echoed by Betty who had worked for StitchCo for many years:

Betty It was different here then. We were all on piecework and we used to sing and have a laff. You can't do that now with these minutes. You've just got to keep your head down and work to your target. Some of them work through their breaks because it's the only way you can keep up.

Sallie But what happened if there wasn't any work?

Betty Well, you took the rough with the smooth. When there was plenty of work, you worked hard and earned your money. There was no maximum like now. I've had my book back with the minutes underlined and *maximum* written alongside. Well, whatever you do over that you don't earn a penny.

Sallie But you have the guaranteed week.

Betty Yes, and you pay for it. When we need time off they want to know where we are going, for how long and you have to prove it. In the old system it didn't matter. It was much freer then. This is much more regimented. We had a lot more fun in the old days. You really have to work to earn your money now. I liked it better on the old system . . . It was up to you then to decide what you were going to do.

Piecework is seen in this and other accounts as a system which offered the workers more control over their own production. But the apparent freedom from 'the minutes' was more illusory than real. The accounts of piecework and the preference the women expressed for this system are bound to a view of its freedom. As Nell put it:

> I wouldn't choose to do this job, nor would most of us here, but it pays you the money. It's very hard work. Years ago we were on piecework. I prefer that – it's not so much pressure. You get paid for what you do on that and no one minds you. But now you've got to work solid otherwise you'll be downgraded: that's always hanging over you like a threat.

The minutes as a system of control is clearly expressed here, as is the pressure that the grading system exerts over the women. They felt as though they were in a school system where being downgraded was a punishment. They were less willing to see the drawbacks of piecework as a system that promoted competition between workers, was equally exploitative and considerably less secure in terms of work and pay. However, there were women who understood this. When I was discussing the preference expressed for piecework by the older women with Cherry – a small, very lively woman – she commented:

> Yes, some of the women do say piecework is better. It's all right when you've got enough work to go around everyone, but when you haven't it's not so good. I was always on short-time at Kerrs so you don't earn your money and you get fights over the work. I'm not so keen on it myself, it's better for everyone to get a fair share of things.

Taruna, a young Indian woman, was also clear in her dislike of piecework: 'It was piecework there. It was terrible. The women used to fight over the work, really fight. I didn't like it. I was no good at fighting, I just left as soon as I could.'

Piecework, then, appeared to many of the women as a fairer system which rewarded precisely what was expended in effort. To the newcomers, it seemed like a barbaric and competitive system which offered no more freedom and control to workers. The experienced women would have fared better in a piecework system, but their accounts left out the disputes that were as fierce about the rate for the piece as those over the minutes. In either system, in the end, the quarrels over the value of labour power were the same.

Skill

As part of their protest against the minutes, the women fought to maintain an element of skill within their work. They saw the MDW system as a system for deskilling them, taking away from them their craft and dexterity. The women discussed the issue of skill often. They were aware that designs were increasingly simplified to allow for cheapness in make-up and that speed, not skill, was at issue. Many of them felt that their skills were not being used. They had been deskilled by the demand for profit. Technically they were classified as 'semi-skilled', but, as Harry Braverman has pointed out, this is a socially constructed category which involves a large degree of arbitrariness.[13] The women saw the process of deskilling as a recent phenomenon, although in actuality it was not. The minutes evolved from a long process of deskilling that had been going on throughout the clothing industry from the time when tailoring was a craft. But the tailor always existed alongside the sweated trades. In the latter, women did not make a whole garment, but were involved in finishing processes and a division of labour which forms the basis of today's production process.[14] They were, in effect, deskilled decades ago. Nevertheless, these women worked for a company that had emphasised quality; this emphasis kept alive the idea that they were engaged in skilled work. Some could remember the time when a training at StitchCo was the best to be received in the hosiery industry locally. Now it was a short period of time before the trainees joined the units.

Louise Lamphere, discussing the 'apparel industry' in the United States, makes the point: 'Despite the "deskilling" of sewing, the women are conscious that their work is skilled, involving a great deal of hand/eye co-ordination, dexterity, attention, and, above all, speed.'[15] Speed for the women of StitchCo was not the same as skill. This view was supported by the union representative who was closest to them, Annie, a former machinist: 'I've just been talking to management about "the minutes". He says they're fair, but I can't get through to him that they reward speed and not skill, so they are unfair. A right set to we've had about it.'

The process the women were involved in was a classic one in which their work was progressively deskilled and degraded so that their labour power was interchangeable. Nell, a woman in her early fifties, described this:

> The way they do it here now, switching us about from place
> to place you can be very skilled and not using your skills,
> that's the trouble with the bonus system it gives you the
> money if there is work and you are quick, but it doesn't
> allow for the skill in the work. You can be really good and
> it makes no difference, it's speed they want. All the older
> women complain about it. It also means that the company
> wants more out of us and we can't do anything about it.

The emphasis by the women on skill was part of their resistance to management control over the labour process and thereby their labour power. Skill implied their value and their control over the labour process. It was part of the dignity of labour that they fought to retain and regain in a system where it was denied. This is expressed cogently by Anya, whom I introduced in the last chapter:

> My back hurts. It's too much work. All we have to do now is turn it out. The last two years the quality has really gone down. Like I told you, I came here because I used to sew at home, just for the children and my husband's friend used to say I was really good so I should go to StitchCo because they made quality goods. That was ten years ago. Then, we used to put our initials on the back of some of the labels because we were proud of our work. Now, I don't even put it on the tag of the work. Because we have to work so quickly the quality has gone. It's the same for the cloth and the cutting, it's rubbish. We make *rubbish* here now and what I wonder is who buys this stuff.

Making time

The MDW scheme offers management both control over the labour process and the workforce and a means of calculating labour costs as a fraction of production costs. The accuracy of this calculation also rests on management's ability to keep the flow of production steady. Equally, the system was not one that went unchallenged by the women, so it had built into it the possibilities of great conflicts. For management, it was a combination of stick and carrot – impossible targets and guaranteed wages.

The targets the women were to meet were set by the work-study analyst in relation to an overall grid of values given to each movement of an operation. These were then translated into dozens, the basic unit used for the clothes, in which they were ultimately produced and sold. Some examples of the targets in operation will serve to show the level of production that was required by the women.

Rhoda, who was an A-grade worker, was involved in the production of a child's waistcoat: she had to join the side-seams of the garment, and attach the rib at the bottom by overlocking them. Her target was 36 dozen and 10 per day. She commented: 'I can do it, but there's not enough work so far, so I never have.'

Across the gangway from Rhoda sat Usha, a star-grade worker, who worked the button-holing machine. She had to make three button holes and trim all the ends of the waistcoat. Her target was 73 dozen and 5 per day. She said: 'To do the target I have to work constantly, not mess around for a minute. It's very hard.' The same daily button-holing operation translated into the other grades looks like this: A, 67 dozen and 10; B, 62 dozen and 2; C, 56 dozen and 7; D, 45 dozen and 3; E, 36 dozen and 9; F, 28 dozen and 3. This gives some idea of the progression in production between the grades.

The times given for the operation in terms of dozens also shows clearly the basis of the earnings system: 1 dozen, 8.76 minutes; 4 dozen, 35.04 minutes; 8 dozen, 70.08 minutes; 20 dozen, 175.2 minutes; 40 dozen, 350.4 minutes; 80 dozen, 700.8 minutes. Consequently, when we come towards the star grade the production time is well beyond the minutes of work available during a day: the worker must 'make' time for the company to earn her pay and the top wages. The working day is timed as 495 minutes: to earn top money the worker must produce two-thirds of the day again.

Star-grade workers can also earn a bonus by producing more and thereby earning time. Jo, for example, had the job of joining facings and then attaching them to the neck of a dress. This was a difficult job because the dress was yoked and if the facings did not lie properly the dress was ruined. As a star-grade worker her target was 15 dozen and 3 per day and she exceeded this: 'I'm doing 140 per cent which is the top – that means 16 dozen and 4 per day.' This meant that Jo was earning top wages. As a star-grade worker her basic was £73.61 and the bonus pushed this up to £81.02 gross wages for the week.

However, the divisiveness of the system was shown up very clearly by a physical fight that broke out in the press area between Bella and Justine, two women who worked on the steam irons. Bella explained to me after the event what the row had been about:

> There's not enough work, you know, so Justine and me we
> are taking it in turns on the ironing. We had a fight
> you know, her and me, over the work. It's hard because
> she's always trying to push me around and I really love her.
> I've taken her like a sister to me, but she don't like it if she
> thinks I'm getting too much work because she is on a

higher grade than me and she don't want me to be on her
grade, so she try to keep the work to herself and I say
that's not fair. I'm just trying to do me work and if it's
there I earn a bonus because I do more than the target, but
she thinks maybe I stop her doin' her grade so she will lose.

The fight itself was a dramatic affair. The other women scattered
to the sides while Bella and Justine attacked each other with fury –
Justine, small and wiry, and Bella, large and strong, shouting
abuse in dialect which only the other Jamaican women could
understand. The fight was much discussed and the others
clearly understood the strains imposed by lack of work. Both
women had only their wages to depend on to keep rent, food and
other bills paid and to look after their dependants. The fight was
also discussed, by both management and workers, as an example
of the volatility of Caribbean women. What the managers
conveniently forgot to take into account was the extent to which
the fight was an outcome of the target system. The minutes, then,
did not overcome the competition over work which the piecework
system encouraged; both systems were but two sides of the same
coin.

The Indian women were as vocal as the others in the protest
against the minutes and they clearly mistrusted the company,
despite its appeals to a common purpose: 'There is no work
for us today. It's a trick, two days' work and then no work
so you can't earn a bonus. The company don't want to pay any
bonus to us any more. They trick us.' In fact, Rekha was packing
knickers but this was merely a fill-in job on which no bonuses
could be earned. That, Rekha suggests, was part of a management
strategy to reduce bonus payments. By not providing a steady flow
of bonused work into the department management minimised
everyone's chances of 'making' time.

Resistance

The women protested and resisted the target and grading system,
individually and collectively, on a day-to-day basis. The work-
study analysts were often marked out as the main enemy and were
constantly discussed – at times, more vehemently than higher
levels of management. These women were seen as the perpetrators
of a system which presented to the shopfloor targets which could

not be reached, let alone surpassed to allow for a bonus to be earned. It is the encounter between the work-study analyst and the shopfloor worker which encapsulates the collision between labour and capital, as this is the point at which the contract for the sale of labour power is realised and where labour power is turned into labour time and, thus, profits for the company.

The supervisors, as I have shown, were placed uneasily between management and workers and the contradictions of their position showed again in relation to the MDW system. They had both the job of policing the system and, as they saw it, of protecting the women on their units against unfair production targets. If the targets were too high the unit would not be able to produce its overall target and this would create more problems with the management.

In the coffee bar Jessie, Eve and Savitri were discussing Christine, one of the work-study analysts, a rather dour woman in her twenties:

> She's just been to my unit. I really don't like her, she never
> smiles and she is never nice to the girls. She's just given
> some really tight minutes on the tee-shirt. She doesn't allow
> any time for sorting out the work, just the sewing – and
> that means it's very difficult for the women to achieve their
> targets let alone earn a bonus. We are supposed to be
> neutral but we can advise the girls to call in the union if they
> think the minutes are wrong and the union can fight them.
> I do it all the time, so does Jessie, but other supervisors like
> Gracie don't do it. She doesn't look after her girls.
>
> It's especially important when you know you have a good
> worker, one who really tries hard. Then, if she is given a
> stupid target by Christine she loses heart or the work will
> be poor. This bonus scheme causes a lot of poor work and
> lot of trouble. I am always having rows with Christine.

Eve's comments were echoed by some of the other supervisors who felt that Christine was both unfair and unpleasant. It was also the case that Eve had noisy verbal fights with Christine which were much relished by the women at the machines:

> That Christine, she's always trying it on with my girls.
> They are working flat out aren't they, Sallie? If she carries
> on like this we're going to have trouble. We had one time
> when she tried to give minutes, before this scheme, and she

timed a woman and didn't ask if she could bring the clock
out. It's against the rules. The girls are only timed if
they agree to the clock coming out and it has to be visible
to the girl. Well, this time it wasn't. She did it on the sly
and when the girls found out they walked off the job. The
nearest thing we've had to a strike here. We had to get
John to sort it out. They have no idea what they are doing
with their clocks and their minutes.

Outside the coffee bar, a row was developing which looked as
though it might erupt into a walk-off. Gillian's unit had just been
given minutes for making a baby garment – a tee-shirt which was
edged, and had pants to match. Gillian was looking distraught and
said: 'I hate this minutes thing; it's the worst part of my job. I feel
sick, I've got a headache. Every time the minutes are given there is a
row, every time.' Lisa, the assistant supervisor, was also looking
very worried as the fury from the women grew. Some sat defiantly
with arms folded while others talked together in small groups.
The unit had disintegrated. Jackie, who was still sitting at her
machine, told me:

I'm supposed to make a dozen tee-shirts, sides and sleeves
in 10.47 minutes and produce 55 dozen a day as an A grade,
and Shanta, as a star grade has to produce 59 dozen and 10
a day. It's ridiculous. Every time the minutes are given they
get worse, they want more from us every time. Well, it
won't work. I can't do that target. Shanta, you should get
the union man.

Shanta, looking perturbed, agreed:

Gillian never questions it. She never speaks up for us. She's
a lousy supervisor. Eve is much better – she always fights
for her line and has rows with Christine. Gillian is
useless.

Shanta was one of the department's union reps (Eve was the other)
and she worked on Gillian's unit. The woman in front of her had
been given a target of 69 dozen a day for putting the edging on the
two small garments and was very fed up: 'It's ridiculous. It doesn't
take account of the fact that small things are more difficult to
work. They think because it's small we can do lots more. Well, I
can't and I won't.'

A few machines away, at the centre of the row, Gillian, Lisa and Stephanie – another work-study analyst – were clustered around Hansa, a large Indian woman in her forties whose job it was to put the labels on the two pieces of clothing. She had been given a target of 97 dozen a day and was furious. Stephanie was trying to follow the laid-down procedure and give Hansa the sheet with the job analysis and time on it so that she could read it. Hansa snarled and threw it back at Stephanie with a toss of her head. Stephanie was also angry and insisted: 'You've got to read it, don't come complaining back to me if you haven't. You're supposed to read it before you call the union rep. Lisa, you read it to her.'

Hansa pushed the paper away and Lisa looked frightened. Shanta moved towards the scene and suggested that Lisa should read it and then she would go and get the union rep. Hansa sighed heavily and looked on while Lisa tried to read the instructions and timings on the job. She read haltingly and the unit was quiet while everyone listened to the instructions. Hansa looked on, arms folded, exuding rage.

Behind Hansa sat Asha, who by this stage was in tears: 'I can't do this target, it's no good,' she wailed. Asha's target was the same as Hansa's.

Shanta made a valiant attempt to calm the situation down: 'I'm going for the union man,' she announced.

'Bah, the union, the manager, they are all the same here, nobody cares.' Having said this, Asha, in floods of tears, raced towards the lavatories. The whole unit was now in total disarray and no one was working. The younger women were beginning to enjoy the excitement.

'I'm not going to work until they change the minutes.' So saying, Suraya folded her arms and sat defiantly in the middle of a pile of work.

In front of her, Taruna shouted excitedly: 'We'll go on strike.'

'Yes, we will, we're not taking this, it's not fair,' Suraya agreed. The rest of the women joined in with this view and started to move away from their own machines to form small groups.

Shanta grabbed my hand and we took off at speed for the union office. Before we had got there, we found Bill (the union representative) and some of the other departmental representatives coming out of a meeting which Shanta had missed because she hadn't known about it. Shanta explained the problem and Bill told her he was a little busy but would try to get along later in the day. In fact, he did not appear until the following week when other circumstances had overtaken the events described: the work dried up.

During the afternoon, both Gillian and Lisa were ill and Lisa left early. The women from the unit moved between the coffee bar and the unit and didn't do any work. The following day, the same situation prevailed: the women talked, worked a little at their own pace and spent time in the coffee bar. Lisa commented: 'It's awful when we have minutes. I wish we didn't have the bonus scheme. It's terrible and it upsets everyone. Look at me yesterday, and Gillian, we were shaking. I just went home.'

Later in the following week, some of the women involved in the dispute were without work and they were sent to Eve's unit to assist with a packing job. They consistently and deliberately got the packing wrong and spent their time chatting about the dispute and the failure of the union representative to appear. The issue had not been resolved because the work had stopped and the women were now being sent from unit to unit to fill in. They were dispirited and angry. It was possible that they were split up and sent to other units deliberately – that the work that had caused so many problems had not stopped, but was being held up. I never managed to discover the truth about this. That the union rep did not appear immediately was not unusual – from his point of view, it allowed for a cooling-off period in which tempers could calm down and the problem be resolved more amicably. For the women, the issue was never resolved: for them, it was yet another example of the way in which the company tried to exploit the workforce, or as they put it, to cheat them:

Lata They try to cheat us. Every time we get a new style they make the minutes worse and every time we complain. When I was working on the last tee-shirt I was an A grade and I had 24 dozen and 6 a day as my target. The star grade was 26 dozen. Now it's a new tee-shirt, but exactly the same job, and they want 28 dozen a day from me. Well, they can't do it like that. They are always trying to cheat us and we complain.

Taruna It's true. They cheat us. The union should never have agreed to the minutes.

Hansa I agree. You know we had all that trouble over the minutes for the baby clothes and the union man never

came. When she asked me to read the paper I said I
couldn't read the paper, the one where they put down how
much each garment takes. I told her I didn't understand, I
couldn't read it, but I can really. They think because
something is small you can do twice as much, but it's not
true. It's difficult to work with and the material is difficult.

Enid That's what bothers me. Who are they? They come along
and tell you how many in how many minutes, but you never
see them doing it. They don't know how, that's why. It's
the same with the supervisors nowadays, they don't know
how to do the jobs they're supposed to supervise. The
management is all wrong here. It used to be better.

The women were furious and they remained so. While we were
having this conversation we were all supposed to be packing
bikinis, but they didn't get packed and we were constantly in
trouble with Eve for doing the job badly.

Later in the week, the baby clothes came back. Management
suspended the minutes as it was a small order, and made an appeal
to get the job done as quickly as possible. The women had a
victory. As part of the management appeal, the unit was both
making and packing the baby clothes in an effort to get them out
by the end of the week. So Lata, Amina and myself were again
packing – this time the much disputed baby clothes. Gillian, the
supervisor, appeared (we were working alongside the unit) and
told us that the orders had to go out that night and so we must be
quick and get finished. When she had gone Amina responded:
'She'll be lucky, slow down everyone, we want this work to last us
for Monday morning. We're not on minutes for this job and it's a
bit boring, but it's nice and easy, innit.'

We all grinned conspiratorially and Lata produced a child's
shirt she was sewing and wanted to finish for the weekend while
Amina started to fill in her pools coupon. Their resistance to the
imposition of what they considered to be unfair targets and,
therefore, super-exploitation was total; they maintained this
collectively and individually over the two weeks that the baby
clothes were being produced. The clothes were not ready for
Friday evening, but were packed by lunch-time on Monday. The
women had fought and won their own time back again.

Gillian, the supervisor, was caught between management and
the women. As a young supervisor, she had none of the power or

confidence to support the women in the way that Eve and Jessie might have done. Her unit recognised her lack of experience and, although they were angry with her, they generously tried to see her point of view. She responded by becoming ill – her way of coping with the pressures of her job.

Although this particular row was prolonged and dramatic, the women resisted the minutes in many quieter ways every day. There were individual strategies: Suraya's, for example, was to work at a pace that suited her: 'I could work faster and do more so that I could be a star grade, but I don't want the pressure. I like to save a bit so I can work the same every day and talk and laugh a bit. I wouldn't like to be a star grade because then I couldn't have any fun with anyone like we have here.'

If the minutes were not the subject of dispute they provided the basis for many of the conversations that women had during the working day. Complaining about the minutes, like complaining about other aspects of their working lives, generated feelings of support in a shared situation. But the complaints did more than that: they provided the women with knowledge about the workings of the minutes across the department. Gracie, who was said not to support the women on her unit, was, in my hearing, one of the severest critics of the bonus system:

> You know, Sallie, the minutes are so hard now that the company can save money. They give out such high minutes that all the girls are getting downgraded, so it's cheaper to employ them to do what an A grade used to do. It's not fair. It's not right that they should treat people like this. Then there's no work, so how can the girls earn their money? In all my years I've never seen it like this.

Gracie's criticism was a clear penetration of what the minutes system was essentially about – cheapening labour in an effort to keep profits. This was not, as she said, 'fair'.

The notion of fairness was expressed in the idea that a fair day's work demanded a fair day's pay – an idea of justice made impossible by the minutes system. The inequities of the system were very clearly set out by Cherry, who had been on Gracie's unit before it was split up.

> Well, I'm here now. We're all split up all over the floor. None of us like it because we always worked well together,

Gracie's line was a happy one. But what can you do? It's
not up to us to decide, is it? We do what we're told, that's
happening more and more here now. It's much more strict
than it used to be. Take the minutes. I'm not kidding,
while I've been here in the last four years they've gone
down and down. They get tighter and tighter and you can't
get the target out. We've had rows all week on this unit
and I'm waiting for Bill or Annie [the union reps] to
come and see about mine. They are impossible. They are
doing us out of our money and the union just come
along and say they're all right, every time. They don't do
much for us, I can tell you. They work for management.
The company is swindling us by making the minutes lower
and lower which means we can't get the target so we are
downgraded, so they have to pay us less to do the same
amount as we were doing last year for more money. I'm not
kidding that's how they are saving money, and they do it to
everyone.

Cherry, too, had cracked the minutes code and she saw beyond the
numbers to a system which increased the power of management at
the same time as it paid her less to work harder. She provided an
analysis of these relations and the role of the union within them,
something I will pursue in the next chapter. Cherry, armed with
her understanding of the situation, was also very clear about what
should be done:

The trouble is that the young ones don't know any
different, but we do, those of us who have been here a bit
and what we should really do is *all* of us get together and
fight against it, but some of them won't do that. Some, like
I said, don't know any different, others are too frightened
of losing their job and, you see, we haven't got a union that
really fights for us. So, it's like if they give us a rise they
will want it back, won't they? The minutes will get even
tighter. I'd rather say stuff the rise and let's have proper
minutes that we can work at and get our target and earn
our money like we used to, not having the company swindle
us out of it, that's what they're doing you know with these
minutes and the rise will make it worse, that's me having
my moan for the day [*laughs*]. But it isn't funny, is it?

Cherry's angry and eloquent account of what it means to labour under a capitalist labour process speaks volumes. Clearly and precisely, she is able to unravel the work-study process and to see its effects within the factory among the women. The point is to fight. But a powerful union is important to success and Cherry, like the other women, was aware that the union lacked power and a will to struggle for its members. For the individual woman, the outcome of the swindle was her wages. Before I move on to take up Cherry's comments on the union, I want to close this chapter by looking at wages.

Wages for women

Friday was pay day; the day when everyone in John's department collected a guaranteed weekly wage which varied with their grade plus any bonus they might have been able to earn. Their wages were the outcome of the bargaining power of the union in the factory and the struggles that took place on the shop-floor. Although there is a national agreement for hosiery workers, StitchCo, like Courtaulds, struck a company-based bargain with their workers, which did not mean that workers received the highest rate for the job. The women worked a 37-and-a-half-hour week (average for women working full-time in the hosiery industry), with 28 days' holiday (including public holidays). Like other factories in Needletown, StitchCo closed down for two weeks in the summer.

On Fridays, the department closed at three-thirty (not a great concession as women in other local hosiery factories often finished at midday on Fridays); from three o'clock onwards the supervisors collected pay packets from the cash office and distributed them to the members of their units. The supervisors were paid first. They, too, were graded – A, B, C – and their earnings corresponded to these bands. Top earnings, which included a £2 'Needletown rate', were £77.40; at the lower end of the scale, a supervisor would earn £64.94. This was the top pay for an assistant supervisor, whose range of possible earnings was from £56.12 to £64.94. The supervisors were classified alongside technical staff on a factory-wide basis; predictably, as these were male occupations, the earnings of technical staff such as the sewing machine mechanics were far in excess of the supervisors'. Supervisors earned only two-thirds to three-quarters of the pay of the men.

The make-up operatives also earned a £2 'Needletown rate', but their earnings were generally lower: a star-grade machinist or examiner had a pay packet of £66.99; A-grade, £61.70; B-grade, £56.04; C-grade, £51.39; D-grade, £43.37; E-grade, £37.71; F-grade, £35.71. The basic rate was paid at 2.058p per minute and the bonus rate at 3.087p per minute. Top earnings for a machinist were £81.02, which included the £2 'Needletown rate'.

The women working on the presses and the irons were paid at a higher rate. The star-grade worker had an average pay packet of £79.19; A-grade, £73.89; B-grade, £68.24; C-grade, £63.24; D-grade, £56.94; and E-grade, £51.57. The basic rate per minute was 2.551p and the bonus rate 3.827p. This allowed for top earnings of £99.96, which again included the £2 'Needletown rate'. Throughout most of my year in John's department, an average 20 per cent of women were earning star-grade rates – but not necessarily with bonuses on top of this. Consequently, those who earned top money were a small handful and average earnings were lower – but reckoned to be 'good' money by a union representative who told me: 'The women earn £60–£65 a week at StitchCo so, I'm afraid to say, it's good money for women.' This was, of course, below the average weekly earnings (gross) for women manual workers in Britain: in April 1981 they were £74.60, or 61.2 per cent of male earnings. So women at StitchCo were earning an even smaller proportion of average male wages.

The wage rates in the department were acknowledged by management to be lower than the wages earned in some other hosiery factories. However, the guarantee of a weekly wage was set against the low level of pay. Women received the graded wage on the basis of a week which comprised 2,400 minutes at the basic rate. Extra speed meant that more minutes could be earned and these were paid at a higher rate in order to provide a bonus scheme. Throughout 1980 and 1981, though, many of the units did not have the steady flow of work essential to bonus earnings. In fact, throughout the lean months of the summer of 1980, supply shortages meant that many women were not able to achieve their graded targets. The company did take this into account: women were not downgraded nor was the guaranteed weekly wage suspended during this time (although it was discussed, an issue I pursue in the next chapter).

The women felt that they paid a very high price for the security of the guaranteed week, both in terms of the targets that were set and in terms of the control that the bonus system exercised over their working lives. Some would have preferred to return to a straight piecework system because they felt they had more control over their own production and their time. Nevertheless, guaranteed wages did look attractive in the climate of the deepening recession and the contraction of the clothing industry. Many of the women had friends employed in other firms who were on short-time; as the year progressed, many had family members who had been made redundant or who were working one day a week.

Women on the same unit were likely to be earning highly differentiated wages. This meant that they often opened their wage packets on their own, away from the other women. The privacy surrounding the women when they were paid was part of the life of the shopfloor. The 'young ones' had more to share; they were among the lower earners and would discuss their wages and complain about their pay in small groups. They were not alone in this complaining. Most of the women were unhappy about their earnings – especially in relation to those of friends in other factories, or in factories where they had worked.

The supervisor brought the wages into the distribution area and Marsha opened her wage packet. This week, because she had had a day off, she earned £39. She was 20, living at home with her mum and her 18-month-old daughter. Angie, who worked on the bagging machine putting polythene over clothes, was a B-grade worker. She had earned £54 basic pay plus £13.96 in bonus this week. Tax and national insurance relieved her of £13.40 so she took home £54.56. Angie, 17, was engaged and living at home, as was Beth, an examiner, who earned even less:

> Well, you know what I think, the money is terrible. I get £43.10 basic and I get £31.40 to take home. What can you do with that, I ask you? I think it's some of the worst money around. They pay you this miserable amount and they expect the earth for it. They want you to be quick and they want the quality right, and they don't want to pay for it. My money has to pay me mam and do everything else and you can't do much with 30 quid.

Frankie agreed with Beth:

> Well, it's got worse at this place. Two years ago I was taking home £52 a week, now it's just over £50. I think

the wages they pay here are terrible and definitely getting worse because the minutes are getting tighter every time they are done.

Marsha chipped in: 'This company is so mean that if you don't count it some weeks it's short. They try to fiddle you here.' The lads, who were also counting their wages, said: 'Yeah, it's poxy money here.'

If the lads had been trainee knitters or technicians or dyers they would have grossed over £58 per week at the age of 18. Young women, at 16, training to be machinists were on approximately £35 a week. They all agreed that, unlike the wages, 'It's good money for training.'

Frankie, Elaine and I discussed earnings in the canteen. I put it to them that women earned much less than men in the hosiery industry.

Elaine You're quite right and it's not fair. The knitters are a
  law unto themselves. They don't have supervisors looking
  them over the whole time. But it's all shift work and most
  women wouldn't want to do three shifts even if they could.
  It's just not possible with a family. You would never
  see your kids. There are a few old women left over from the
  war, that's all.
Sallie Knitters here earn £120–£130 a week.
Elaine Yeah, and they earn a lot more in other places.
  My husband earns £140–£150 a week as a sock knitter.
Frankie Yeah, Jack earns £155 a week where he works, so the
  wages even for the men are low here.
Elaine The other thing they don't do here is pay your holiday
  money as a percentage of what you've earned. In a lot of
  hosiery firms you get a percentage, say 10 per cent, that's
  what my husband gets, for every £1,000 you earn. So, his
  last holiday pay was £600. You get paid on what you earn
  so the more you earn the better it is. It works like an
  incentive, not like this guaranteed-week business where you
  get £50 a week, finish. If you work in the big firms in the
  hosiery you earn a lot of money, but not here.
Frankie I tell you the money we earn here is *scab labour*,
  that's what it is. The bloody union should be doing
  something about it, but they are so pally-pally with
  management they let our pay go to the dogs.

At this time the union was fighting for the 1980–1 pay rise; as Shanta explained to the women, the negotiations were not going well: 'Well, the company has offered 2.5 per cent, but the union says "No" it must be 4 or 5 per cent because everything is going up. But it's difficult because the company doesn't have much money and we don't want to lose jobs, so we can't expect much.' The women grimaced at this news.

Jackie It's ridiculous, 2.5 per cent, *hah*, you might as well not
   bother. Look at the way everything is going up. We have to
   pay more national insurance in the new year and with the
   prices so high our wages will soon be worth nothing at all.
Bridget You're right, electricity is going up, gas is going up,
   the phone is going up. I tell you the only thing that is
   going down is the minutes.

The other women laughed but Bridget said, more soberly: 'It's not funny really, we are really out of pocket now.'

The women were generally pessimistic about the future of the industry and worried about job losses. They saw little hope of a major improvement in their wages. Tula spoke for many when she said:

> I still don't know how they're going to give us a rise. The
> union must be negotiating at the moment to get the next
> one. What they will be asking for and what StitchCo are
> going to come up with the way things are we don't know.
> The trouble is we never hear until it's all over, and we are
> then told what we are going to get. I don't see how our
> wages are going to go up much.

Eve, who represented the supervisors, replied:

> My view is we should have as little as possible and keep our
> jobs. It's the view of a lot of the women. But, on the other
> hand, no one is saying to the shareholders don't get any
> dividend, are they? It's not a thing I dare say downstairs at
> the union meeting.

Eve's comments suggested an astute understanding of the way in which the recession demands different things from different sides on the capital–labour divide and how these differences are not on the agenda for open discussion by the union. This ability to situate the struggle for higher wages within the wider economic situation was also expressed by other women, like Elaine, who commented:

The hosiery is in such a bad state that the employers haven't got money for rises and if the gaffers haven't got any money then we certainly won't get any. It's this bloody Thatcher. The companies can't afford to pay off their loans and all companies have to borrow to invest. Then they get to a point where the money coming in won't meet the money going out and they're stuck. That's what happened to the company I was working for when I was made redundant.

The wage negotiations settled finally on a split settlement which spread the rise over two financial years. An initial 3 per cent was followed by another in the spring. In addition, the union fought for another day's holiday but failed to affect working hours or to win extra payments for extra responsibilities. It was, as in previous years, a low settlement and did nothing to counter the view among the women that 'You can't live on this money.' Thatcher and the company were all to blame, as Tessa said: 'How we're supposed to live on these wages I don't know. And the budget will put everything up. It's really bad isn't it, Sal . . . This bloody Thatcher, she couldn't be worse could she?'

Very few women quarrelled with Tessa's comments on Thatcher; for them, Tory policies were responsible for keeping wage rates down and putting women out of work.[16] But the history of women's wages as non-living wages is longer than the life of Margaret Thatcher's government. As other writers have clearly shown, it is a history of the relationship between capital and male trade unionists who, together, conspired to create the family wage thereby depressing the wages of women workers.[17] Current wages for women are the outcome of a long patriarchal history which has celebrated male wages and the male breadwinner while the woman worker has been seen as someone who works not for wages, but for pin money. The women of John's department were acutely aware of this, and their response was unequivocal: 'Pin money, *rubbish*. I work for money and so do all women. This nonsense about pin money, it's all rubbish, women have to work to keep the family going and that's been going on for years.' Eve was also very scathing about the romantic view taken by some of the young women towards the male wage: 'These young ones who think they are going to be at home on their husband's money are dreaming. Life's not like that, it's too costly.' The dream, of course, was built upon the notion of the family wage which the women understood to be a myth because it didn't cover the costs of reproduction. Additional resources were necessary and these came from women's work, paid and unpaid.

Wages for women, then, like the minutes, were discussed in relation to a much wider and deeper understanding of what wages actually represent. The women were acutely conscious of the fact that they didn't earn a living wage and that this imposed severe limitations on their ability to claim economic independence and personal autonomy. Instead, women looked to the family and saw their wages as part of the way in which working-class people sought a viable standard of living in the low-wage economy that Britain had become. They protested about their wages. Central to their protest was the sense, expressed here by Rekha, that the union was failing them: 'The union has raised the union fee from 35p to 38p. That's all they can do, get more money *from* us, not *for* us.'

As this chapter has shown, women fought against low wages. Nevertheless, they genuinely felt that the most important weapon in the struggle – the union – was not with them. The story of the union and its relations with women workers begins with the day of action in Needletown.

4

Big brothers and little sisters

The year 1980 was a bad one for manufacturing industry in
Britain; the knitting industry suffered large numbers of bank-
ruptcies and thousands of jobs disappeared.[1] The deepening
recession, coupled with the growing volume of cheap imports
from overseas and the Italian penetration into the quality-end of
the market, showed in falling profits, empty order books and
redundancies. Consequently, both unions and employers had an
interest in drawing attention to the fate of the industry and they
came together to stage a series of one-day events in the major
knitting towns. Marches and rallies were held by unions throughout
the Midlands in November 1980, with the full backing of company
managements.

The employers, of course, had much to gain from supporting
the marches and joining with the union initiative. Management at
StitchCo thought the march a splendid idea and John did a lot to
drum up support for the event in the department. But this
enthusiasm did not extend to the provision of paid time off for
those who wanted to join the march. Women on the shopfloor saw
the contradiction clearly. They wanted to march but were not
prepared to make up the time in order to keep their wages: 'Well,
I'm not going because you have to make up the time. If it was paid
I would go along. I support it and I've got all the songs for singing
on the march.'

Elaine disagreed with Beth: 'Well, I think we should all go. It's
no good the union organising this if we don't support it. Our
livelihood is at stake, you know, the jobs of thousands of people.
So many have lost them already and it's going to get far worse after
January.'

Her words convinced Beth and many of the women who worked
near her and they all joined the march. Their discussion was
echoed elsewhere:

Tula I'm not going. They want me to make up the time. I
  haven't got time to do that. They've given me some songs
  to sing, better to give me the money for the time I lose.
  The supervisors will go because they don't have to make up
  the time.
Carol Yes, but we will, we'll probably come in early a couple
  of days.
Eve You see, I'm trying to rouse this lot. It's their jobs at
  stake but they want the company to pay them for going. It will
  never do that, but they can make up the time.

At midday there was a sudden wave of enthusiasm for the march
and women on Eve's unit were the first to line up, ready to go.
They were joined by other women, including all the supervisors
and assistants, and the mood of the department became festive as
the women began to sing songs and don mobcaps, made from
waste material, in nationalistic red, white and blue, and to wave
Union Jacks. Gina carried a cuddly teddy bear with a Union Jack
under its arm, which she waved at everyone. As we gathered
together, Gracie looked across at the press area where the women
were not preparing to join us and said: 'It's typical. These
coloureds won't come, but it's their jobs and but for them there
might be jobs for all of us anyway, I've got no time for it.'
  Gracie's comment cut through the solidarity generated by the
march because she suggested a conflict of interests between black
and white women over jobs. Her racism ignored the real situation
and the struggles waged by black women; they confounded her by
showing up in large numbers for the march. Between 60 and 70
women left the department; at least 30 per cent were Indian
women. Many of them came from Gillian's unit where Shanta had
encouraged them to join in. Some of the Indian women were older
and had difficulty keeping pace with the march. As they told me,
though: 'It's important. We have to save our jobs, we will go all
the way with the march.'
  We assembled on the main road outside the factory and the
union stewards gave us stickers. We were joined by a group of
Right to Work marchers who set up the chant, 'Maggie, Maggie,
Maggie, Out, Out, Out'. The women around me soon took up the
chant and joined in, in good voice, waving their stickers and their
hats in the air. There was a carnival atmosphere as we set off; a
band would not have been out of place. The women stuck stickers

all over me, each other and any passerby they could find. We linked arms and moved forward at a halting pace, our line stopping and starting every few minutes because some of the women kept losing their unsuitable stiletto-heeled sandals along the way. We were jostled and overtaken by marchers wearing flat shoes and travelling at speed while they laughed at our slow progress. As we came into the centre of town we were met by cheers, waves and claps from shoppers and by-standers and this encouraged everyone to sing more loudly and to laugh and shout at the people on the pavements. The younger women, especially, were full of excitement and became more energetic and more boisterous as we marched, pushing one another around, falling over and running from the back towards the front of the march. Everyone was enjoying the event and the lunch-time revelry.

The Right to Work marchers had travelled along the route with us and were trying to give out leaflets when they were rushed by the police, who charged towards them and tried to move them on, away from the march. Our group hissed and booed very loudly and shouted at the police to 'bugger off'. The Right to Work group set up the 'Maggie, Out' chant again. Everyone joined in, shouting at the top of their lungs with great passion, while they turned to one another and said, 'I hate her.' But management, who were now walking close by, were very bothered by the Right to Work marchers and tried to tell the women that they were not connected to the hosiery industry and that the women should not support them. Management's attempts to distance the women from the anti-Thatcher chants and problems with the police were wholly unsuccessful: no one listened.

At the main hall in town, there were speeches and telegrams of support to conclude the march. Women from John's department had to leave quickly to get back to work, though they were loath to go and would have preferred to have marched back to the factory. Instead, the young women linked arms and sang as they moved off, while the older women drifted back more slowly.

I stayed on to listen to the speeches which were deadly, slow, laboured and not helped by the mayor who had forgotten both his lines and who the other people on the platform were. The situation was saved by Ada, a popular local trade unionist, who was given a loud cheer. Unlike the men, she did not deliver a lecture on the economic ills of Britain, but made an impassioned plea for the employers and the government to understand the fear of redundancies on the shopfloor and the misery brought to families by unemployment which was wasting the talents and energies of a whole generation. The audience applauded long and loud when she left. They, too, began to leave.

Back at the factory everyone was recounting their own version of events. The young women, especially, never having been involved in a march before, were fired with the experience which they tried to prolong by singing and chanting slogans through the afternoon and occasionally waving the hats they had worn. The march generated a tremendous spirit of unity on the shopfloor, coupled with a sense that perhaps the women could do something to stop the decline in the industry, after all.

The realisation of this power, however, was crucially related to the union organisation to which the women belonged. This was a responsible union which enjoyed good relations with the employers – so good, in fact, that the union could get workers out on a march to save an industry which was not prepared to pay them for the hour they spent marching in defence not only of jobs, but profits. The march sets the scene for the discussion in this chapter which follows the relations between management, the union and the shopfloor, and looks at the struggles that the shopfloor representatives engage in, in an effort to generate a strong union.

All together now

The fact remains that for all the inadequacies of the trade union movement, it is men, not women, whose voice is heard, whose strength is felt, whose investment in the organisation yields the greater dividend.

– Anna Coote[2]

The union which organised the factory is a typical example of the situation described by Anna Coote. Though the women were not unaware of this, 'the union' seemed so impenetrable, so immovable and so deaf to their voices. Women, it is clear, show a great willingness and ability to struggle and resist on the shopfloor, and to do so in an informed and articulate way. They are united in a fight against a labour process which seeks to deskill and degrade their labour and which divides them into units separated by machinery, by distance and by break-times. Thus, the shopfloor has little opportunity to come together as a whole. All the women at StitchCo were members of the union: the problem is that unionists are brothers not sisters. Like the construction of the skilled worker as a white male, the trade unionist who emerged so clearly from the craft unions is also a white male.[3] The language and organisational forms of trade unionism are more than simply male; they are patriarchal. Men in general hold power and exercise authority; older men exercise both in relation to women and to younger men.

As Sarah Boston has shown, there is a long history to the exclusion, denial and separation of women in the trade union movement.[4] Her historical picture of the trade union movement is reproduced in the hosiery unions where fears of dilution, unequal pay, appeals to the family wage and the construction of the breadwinner as exclusively male may all be found in the official history.[5] As a consequence, when the phrase 'a woman's place is in her union' is put to women their response is likely to be that the emphasis must be given to the words *her union*, not the idea that women should come into the unions. They are in unions in large numbers, yet current organisation and practices do not take account of this. Such a situation will continue until women have finally and successfully laid the ghost of a trade union world which is constructed on the assumption that the 'normal' equals the 'white male'. Similar assumptions also underpin the treatment of the unemployed where job losses among women have been too easily ignored in the statistics and by the trade union movement.

Nearly 13,000 jobs, or 12 per cent of the labour force, were lost in the hosiery and knitwear industry in 1980. Additional jobs were also lost in the allied areas of dyeing and finishing and lace-making.[6] Losses such as these had a major impact on the union's membership which fell by over 8,000 during this year. In December 1979 the union had 70,484 members, of whom 51,026 were women; by December 1980 it had 61,837 members, of whom 44,566 were women. The total loss was 8,647 members, of whom the greater proportion, not surprisingly, were women.[7] The union is clearly numerically dominated by women; predictably, the full-time officials, the executive and workplace representatives are predominantly male. Only three of the 23 members of the national executive committee were women and this 'large' number was very new (one woman member had been the norm for years). Recently, the idea that a full-time women's organiser should be appointed has been discussed by the union; lack of funds now makes this unlikely. The same constraints also apply to the work of unionising the growing numbers of homeworkers – or out-workers – who are, of course, women.

The union had two full-time officials on site at StitchCo – Annie and Bill, both of whom were paid by the company. Bill was a good-humoured man in his fifties. His style was avuncular (which suited the paternalism of the company) and he never seemed to be ruffled by the dramas around him; Annie, on the other hand, was more assertive and energetic. In addition, the union worked with departmental representatives who attended the factory meetings and supported the women on the units. Eve was the rep for the supervisory staff and Shanta for the rest of the department, the 'operatives'. They also worked as the health-and-safety represen-tatives in the department.

The union and its officials were well integrated into the company. They were present at monthly grading meetings and signed the warning letters alongside management in the case of disciplinary actions and downgradings. At the same time, it was the union officials who were called in to mediate in disputes over the minutes. As the last chapter showed, they did not always rush to take up such cases – undoubtedly part of a strategy which allowed for a cooling-down period before they came to the department. There were only two people to cater for a factory of over 2,000; they were also required to advise branch factories, attend meetings with management, advise safety reps and maintain their own contacts with the union. So it was not surprising that they did not always arrive immediately they were called. It was easy for me to be reasonable from a distance – it was not my bonus that was threatened nor my job that was at the centre of a dispute. Women on the shopfloor were understandably angry and frustrated by what they conceived as lack of interest on the part of the union, generally, and the union reps, specifically. Union dues were deducted by the company finance office; contact between union officials and the shopfloor was thus minimised – a point not lost on Annie.

For many of the women, the union lacked credibility. The officials on site were, after all, paid by the management and the women had a very healthy suspicion of this arrangement. Their view was that this inclined the union officials to answer first to management and only second to their membership. The union seemed as far away as management, locked into an alien world of meetings and men which somehow never seemed to relate to the world of women in the department. Of the two officials, it was noticeable that Annie had much greater credibility than Bill. She had been a machinist and was acutely aware of the ways in which the union failed its membership and the ways in which this failure was bound to its sexism. Annie was a very able, lively woman whose opinions and judgements were trusted and valued by women. She was one of 'us' and it was her name that was called out when a union official was needed. It was Annie who was most able to articulate the feelings of unease that many women had about the union. They felt strongly that they were locked out by their 'brothers' – not only from positions, but from discussions, as well. They were not consulted; their words were not listened to. Yet, as we have seen, so many women were crystal-clear about their position on the shopfloor in a time of ever-deepening recession.[8]

Though Annie was an incredibly busy woman, she was always willing to discuss with me the question of the union and women workers. In these discussions, she tried out her ideas and her analyses of some of the issues which she felt were important. She then went to the members and engaged in discussions on the shopfloor, unselfconsciously, as a woman who understood the power and potential of other women.

One day I encountered her and she asked me whether I had seen an article in the *Financial Times* on women in the hosiery industry. The journalist had come to interview Annie and some women who were in danger of redundancy at a local factory. Annie was furious and told me:

> She was writing this article on unemployment and
> redundancy among women in the hosiery and she was saying
> that the women were working for pin money. We were
> really furious with her. She had been to see management
> and she just took their part. We wanted to see what she
> was going to write before it went into print. She was sitting
> there, telling us to move to a new job, no thought for the
> girls' families, their husbands' jobs. We can't move like
> that. It's all right for her maybe. We got the idea if she was
> married she certainly didn't have any kids to take account of.
> We said to her: 'Do you work then, for pin money?' And
> do you know what she said? 'It's not the same, my *career* is
> rather different,' meaning I suppose that we don't have

careers, that women in factories are not serious about their jobs. Huh! Well, we shouted at her on that one, treating us like we're rubbish and she's some high falluting person. We're not having it. I must find out who she is, she was a real case.

Annie's indignation and anger at the suggestion that women worked for pin money, or that factory work was not real work in which women were involved and to which women were committed, was an attack on the trivialisation of women workers and the class bias which she perceived in the journalist. Her understanding of class issues came together with her feminism when she confronted this journalist on the notion of 'pin money'.

Earlier in the year, Annie and I had been discussing the level of redundancies in the hosiery industry and the conversation moved towards the general issue of women in the union. Annie said:

It's impossible, these men still believe that women are working for pin money. I keep telling them that they aren't, no woman works for pin money. These women have families to support, lots of them are on their own bringing up children as single parents, or they are divorced, or, like me, they are looking after their parents and as jobs get more scarce their wages are all the more important. But we mollycoddle the men in this industry. They like to believe that they are the breadwinners and they alone – well, if it was ever true, and I'm not convinced it was, it certainly isn't now. The men get away with murder in this company. Just for example, every night the women leave here one or other of them is checked by security. But the men, they get into their cars and off they go, especially on the night shift. They get away with just coming and going as they please. You see on the night shift there are only two managers and one of them has been away a lot because he was ill. The men are not supervised like the women. The knitters look after their machines and that's that. They aren't on units like in A department.

Annie made these comments without any prompting, she didn't need any. She knew the history and contemporary situation in the hosiery industry and made a clear connection between male privilege and the construction of the male breadwinner. She also took the point into the area of control: male wages and privileges meant more freedom for men and less for women.

Sallie So, the women are more tightly controlled than the men?

Annie Oh, yes. The units are a different way of working. The men in the dyehouse, the cutters and layer-uppers are just doing their own thing most of the time, in my view. They are really spoilt in this industry and remember it's female dominated, by numbers anyway.

Her final comment shows that she understands the constraints upon numbers as a source of strength. Despite the high number of women, the hosiery industry gives power to men, supports male wages and the men's ability to 'do their own thing'.

Sallie Do women have the same opportunities as men?

Annie No, they don't. Take the knitters, they work three shifts, so the women can't do the job. They [women] are only allowed to work two shifts in this industry. We used to have women knitters – a few anyway – when it was only two shifts, that was 15 years ago. Women are not allowed to work nights, so they can only work two shifts. So, some work in central cutting on the laying up, but not the actual cutting. Women don't have the same opportunities as men in this industry and they are not treated equally, either, because the men control things.

Sallie In the union as well?

Annie Absolutely! Our membership is more female than male, but the union is controlled *by* men and run *for* the men. We have one woman on the executive. We always have *one* woman on the executive, but that's it. They decide who they are going to have and, quite honestly, if your face fits, you're in. I did apply once and so did Ella [the woman who preceded Annie] but she said they wouldn't take you from StitchCo. They never take anyone from here. Well, I did get through to the short list which no one else had ever done. Then I went for the interviews, a medical and before that they make you write papers for them. I got into the interview – well, I didn't know who these people were and they never introduced themselves to me. They made me feel as though I shouldn't bother them. I didn't get it. StitchCo

is part of it, not knowing them was the other. You see
StitchCo pays us, helps with cars so it's useful to the union
to have us here because StitchCo is so large. It means the
union can leave StitchCo to itself, they come up here
sometimes but it's mainly for a social chat.

Annie continued: 'Well, they are the men who are supposed to be
organising us, the women. They don't know what women want
and the problems that they have. Quite honestly, they don't have
a clue about what women want or how women understand things –
and maybe they don't want to know.'

Annie's comments are a severe indictment of the men in
positions of power within her union. Their lack of interest in the
membership and the priority they give to the male knitters is a
demonstration of the situation of big brothers and little sisters:
women's work and contribution are minimised, trivialised and
viewed as peripheral in relation to the work and contribution of
male members of the union. Annie's critique shows a union
organisation which reproduces the patriarchal forms of the factory –
hardly a promising vehicle for presenting the views of women and
representing their interests. But as Annie later pointed out, all was
not lost because those women who were in a position to do so,
spoke out for women and women's interests. In fact, she was
encouraged by recent developments:

It's much better now because being on the district helps
you to know what's coming off in the union, so now I
know more of the people who interviewed me and much
more about the union and how it operates. The district,
because there are us couple of women, takes women more
seriously. For example, we had a long debate over the
maternity arrangements. All firms must give time off for the
first antenatal appointment and the woman must have
a card for the others, but not all the clinics give
appointment cards. We're much better off here than some
of the firms because pretty much they let you go, but
leaving it to management's discretion doesn't help women
in the smaller firms. We didn't make a decision about what
to do about it, but at least we discussed it. Then, recently,
I went to a day school on the new Employment Act because
that has new rules about maternity leave and how you get
your job back. You would think with all the women

workers in the industry the union would have organised some leaflets or information for us, but there isn't any. I rang the office this morning to get some stuff from them and, nothing.

The lack of attention given by the union to changes in the law surrounding maternity leave is another instance of the lack of interest in women's issues articulated by Annie. She can see quite clearly the way in which the woman worker in the hosiery industry is disadvantaged by the emphasis upon the male breadwinner and the consequent lack of attention to women's concerns – in short, the assumption made by male trade unionists that the world of *labour* is a *male* world.[9] It is the sons of the working class who are celebrated as folk heroes; the women who are expected to line the streets to applaud. The surprise is that women like Annie have the patience and the will to work with these men, while remaining firmly tied to the membership and the world of women.

In its concern for skilled male workers, the union contributed to a social construction of woman that was firmly tied to an outmoded – but, for them, useful – view of women as adjuncts to men, as dependent and domesticated. It is therefore hardly surprising that the women on the shopfloor tended to write the union off: Asha's comment – 'The union, the management, they are all the same' – was a view generally held. Trying to discuss the union with women generated some of the shortest conversations that I had. It was not that the women were not interested; simply, they were frustrated by the lack of consultation. They participated little in their union because no one ever asked them or suggested that they might have a voice:

Tula The union must be trying to negotiate our next rise at the moment. The trouble is we never hear anything until it's all over and then we are told what we are going to get.

Maria Yes, that's right. My husband is always going to meetings about redundancies and their pay, but we never hear anything here.

Tula The problem is we're not properly organised. We just take it – minutes, targets. We don't have a proper union here. The union is great for StitchCo. Bill knows all the managers. Do you know we used to go to union meetings and the dyers and finishers and the cutters would come well organised and make demands and there was Bill and there were we without anything properly organised or any demands to make? The union doesn't help us here. The union doesn't fight the bonus scheme and it doesn't insist we keep our own jobs. Here we are doing this and that, moved around here and there. I tell you, if you call the union official he lectures you, that's what he does. The union is useless. They are going to make people redundant in the knitting, maybe 25 per cent of them. What's the union saying about that, I will tell you: *nothing*. They have their rules and their agreements – that's all you hear about and they go by these.

Amina agreed with much of what Tula said:

Amina The union works for the company, not for us. I told Bill I wasn't going to pay the union because he never helps us. When you call them for the minutes they don't come. If you are sick, you have to ask Annie so many times to get your sick pay. If you are in trouble, they are in the office – but they never try to help you. They just don't say anything; you just have to present your opinion yourself because they don't speak up for you. They do what the company wants them to.

Sallie Have they assisted the Indian women at all?

Amina Indian, English, it's the same. The white women get the same treatment from Bill and Annie as we do. They don't do anything for us. They don't tell us what is happening. They don't fight for us. It's not worth paying to be a member. All they do is collect your money and that's it.

Sallie But they negotiate your rises, your wages.

Amina Huh, have you *seen* our wages?

The union and the shopfloor were miles apart. This distance was increased by the interventions of the anti-union views held by some of the women. Their views were deeply ambivalent and were summed up in a coffee bar discussion, when Norah said:

I don't hold with unions, they are full of agitators. They do some good things I suppose. We're all in the union here. You don't get a choice now. At one time you could opt out, now we all pay our 30p. They did do good things in the past when things were really bad for working people.

The contradictions were not just part of the perspective of the membership. For example, one male union official told me, in contrast to the general union view that women were unmilitant: 'Women don't accept compromise the way men do. If we've put in a claim for 10 per cent and we get 9 per cent the women will strike for the extra 1 per cent. I don't know what it is, if they've decided on something nothing will budge them.' It is also interesting to compare this notion with the earlier views on women expressed by management, that women are somehow more amenable. The two views, it seems to me, come together in a hidden assumption about women: that they are *irrational* and the fact that you can't budge them is part of this. The union might have celebrated the solidarity of women workers as activists; instead, there was an implied criticism in the above statement.

Sisters

In the middle of this minefield of contradictions and misunderstandings were the two departmental representatives, Eve and Shanta. Somehow, they had to deal with the sense of powerlessness and mistrust which translated itself into the instrumentalism which most women settled upon as the only viable relationship to have with the union. The union would be called upon on matters of the minutes, wages and issues which were essentially economic ones.

Though Eve was considerably more experienced in union matters, Shanta spoke Gujarati and this it was supposed would assist in getting the union message across to those Indian women who knew little English. While this was an important consideration, the union should perhaps have realised that, for Shanta, the union was a novel and alien environment and that she needed help from union officials. They didn't assist her. Instead, Eve was left to try and fill this gap. Shanta often discussed with me issues which she saw as problems for her union work. Most of all, she wanted ideas on how best to put the union case to Indian women in a way which would generate support for the union. Her task was a difficult one, partly due to the general lack of support for the union, but also because she was a young woman trying to put the case to older women. Her union role reversed a cultural hierarchy in which she was a daughter. She was not yet a married woman, nor a mother – her status was ambiguous. Nevertheless, she tried valiantly:

Shanta I try to tell them about the union and how it helps us
as workers, but they always ask: 'What has it done for me?'
They don't understand it, especially the older Indian ladies
because they came from Uganda and such places. They have
never worked before they came here and there are so many
things they don't understand.

Sallie What do they want the union to do for them?

Shanta Once they asked me to ask at the reps meeting
whether they can wear saris to work. We are not allowed to
wear them because of safety. I told them this. It is also the
case that we younger ones don't want to wear saris to work,
and for the married girls if they could wear them then their
husbands would make them do it. So, we don't want it
anyway. But these older ladies said, 'You ask because at
other places they can wear them.' Well, I ask and the
management say no because it is not safe at work. So, the
Asian ladies say to me, 'Ah, your union is no good, I want
to come out of the union, bring me the forms.' Anything
they don't like, they want to leave the union.

The contradictions in this situation were enormous. Shanta was
much closer to her own age group and they would have made quite
clear to her that they did not welcome the opportunity to wear
saris at work: they didn't want to inhibit their freedom of choice
about dress. The older Indian women wanted a recognition of
their culture and their status as women in the Indian community.
They very much disliked wearing Western clothes and most wore
trousers with smock-like tops in order to retain their propriety.
This older generation of women also came from a domestic
environment in which unions were not necessarily supported.
There was nothing in their experience or the ideology of their
community which lent support to trade unionism – although this
has not stopped some of them being in the forefront of union
struggles. Their request for 'the forms' does at least suggest that
they had grasped the importance of bureaucratic means in union
affairs.

Shanta continued:

Another case was when we have Diwali. They said they
wanted to have a day off because it is our Christmas, a big
festival for us. So, I go back to the union and I ask about it
and the union manager [*sic*] says collect some signatures on

a piece of paper which says that you want that day off. So, everybody signs and I go back to the next meeting and they say all right. I think this is good and go back to the Indian ladies and they said: 'We want to be paid for the day off.' But, the company can't do that because they pay us to be away at your Christmas. It will be ten days this year and it is Christmas for the whole country and we live here so we have to take that holiday. Anyway, they said, 'Bring us the forms, your union is no good, we want to leave.'

I was so fed up, I said, 'Leave the union and then if something happens and you need some help, don't ask the union to help you.' I was really angry. You know I talk to them in our own language but they still don't understand. They get an idea about something and if it doesn't come right for them they just say the whole thing is no good.

They come to me to explain things and the union manager comes to me to explain things and they don't understand. I try, but it's like Jayaben, she was on the sick and then she came to me and said she didn't get the right money. The problem was she didn't have a sick note for all the time she was away. Finally, she realised this. Another one was sick on holiday and couldn't understand why she didn't get sick pay *and* her wages. I try to explain, but it is very difficult.

Shanta often seemed overwhelmed by the task and this was not surprising. Her own reference to the union 'manager', while it expressed the view the women held of the union representative in many ways, was a terminological confusion which expressed Shanta's own difficulties in understanding the union position generally. She was not incompetent as a union representative, but could have been much more effective if the union had supported her better. Too often, for example, she missed the departmental representatives' meetings and she could never understand why or how this happened. Similarly, she was not kept in the picture on negotiations or disputes. Obviously, this helped management but it did nothing for women in the department or for the union and its relations with its membership. At the same time Shanta saw clearly that the union was a potential source of support for workers. She told me that she had tried to explain the 1976 Grunwick strike (which involved mainly Asian workers) to the women as a strike about having a union 'like we've got'.

A system of properly elected union representatives would, of course, have meant a different level of engagement by members and the union, but there was no pressure for this. It was part of the cosy accommodation that had been forged between union and management in the factory and enforced by MDW. Many of the problems Shanta encountered were a consequence of this. Such an accommodation left out of account union reps and members. Annie and Bill, while not unaware of the difficulties which Shanta faced, seemed powerless to assist her. When I talked to Annie about the relationship between the union and the Indian women in the factory she replied:

> They don't understand what the union is all about. It's not surprising is it? These women have never worked before and they come here and suddenly they are in a factory. The trouble is they quarrel so much between themselves. We've got Indian reps like Shanta and Jyoti in socks and they are nice girls, but quite honestly they don't know what is going on and when they try to explain the other girls don't listen, or won't listen. They always come back to me, 'Annie come and tell them.' The trouble is the other women call them names. Jyoti has left her husband and they say she is a loose woman and all that, and Shanta has similar problems.

Lack of support from the shopfloor was an issue raised by Eve, the departmental rep for the supervisors, but it did not stop her taking up issues in relation to wages:

> I became involved in the union about four years ago, but you know, there's no support from the other supervisors. They don't want to know so you get fed up. The first thing I discovered was that Gina had not been paid properly for three months so I went straight to Bill and to management and we had a few rows about it, but she's getting paid properly now. It was the same with Geeta, she was the lowest paid on the whole floor until I made a big fuss and they put her on the right grade. It's not right: she's doing the job, she should get her money.

Eve was known as a fighter, both as a supervisor and as a union representative. As the safety rep she consistently pestered management about hazards in the department; she was also critical of women in the department:

Eve These women don't try to understand what's happening.
   They just accept things. It's the same with the union. Any
   union is only as good as its members and they say to us,
   'You don't do anything.' But when we go to the meetings
   the other departments are ready and they fire away and stir
   things up, but not our lot.

Sallie Why aren't the women more interested?

Eve The main reason is that Bill and Annie are paid by StitchCo
   so they see them as management, they don't trust them, so
   they don't bother and that means you don't get support for
   the union work, and you're working for them.

   Do you know it was only when we had the new bonus
   scheme and I was explaining how the lowest rate couldn't go
   down that Carol came over to me and said that her money was
   nowhere near this. It was £6 down. StitchCo don't pay their
   supervisors properly and if you don't ask they will go on
   paying you less than you should have. I went into the office
   and saw management and told them Carol needs her money
   made up and some back pay. They said it wasn't possible,
   they'd see about it, or something. I told them, right now,
   there's nothing to see about. Anyway, John came in and said,
   'It's simple, pay her what's due and some back pay and get her
   in here to sign for it.'

Eve was very clear about the role of the union and the workplace
reps:

   The trouble with Shanta is she doesn't have a clue really
   about the union, how unions came about, all that. It's not
   surprising is it? I don't want to be unfair. I've got nothing
   against Shanta, it's just that she's not right for a union rep.
   She's too accepting. She will never be a shit stirrer and
   you've got to be to get anything done. Poor Shanta wants
   to please everyone all the time. Well, you can't and I'd
   really fear for her if she went on the shop stewards' course.

Eve was an effective 'shit stirrer' and she did assist Shanta in a way
that I have suggested the union might also have done. Eve's
understanding of her role had grown out of her experiences when,
as a young woman, she had come from Ireland: working among the
weavers in the North of England, she had seen, she felt, the kind of
solidarity which she missed among women at StitchCo.

I have concentrated here on Eve, Annie and Shanta, each of whom brought into sharp focus the complexities of the situation among women in the factory. It seemed important to present the union not simply through the frustrated eyes of women on the shopfloor, who so clearly mistrusted the union. It was rarely referred to as *our* union because women felt it was not theirs. Discussing the union unleashed the kinds of comments we have heard in this chapter – and which could have been reproduced many times over – but this alienation and sense of powerlessness needs to be set against the work of women like Annie, Eve and Shanta, who struggled to keep resistance alive in an unpromising situation. They were not simply incorporated elements of a cosy relationship between management and union: they fought on all issues and within the union for recognition of the problems of women. They faced management sometimes alone. Needless to say, this was sometimes unpopular with both union and management; the three women remained undeterred. In fact, Eve fought more battles than I initially recognised.

The union sent Eve to a meeting of other supervisory staff reps and she came back very excited and keyed up by the experience. We were talking about this in her front-room:

> It was really interesting, meeting all the people and finding out what's going on at other places. The union want me to do more and to go on a reps' course, but I'm not sure I want to be that involved. Mike [her husband] wouldn't like it, he's not so keen on all this union stuff, but he wouldn't stop me, mind. It's just I'm not sure if I want to do it, though I'm sure I'd do just as good a job as Annie and Bill – not Annie so much, but Bill. He's useless. The staff rep isn't like him, he's not full-time like our Bill, he talks to you in language you can understand, not like Bill – I never understand a bloody word he's saying. So I don't know, I'll have to think about it. John is keen for me to do it but I'm not sure my husband is.

Eve continued to think about, but could not resolve, the dilemma. It was another instance of the way in which the domestic world becomes enmeshed with the world of production and the factory. Eve the union rep was also wife and mother and held within the family.

Down among the members

The encounter between the shopfloor and the union was brought into sharp relief on the day that Bill came to the department to discuss the guaranteed week. Bill was joined by Annie and they stood in the middle of the floor and beckoned the women to join them. Once they were assembled, Bill told them that, due to the worsening recession, there was a distinct possibility that the guaranteed week would be suspended from January:

> The point is that the company cannot go on paying for no work and there are various things that might be done, but the company wants to ask for suggestions. There are a number of options, one is redundancies, but the union doesn't want that, no one wants that. The other option is to abandon the guaranteed week, but again, if we do that we would have to negotiate it all over again and we might not get it back, so the union doesn't want that. The guaranteed week can be suspended due to industrial action elsewhere which affects production here, or if the company's production is falling, which it is. So it is possible to suspend it and we may have to have shorter working weeks.

Some women frowned, others looked bemused because, as they murmured, they couldn't tell whether it was on or off. Anya broke the silence that had fallen: 'Come on, there is no option. What you are saying is redundancies or no guaranteed week. It's not a choice, the decision has been made.' Other women murmured agreement with Anya while nodding their heads.

Bill I have to go all round the factory explaining this, so I can't stay long. The company and the union want you to make any suggestions you can. Talk about it among yourselves and write down any suggestions and give them to Shanta. She can also explain more about this. [*Shanta looked baffled*] Shorter working time will be done fairly. Let us know what you think is the best way to organise this; that's what we're asking for, suggestions.

Marie I don't understand this. Are you saying redundancies or no redundancies; back to piecework, or what?

Anya He's saying it's either redundancies or no guaranteed week, that's it, that's what he's saying.

Bill You must talk about it among yourselves and let us know
after the holidays.

Annie nudged Bill and said, 'Say something about the vote, the
political affiliation vote.' Before he could, more women intervened:

Roxy Are we going to be laid off? Well, are we?
Beth Is it going to be short-time working, one week off, one
week on?
Voices Christ, this is terrible. We'll all be on short-time in our
'ouse, now.
Bill What can happen if you are laid off for a week you can go
and claim unemployment benefit for the week you're off, so
you still get some money.
A voice That's all right if you've paid a proper stamp. What
about us married women?
Yvonne Let's face it, you've come to tell us we're going to be
laid off and that's that. We've got no decision to make.
There isn't any option. You've come to tell us what *is*
going to happen. I don't see why we're being asked to send
in any suggestions at all.

Many women agreed with this view and they edged closer to Bill.
They no longer looked bemused. They were angry.

Bill Hum, no, really. There are a number of ways we can go
and we have until the new year to decide what is going to
happen. I really must get on. I have the whole factory to see.

Annie nudged him again, 'The affiliation vote, Bill,' and said to
me, 'He keeps forgetting the ballot'.

Bill The second issue is about the union and its political
affiliation. It was agreed, I regret to say, at the conference
that all members should decide whether to provide a
subsidy for a political party. It's a pity, but there it is. No
one is going to force you to do this. It is a matter of
conscience and you decide as individuals, each one of you,
whether part of your union dues will go to a political party,
but you are not bound to do this. You must decide for
yourself whether you want to and you can discuss it.

Not surprisingly, the women looked baffled again and they turned
one to another. 'What's political affiliation?' murmured the young

women. Others answered 'The Labour Party, you give some money to that – *not* the Tory Party, *not* Thatcher.'

A voice Is that what you mean? Give money to that lot, no fear.
Jessie No, it means to the other lot. You give money to the
    Labour Party.

There was a buzz of conversation and Bill interjected: 'I really must go. Political affiliation just means that when we collect your union dues, part of that if *you* want it to will go to the Labour Party, that's all, now, I must go.'

Bill's words had initially shocked the women; then, as the day wore on, they became more and more angry. His attempt to explain the issue of political affiliation was a complete failure and it seemed from his performance that this was intended. There was no suggestion of winning support for the idea, putting a case for or against the affiliation – explaining, for example, which unions supported the Labour Party in this way. The issue was made as clear as mud. To juxtapose it with the issue of redundancies and short-time working could have been useful, but it wasn't. Political affiliation was lost in the general concern over jobs, short-time and the possibility of redundancies.

The encounter only served to fuel the view that Bill was a management agent:

Anya It is not worth discussing. They send Bill up here when
    the decision has been made, not before. Does he think we're
    stupid, or something?
Phyllis Yes, that must be the case, the issues have been
    decided. I wonder what's happening to all these company
    cars. They could cut those out for a start.
Tracey Great, isn't it? They wait until the start of the holiday
    fortnight to tell us this, the sods.

The suggestion that women could intervene in the situation was treated as a joke.

Dee Well, Laura, have you found a way to save StitchCo?
Laura Ehem, well, I've been thinking about it all morning,
    but nothing's come to mind so far!

And the idea that the union would fight redundancies was quickly dismissed:

Dee Well, I hope we don't get redundancies because the union

won't fight it. They only know how to say yes to everything.
Bill doesn't tell us what is happening because we might make a
fuss. It's not good at all. People here don't bother about the
union because it doesn't do anything for us.

Tula You see, Sallie, they come up here and they ask us,
but they know what they're going to do and they'll do it
and Bill will let them because he's a company lackey, a
manager's man. He won't fight them. He's got a company
car and he's like them, not us. They could cut some of
those things first – cars, petrol, lunches that they have –
before our jobs.

A few weeks after the holiday, at the departmental meeting, the
subject of the guaranteed week and its future was raised by John,
the manager:

John By the way, has there been any more discussion about
the guaranteed week? Wasn't it before the holidays that Bill
asked for suggestions about this? What's the general feeling
about this? How do people see the future of this? It is a
moral dilemma for us, of course. We are proud of the
guaranteed week and both the union and management are
not keen to let it go. It means security for people and that's
a good thing. We have had the guaranteed week when the
other factories never have, but the problems are quite real.
In the changeover it does mean paying people when they are
not working, whether that is our fault or not, with the
present climate, it is very difficult seeing us being able to do
that because we can't make money that way and we have to
stay alive. The other thing we don't want is the possibility
of putting people out of work. It is an economic problem,
but it's also a moral problem, as I see it. Tell me, what do
you think?

Cherry Well, speaking personally, but I know other people
feel the same, I'd rather see us on a three-day week than
anyone be out of a job. It's better to have a little work than
no work at all and I think we know that we can't get paid
for doing nothing. It's been that bad until these last few
weeks, but I don't think anyone wants the guaranteed week
to go. It may have to be put off for a bit, or something like
that. But we don't want it to go for good, while we don't
want jobs to go either.

The other women murmur assent to this view and nod. Cherry has opened up the discussion in a way which gives the dilemma back to the manager, but which also emphasises solidarity. Phyllis then shows management that she knows the basis of profits and asks that they come back to the workers:

> I don't see why it has to go. You say we made a profit for this six months. Well, if people are working really hard to earn that and then there's no work, it's not their fault. They've already earned the guaranteed week; it should be paid to them. There's nothing we can do about the work coming through. But if we have worked and there has been a profit, we deserve to be paid all year.

Cherry agrees:

Cherry Yes, that's right. I mean we can't do anything about the way the work is coming through or how the trade is going.

Freida Well, I think it's right that no one wants people to be made redundant. The girls would rather work less if they have to than anyone lose their job, because it's not like you can go somewhere else at the moment. The other places are worse off than us. But neither Bill nor Annie have been round again and we haven't heard anything about it from the union. It just seems to have got dropped.

John So, what you are saying is that if we've got 3,000 workers and only work for 2,500 we should share it out rather than get rid of 500.

His comment neatly sidesteps Phyllis's point but she is quick as a flash to respond:

Phyllis No, I'm saying that if the 3,000 have worked for six months and the company have made a profit then that's their work and they have done it and they shouldn't be cut because there's no work. They've already earned the guaranteed week.

John withdraws from the battle by saying:

John Yes, ideally um, we would say that, but the industry is not so healthy and we are better off than most. But let's leave that and see if Bill and Annie bring any more news of it.

From the way events unfolded it looked as though the company was trying to test initial reactions to the suspension of the guaranteed week, using the union and the departmental meetings as a means to find out what level of resistance there might be. It was clear that resistance to redundancies was high and that some women – and not just Phyllis – understood that they had earned their guaranteed wages for the year after six months of work. They could see that they were the source of company profits, even if, as in this half-year, they were not large. Their labour had, however, contributed towards the enormous profits enjoyed by one of the major chain stores in the country.

This meeting provided yet another instance of the understanding the women brought to their situation as workers in the production process. It was this clarity and comprehension that the union completely failed to relate to or build on. Consequently, it could be said that the union worked to disunite and disorganise its members, rather than to listen to them and to learn from them. These were not women who lacked an analysis of the problems faced by workers in the hosiery industry in a recession. The departmental meeting showed that there were women who could speak on behalf of others from a position of knowledge and that they spoke of 'solidarity' and 'exploitation'. Words, it would seem, that were not common in the vocabulary of the union. Had women such as Phyllis or Tula or Cherry put the case for political affiliation it would have been carried; instead, it was lost. The vote should have been won because the women saw a very clear link between politics and trade unionism: 'Thatcher can't go on blaming the unions. It's not their fault all the jobs are going. What were the miners supposed to do, say thank you for being put out of work, Bah, she's a bloody disaster. Everyone is just fed up with it and they won't take it.' The issue of the guaranteed week being suspended faded from view as production picked up in the latter half of 1980. It was, however, a lesson to everyone in 'A' department. Their security was threatened and they responded by consistently emphasising that 'an injury to one was an injury to all'.

Listening to voices on the shopfloor I was never far away from women who were able to see through a situation and plot a course in relation to a well-grounded notion of their own interests. There was nothing here to suggest that women were less militant than their trade union brothers. There was still a problem: how to get the union to take note of their views and concerns?[10] It is an issue that women trade unionists are concerned about; they are, though, up against a more complex situation than that of a trade union bureaucracy which suppresses the radicalism of the rank and file. It is clear from all that Annie has said that the trade union hierarchy operates differently in relation to the control of male and female members. Women are facing the economism of the trade union movement which is expressed in its attention to protecting skill, bonuses, and the family wage – all of which relate to male workers. The complement to this exaggerated concern with the male worker is the silent woman. These facets of the movement are all part of an organisational and ideological complex which fails to support us and which ignores the wisdom of women on the shopfloor.

There are other ways to resist, and these were much in evidence at the factory in the form of an elaborated shopfloor culture, nourished and sustained by the department. As I have already suggested, this culture fashioned by and for women was a contradictory whole: it resisted management control and the union hierarchy, but did so by using notions of femininity which colluded with a subordinate and domesticated version of woman. These are the issues which are tackled in the next chapter and those that follow.

5
Shopfloor culture: resistance and celebration

It was against the background presented in the preceding chapters, and within the context of a society in which capital and labour are divided, that the women fashioned their culture: a culture born out of the shared experience of being women and workers in an unequal system. The culture that they created and sustained day by day, week by week, was a marvel of ingenuity and creativity. It was also a complex and contradictory whole: oppositional in terms of the demands of their employers; collusive in its emphasis upon women's traditional roles in the home and the family. A culture of this type is undercut by the ideological constraints in which it is born because no culture is a spontaneous event divorced from its social and cultural landscape. A culture is most simply a way of life, a set of shared meanings with specific symbols that signify membership of the cultural group, a language or its specific use, particular rituals and events in which all can share and thereby reaffirm life as it is lived.[1] Cultures in this sense are bound to a common-sense understanding of the world through what we now call practical ideologies.[2] Common-sense, as Gramsci reminded us, has many pitfalls in a world which is fragmented and where understanding is partial, but, on an everyday basis, common-sense provides answers to the growing complexities of the world.[3]

Resistance to the minutes, the critique of trade unions and political parties were all part of the way that the women at StitchCo sought to reassert their control over their lives. This was not the end of the matter: as this chapter and those that follow will show, there were other forms of resistance. In her study, Anna Pollert has discussed the contradictory nature of shopfloor culture among women, and has detailed the way in which gender intervened as a key factor.[4] The women she researched used their 'femininity' and their sexuality as a means of confronting management controls and the sexism of male supervisors. In using these weapons, the women themselves colluded in the definition of woman as a sex object. Anna Pollert emphasised the view that shopfloor culture was a form of symbolic resistance which remained at the level of style rather than developing into organised resistance to exploitation.[5]

The women of StitchCo would probably dispute this analysis in their own case because they saw in the informal organisation of the shopfloor the major resistance to management controls, given that the union was not playing the part that many of the women felt that it should. It was also the case, as the next chapter will show, that the elaborate rituals surrounding weddings and brides meant that company time and resources were used not for profit, but for the women on the shopfloor. Their rights to this time and these resources were acknowledged by management who knew from experience that if they attacked these spaces they would have a walk-off to deal with. This is not to dispute the importance of style and the level of disorganisation and mystification on the shopfloor. However, these negative elements should be set against a cultural response which emphasised friendship and solidarity and which was oppositional, energetic and potentially very powerful. Women on the shopfloor attacked life with great energy and verve; there was nothing to suggest defeat or submission or that they were cyphers or puppets. Life was difficult but funny, colourful and punctuated by the quick repartee and the jokes and pranks that friends and mates contrived.

Friends

Friendships were an essential and vital part of life on the shopfloor; they made work tolerable and at times even fun. Friends were the major antidote to the pressures of work: 'Well, we don't like the work that much, but we don't like to move around either. You get friends here who keep you going, so you say, "It's not so bad, really".'

Taruna's views were echoed by other women like Avril, a relative newcomer: 'I like working here. People say factories are terrible, but they aren't, you know. If you've never been in one they seem bad, but working here you see all your mates and you get good money.'

Laura, too, emphasised the importance of the people at the factory: 'It's the people who make StitchCo. You're never bored because there's always something happening and the other girls are so friendly we're always having a "laff". I really missed it when I went to do that nanny job.'

The things that were 'happening' varied from scurrilous gossip to organised pranks, but they were given life through the network of friends. There were no 'laffs' to be had on your own: bunking off to the toilets, spending too much time in the coffee bar made no sense if it was an individual activity; there was no way to organise a prank without your mates or to have a laff at a pornie picture or a coarse joke. The material base for all of these was the friendship group.

Pranks were not uncommon and were enjoyed by everyone because they relieved the monotony of the working day. Julie, Sally, Avril and others were always eyed very suspiciously when a joke was unleashed on the department. It was they who invoked the fury of management when, to everyone's delight, one or more of them set the buzzer off and emptied the department ten minutes before the end of the day. The glee with which women grabbed their coats and bags and left early, disappearing in a flash, said a great deal about the level of job satisfaction enjoyed by 'A' department workers. The next day management instituted an investigation into what was termed 'the incident'. The shopfloor was absolutely delighted that their speedy exodus had caused such obvious pain to management. Everyone who was asked about it shook their heads wisely, at once 'agreeing' with management's view that this was a very serious matter, while keeping quiet about the identity of the buzzer-pusher – as did I.

Another favourite joke with Beryl the Peril and her gang was to draw lewd pictures of penises and naked men and women, give them captions and send them around the units hoping that they would embarrass some of the other women and provoke a response – which they nearly always did. The older Indian women were particularly sensitive and complained to management – which, in turn, listened sympathetically and did nothing. Among themselves, written jokes were passed around and sniggered at through the working day. It all added excitement and 'a bit of a laff' to the factory days. Sex, of course, was a crucial ingredient and always managed to spice up the end of the day.

Friends stuck together and supported one another both inside and outside the factory. This meant, of course, that other women were excluded and that, on the whole, friendship groups did not cross either the age or the racial barrier. Black women, like Marsha and Tula, mixed more easily with white women than with Indian women. Tula, for example, spent her breaks with Laura, Carol, Jessie and Freida, who formed a core group because they had joined StitchCo at the same time, they said. Although they spent most of their coffee- and lunch-breaks together playing cards and discussing current affairs, politics and the state of the company, they rarely met outside the confines of the factory. They were unusual in this.

Visits to discos and eating out were common events for groups of women who also saved up to go on charabanc trips to Skeggie and Blackpool. The age difference and the division between the friendships of black and white women were very clear on these outings. Rarely did black women participate and those who did were younger. Indian women either regarded the trips as irrelevant or were deterred by the cost and the sense that such outings were not 'respectable'. Some younger Indian women did want to go on a trip to Blackpool, but they either didn't have the money or were refused permission by the family.

That trip was marshalled by the ever-energetic Eve whose presence actually deterred some of the newcomers to the department. Some of the older women wanted to take their husbands along, but Eve was quick to point out that 'there's mainly women who's coming' to Norah. She confided to me 'We don't want the men around. Christ, I see my husband every bloody day I don't need to see him in Blackpool, as well. We want a day out on our own for a change, get away from the kids and the house, not have them hanging around and findin' out what we're up to, up there.' Blackpool was to be an adventure away from the constraints of work, husbands and family and Eve managed to keep the trip a women's trip. Everyone, freed from the control of management and men, could be loud and outrageous if they chose to be. Some, the younger ones, got drunk and met new men they spent the day with; others gambled and drank and enjoyed each others' company. Whatever way, it was a women's event and they made the rules.

Friends were more than just good for having a laff with. They were the supports so essential to women's lives, whether it was by way of assisting a friend at her marriage by being a bridesmaid, or baby-sitting, or providing cover for illicit relationships. Without friends to help you along the way, life was so much more difficult. Shanta, for example, could not possibly have developed her relationship with Vijay without the cover provided by Rekha and others.

Food

Solidarity and friendship on the shopfloor were expressed through the sharing of food, most of it crisps and sweets from the machines in the coffee bar. A woman rarely ate a bag of crisps on her own; it was a way of showing friendship to send it around the unit or offer it to those nearest. Breaks to get sweets and drinks were an important antidote to the boredom experienced by everyone; they also provided a way of pacing the working day. It meant that vast quantities of junk food were consumed in any one day, although everyone agreed it was 'rubbish'.[6] Dieters were notoriously unsuccessful and it is hardly surprising, given the amount of calories needed to get through the working day and the monotony of the work itself.

Partly, food provided an excuse to go to the coffee bar and see your mates and spend time hanging about; on the larger stage of the factory canteen it provided the potential excitement of meeting men or engaging in mild flirtations. The food in the canteen was good and, as it was subsidised, everyone could afford a hot lunch if they wanted. Shanta, Suraya, Rekha, Taruna and Lata and I often had long lunches in the canteen – not a very exciting place in terms of the decor, but a dramatic space offering great adventures in relation to food and men. Shanta and her friends came to experiment with what were for them forbidden foods – bacon sandwiches, for example, which they ate with giggles and great relish because at home they were all vegetarians, more or less strict, depending upon their husbands or families. Taruna's husband was very strict and she impishly worked her way through the whole English menu day by day, week by week. Chips were a great favourite, and were given some zest with the addition of chilli which also cheered up bacon, sausages, eggs and everything else. Lata and the others took it in turns to bring a pot of fresh chilli with them. Chips with salt and chilli are a winner.

While we munched our chips and they tried to tell me about their home lives and teach me some more Gujarati, we watched the people in the canteen. Sometimes Shanta, who seemed to see more Indian films than anyone else, would describe the one she had seen most recently in minute detail – which often meant that the story line took from lunch-time to the final buzzer. The complicated plots and sub-plots were told with great skill by Shanta, who clearly enjoyed the role of raconteuse. The narrative was only part of the importance of the films. The stars were also described in great detail – what they had worn, how their hair looked, what their make-up was like were all important cues to style and fashion among Indian women. Interest in the Bombay film industry was also fed by film magazines which concentrated on the affairs of the film stars and printed vicious gossip about them in turn. Locally, the Indian cinemas were being decimated by the power of video which brought films directly into the home and, as Taruna pointed out, meant that parents could watch the film and judge its suitability for the children. Some of the films were so painfully sad, taking off from the classic Mother India, that they had Rekha and Lata in tears by tea-time.

Films and their stories were one part of the lunch-break in the canteen, but there were other things going on as well. The Indian men who took their lunch in the canteen tried their best to flirt with Suraya and the others. Taruna and Lata responded by looking in the opposite direction, but Rekha, Shanta and Suraya were bolder and returned the banter of the men in an effort to shame them. They also gossiped about some of the younger men. 'You see him, that one over there, he dyes his hair, yes, it's true,' whispered Suraya in relation to one of the best-known men, a singer in a local band. Her comments were greeted with peals of laughter from everyone who looked at Ramesh with renewed interest. He was a cheerful flirt who liked to chat to the women; he also spent most of his lunch-hour on the telephone having very public discussions about gigs for his band. He clearly enjoyed his notoriety and never seemed to mind the women joshing him and teasing him about his music, his women, his hair. All of this, plus the attentions of older men who would smile and chat to us, added excitement to the working day. Everyone, though, was careful in the way that they handled these encounters. Needletown was a small place and people would talk: Taruna, Lata and Rekha were all married women and were supposed to behave 'properly' – this did not include flirting with men at the factory.

Celebrations

Women, of course, have a special relationship with food. They spend a great deal of time and effort in its preparation and the gift of good food to a family is an essential part of what it means to be a wife and mother at the centre of home life – a discussion pursued later in this book. Given the importance of food in women's lives, it was not surprising that its provision and sharing were essential ingredients in all the celebrations of the shopfloor.

Birthdays, for example, were celebrated by everyone and each unit had a list of dates so that no one was forgotten. Women exchanged birthday cards and, those who were close, presents. It was the responsibility of the women with the birthday to buy cakes or sweets, or both, for the unit and other friends. It was important to demonstrate generosity on your birthday and all the women would buy goodies to bring to work – a birthday was an expensive time. Shanta, for example, bought sweets for the unit and her friends and spent over £10 on small bars of chocolate so that everyone could have one. Birthdays usually meant that women left their machines and spent some time in the canteen – as they did with all forms of celebration. Although the supervisors tried to keep the time lost down to a minimum, everyone knew that this was one way to subvert production efficiency: time for celebrations was, therefore, jealously guarded. On the whole, the company took a tolerant line but this had limits which were reached on Sally's birthday.

Sally was 18 and she had bought a huge cake which she spent the whole morning cutting up and distributing to her friends and co-workers in the canteen. Women came and went from the coffee bar all morning, younger ones staying as long as possible. They then went off to the pub in the lunch-break and Sally consumed a large amount of alcohol in a combination of vodka and cherry brandy. When she reeled back to the department, she refused to go back to work and, instead, ran up and down the machine lines chatting and giggling and cracking jokes. Gillian, the supervisor, and her other friends tried to get her to sit down, drink black coffee and sober up because she had an appointment with Clare, the personnel manager, about her poor time-keeping and pro-duction record. Sally was unimpressed by the suggestion that she was going to be warned and soon out of a job: 'I'm leaving anyway, I don't want your fuckin' job,' she countered. Lisa and others tried to sober her up, to no avail, though Gillian did manage to get the interview with Clare put back. Sally continued to disrupt the work of the unit throughout the afternoon – running about, shouting and throwing sweets around, she declared: 'I'm going to get married and have a baby.' This was what Sally really wanted to do; working at StitchCo was an interruption in the real business of life.

Like other celebrations for weddings and babies, which I will discuss in later chapters, this celebration was used to resist the imposition of work discipline and management controls. Sally fought to regain her own time in a dramatic way, but it was the final outburst that she would make. She was sacked after another warning and when I last saw her she was still unemployed and waiting to get married.

While weddings and babies marked life-cycle changes in women's lives, retirements marked not only a change in status at home but the end of a working life. They were bitter-sweet affairs which showed the contradictory nature of women's working lives. Early retirements were already an accepted practice at the factory and women spent one day a week for four weeks on a short pre-retirement course which gave them advice about money and leisure, as well. The courses also contributed to the process whereby women came to adjust to the idea of leaving work. Ada and Dol left together and on the day they were leaving they arrived at work in their best clothes, wearing more make-up than usual. This marked the fact that the day was special and at some distance from the normal run of things. They had bought cakes and drinks and we spent most of the afternoon sitting in the coffee bar talking over old times and eating and drinking. Prior to this, John had made a speech warmly thanking Dol and Ada for their loyalty towards the company and their efforts in the department. By the end of the speech, both Dol and Ada were in tears and their friends also started to tremble at the lips when they gave flowers and gifts to the two leavers. They left the factory early on their last day, clutching their flowers and weeping into them – no longer wanting to go, and filled with fears of isolation and idleness. Phyllis, who was their close friend, dabbed her eyes and said sadly, 'They were like sisters to me, I don't want to work here any more if they're not going to be here. I'm glad I'm next to go.' The tears cleared a little, because as we were helping Dol and Ada to the car we got stuck in the lift. It just rumbled to a halt filled with crying women, flowers and suitcases stuffed with presents. After a moment of panic when we all held our breath, everyone started laughing and shouting up the shaft for help which eventually arrived. Most of Dol and Ada's close friends did nothing for the rest of the day. It was a sad day, a day of parting.

One of the other women who retired during my year at the factory was Joan, who was in charge of the stock-room which held the cotton, buttons and the like. Management and supervisors colluded in an elaborate plot to give her a surprise retirement party at the company social club because she had worked for the company for over 25 years. She spent her last day at work innocently selling raffle tickets for a raffle which would be called at her own party but which she thought was for old folks in the community. Her husband had the task of suggesting to her that she might like to go 'up the club' for 'a quick one'. Once at the club, she was greeted by management, supervisors and friends from the shopfloor holding a huge banner and offering her an enormous bouquet of flowers. She was completely overwhelmed and had to sit down to recover before speeches were made and the party went ahead.

Informal economics

Celebrations were one way in which the shopfloor wrested their own space from the company, but it was not the only way. The women reappropriated the department and used the space as a market-place for goods that they brought to work. Hardly a day passed without someone having a new line in tee-shirts, brushes, pens, watches, make-up, baby clothes or soft toys; lime green elephants and orange teddy bears sold at £4–£6 a toy and were very popular. The sale of clothes in the factory was an interesting comment on the goods that the women made and the price of clothes even in the factory shop.

The women got most of these things from a family member who probably needed a bit of extra cash and this was easily generated from the shopfloor. Baby dresses, although they were usually £3 each, disappeared very quickly. Buying something at some point during the day helped to brighten up work and help a mate who needed the extra money, so everyone joined in. To my knowledge, management neither commented on these booming side-lines and examples of entrepreneurship nor did they try to stop them. In fact, these *ad hoc* sales were probably less disruptive to production than the catalogue sales.

Amita had a steady flow of customers for Avon cosmetic products. Time was spent looking at catalogues, making decisions and consulting friends about this cream or that, and, in the case of the clothing catalogues, this dress or that sweater. Catalogue agents found a ready market among the women. Some of my friends, like Suraya, could in this way buy clothes before their wages became part of the family pot. Suraya regularly lost £15 out of her wages for goods she was buying from catalogues. Many catalogue items seemed to me to be more expensive than goods in the shops. Even so, buying from a catalogue allowed Lisa to spend £20 on a flashy black-and-gold swimsuit she would never have been able to afford in the High Street.

The market-place in the factory was extended into the homes of some women who were agents for other goods, like jewellery. Every month Eve, who was an agent, would dragoon someone into holding a jewellery party and one month it was Laura's turn. She had just moved to a new flat and was keen to have friends come along, a jewellery party making a good excuse. About 15 of us gathered at Laura's to drink tea, eat biscuits and look at gold and silver jewellery – rings and bangles, earrings and necklaces – while the mimics in the group made quick work of the managers at StitchCo and some of the other supervisors. Eve was in her element, telling jokes and laughing loudly while she encouraged the women to spend their money. She, too, complained about the department and the stress which supervisors, like the other women, experienced. This generated a strong feeling of togetherness in the room. By the end of the evening we had spent £200 and Laura had earned a commission which she put towards a silver ring.

The interesting thing about these shopfloor transactions was that they set up a system of indebtedness whereby parts of wages circulated between women on the shopfloor generating some, albeit very tiny, income for the agents of Avon or Grattan or jewellery companies. There were, of course, less legitimate ways to obtain goods and services via the company and these too were part of the way that the women tried to get something back from StitchCo.

Everyone I knew seemed to come to work with a bundle of clothes to be pressed or ironed or altered at some point during the month and these were fitted in alongside regular production. In addition to this, women made clothes for themselves, their children and their friends which was, in part, legitimate, so long as it was done in the lunch-break. But a coup like the manufacture of six bridesmaids' gowns in a short period of time meant that company time was also used. Small electrical goods were also brought in for repair or service by the mechanics. Women carried irons, hairdryers, kettles and the like in and out of the mechanics' office and the mechanics seemed very happy to fix them.

While the company seemed to have no trouble tolerating this informal use of machinery and mechanics, however, they took a much firmer line on theft. If women were caught stealing, the company security officers made public examples of them and they were both dismissed and taken to court, which some of the managers thought was excessive; losing a job was felt by them to be sufficient punishment. The women who were caught during my year on the shopfloor included Connie who was chased from one end of the department to the other and grabbed unceremoniously by the security staff in a public shaming which made everyone cringe. The other women did not suffer this and one older woman who had been with the company a long time left quietly. They were unlucky. All kinds of things disappeared without trace – cotton and clothes, machine needles and other small things which were slipped into a pocket and not missed. Certainly, the company lost a large quantity of baby vests from one of the units and, between them, a number of young mums liberated a quantity of baby and children's clothes. One single parent who stole some of the vests was caught, but there was a lot of sympathy for her situation and one of the managers suggested that if she had asked for the vests the company would have given her some of the seconds from the line. Some women found the pilfering very funny, 'I ask you, who would want to wear this stuff anyway?' was Anya's view. From the tales that were told, it was clear that somebody, somewhere, did. The most daring thieving deeds – involving a group of men on night shift, not the women from the department – entered shopfloor mythology. The men had bundled clothes from the racks into vans by throwing them out of the window to the waiting vans below. It had taken some time before they were caught. Everyone enjoyed this story.

Chance, Fate and luck

Kate Purcell, in a very interesting analysis, has emphasised the importance of fatalism in the lives of working-class men and women, and especially in relation to women who have less control over their world at home or at work than men.[7] Certainly, my friends enjoyed the horoscopes and the Indian women, especially, would read hands and see the future in the lines of a palm. Horoscopes, of course, are a crucial element of Hindi culture and are acted upon; Fate is ever-present. Still, in other ways, as I have suggested, my friends tried to exercise some control at work and in the home: they were not passive recipients of life's blows and so the chance to win on the pools or the horses, to have a 'flutter' on a raffle was enjoyed by everyone. Indian friends sat side by side with English ones to fill in their pools coupons and a major win was held out as an escape route. This is, I think, the important point about luck, chance, and gambling: they offer an alternative which is not available in any other way. Domesticity, marriage and motherhood were the alternatives to the factory, but when we talked about other options we always seemed to come down to someone saying: 'Well, there's nothing for it, we'll have to win the pools like those others did, £75,000 a piece.'

Sallie What would you do with £75,000?
Chorus Give up work [*laughter*].
Flo Seriously, I wouldn't stay a minute longer. I'd buy my
   bungalow and put the rest away so it gave me an income. It
   would be a fair amount of money.
Norah That's right, no more working for a living.

The interesting thing about this conversation was that it was going on within the hearing of Nancy, a woman who had indeed won a large amount on the pools – close to £70,000, in fact. Nancy was famous for her win, which was one of the largest, but there were others that were celebrated from time to time. I wanted to know why it was, if everyone else in the coffee bar thought a win meant giving up work, she was still at StitchCo. The answer was very easy: 'Well, when I won I went to visit my brother in Australia and had a really good time for a couple of months and then I came back and we bought our house, but I missed me mates, I mean, the house is nice and it's nice to have it all paid for, but it's no fun bein' on your own all day.' Flo considered this and agreed that it wouldn't be any good to be lonely all day.

The pools win was not just an idle thought in John's department: women did win small amounts regularly and this encouraged everyone as most of them seemed to enjoy gambling. It was part of the way that life was spiced by uncertainty and chance and it was always possible that the jackpot would turn up. Women, young and old, went to bingo and fed fruit-machines and backed a horse every so often just in case luck came their way.

It seemed to me to be part of the whole attempt to take life on with a degree of adventure and courage rather than passively accepting it. I think it is dangerous to over-read the interest in chance and luck as simple fatalism. The point is that Fate is not a simple, unambiguous notion in this culture or in cultures where it plays a more prominent role. People struggle with Fate and try to make it bow to them in the same way that they struggle with employers, poverty and disease. Consequently, the invocation of Fate, chance and luck and its consequences in gambling or a visit to a fortune-teller are not a quiescent response; they are, rather, an attack on the vagaries of working-class life made by both women and men. Similarly, what may be regarded as superstitions may be part of a folk wisdom which is tried and tested and which reminds people that all the answers do not come from the experts.

The resistance generated and sustained by women on the shopfloor was a clear indication of the level of tolerance that they extended to the factory regime and management's authority. But more than this, it was a statement about the strength of collectivity and the importance of creativity in the lives of working-class women. Although the elements of shopfloor culture were shot through with ideological components which linked shopfloor culture among women to an ideology of femininity and a patriarchal definition of womanhood, they also contained a message about sisterhood and strength, both inside and outside the factory. In this respect the culture was a powerful threat to gender inequalities and patriarchal assumptions. Girls coming into the factory were inducted into a culture that was deeply contradictory. Girls became women on the shopfloor and women were strong, active and creatively trying to control their lives; at the same time, as the next chapter will show, they were enmeshed within a world of romance and sexuality which took its cues not from solidarity and strength, but from the myths and stereotypes which surround men and women and their relationships. The discussion that follows highlights the way in which women manage the tension between sisterhood and strength and the picture-book romance.

6
You sink into his arms

Marriage was booming in John's department. If there was one area of excitement which never seemed to wane, it was the glamour of a white wedding. Everyone was excited by the prospect of a wedding because it kept romance and sex alive through the boredom of sewing side-seams day after day. It made real the world of Hindi films and Mills and Boon romances with their gallant heroes and beautiful women who sailed off into the sunset together. The heroes and the brides were an essential part of the culture of femininity on the shopfloor and this chapter follows the fortunes of some of the young white women who married during my year at StitchCo. With them I shared some of the experience, while I struggled to understand the sense of liberation they felt as they walked down the aisle. Prior to this, there were complex ritual processes to be undergone which transformed girls into women – 'women' being defined in relation to domesticity and biology, as wives and mothers. These rituals are described in detail in this chapter. Whether the bride wore a white dress and a veil or a red-and-green sari shimmering with gold, the patriarchal assumptions about the bride–woman were the same.

The next chapter follows the stories and lives of Indian women in particular. My reasons for starting with white working-class women are that the celebration and rituals which surrounded brides on the shopfloor were historically generated and sustained by white women in the hosiery industry. Indian women have come into this alien culture and tried to connect with it to join in the celebration; at the same time, they have invited their white friends from the factory to come and join with them in their celebrations of marriage.

All young women share the status of daughter and the subordinate status implied by that. However, the parameters in which daughterhood is lived are not necessarily the same, as this chapter and the one that follows will show. The cultural level intervenes to form the context in which women live their lives and the freedom that they have within these contours.

Getting it together

Girls coming into the factory as trainees arrived starry-eyed, bringing dreams of their latest heart-throb into an environment already heavily saturated with the themes of romance and sexuality. They wanted to talk to me about Wayne, Mike or Darren rather than answer questions on their school experiences, the careers advice they had received, or their contributions to the family budget. My questions were always answered, but a lull in the conversations would allow Trish or Nikki to intervene with: 'Come on, Sal, let's talk about something interesting. Mike, eh?' I tried to coax from them their vision of the future and they presented me with a picture of the next ten years of their lives: they could see an engagement at 17, marriage at 19 or 20, followed by two children – a boy and then a girl. The future, in fact, looked like the past. It is easy, of course, to judge the visions presented here as myopic and restricted, but it is more important to try to understand the nature of the constraints within which the next generation of wives plot a course or conceive a future. I came slowly to appreciate, as they did, that the ideological and material parameters of their lives presented marriage and children not as burdensome and oppressive, but as liberating events – part of the great adventure of life. In taking hold of these moments, young women locked themselves into domesticity and subordination in just the same way that young men, taking hold of manual labour as their moment of liberation from boyhood, locked themselves into dead-end jobs with low wages.[1] For the women, there were very good reasons why they should embrace both marriage and men.

Nikki and Trish, like their older sisters and friends, lived at home as daughters and it was not economically possible for them to do anything else. They did not earn a living wage nor could they expect to; instead, they paid £10–£12 a week to their mums for their 'keep' and dreamed of the day when they would be able to leave home. The only way out of the family and into a house or a flat of their own was to join hands with a male wage and, therefore, with the man who went with the wage packet. The contradictions in this situation were very clear: on the one hand, the possibility of independence from family and home; on the other, the actuality of dependence, of being 'tied down'. The contradictions deepened because the young women felt that, in choosing a boyfriend and getting married, they were exercising some control over their lives and joining the adult world. In addition, they suggested to me that, as women in a society controlled by men, the possibility of being linked to one man offered at least a chance of exercising some power in the world. So engagements and weddings were emphasised.

This meant that sexual relations were invariably taken to mean relations between men and women. Sex in all its aspects on the shopfloor – from 'smutty' jokes to discussions which expressed fears and joys – was invoked in a heterosexual context and thus women's sexuality was bound to be explored in relation to men. Gay women were quiet and hidden: to be thought 'queer' and discussed as though you were was to be insulted and stigmatised. One older woman was accused of being 'queer' and this, everyone said, showed in the way that she changed her overall in full view of the department and, worse, in the way that she touched other women. Perhaps because she knew such things were said about her, she countered with a steady supply of sexual jokes and innuendoes that were determinedly heterosexual. This did not alter the opinion of Tessa and Julie and others, who finally decided that she had 'a hormone problem' shown by her childlessness. Gay women in such an environment must have suffered a silent agony that I never uncovered. Trainees were soon engulfed by a culture which encouraged them to want what Tessa and Julie already had – a steady bloke, a husband-in-the-making who would help them secure a place of their own.

Romance and realism

Although romance breathed life and energy into shopfloor culture it was not a simple notion, but a complex and contradictory element in women's lives. Their commitment to love and marriage and their insistence upon heterosexuality were underpinned by the economic constraints which necessitated an 'alliance' between men and women if they were to enjoy a reasonable standard of living and some of the freedoms of being away from their parents. Marriage was part of a strategy adopted by women to realise some of the benefits of our society. It was not, however, simply material benefits that were at issue. Womanhood, as it was understood on the shopfloor, was realised through marriage and motherhood; the celebration of engagements and weddings was part of the confirmation of this. Alongside marriage was the network of friends and relatives who provided a system of support for women and these relationships among women were not denied or diminished by the emphasis upon romance and weddings. On the contrary, relations between men and women, womanhood realised through marriage and motherhood, were validated by friends, sisters, mothers and aunts who provided a vital cultural context. The tensions between romance and realism existed and were skilfully lived out on a day-to-day basis and when women looked to the future. The effect of all this was, of course, to reinforce the importance of the family and all the attendant inequalities that go with it.

Romance was not only brought through the factory gate; actual romances might begin at work. Flirtations in the factory canteen were usually initiated by the men whistling and calling to the women, who played it cool until they were back in the department where they made an appraisal of the men. Some of the men were known to be womanisers and newcomers to the department were told about them. Mick, one of the mechanics, was notorious in this respect. He had a prolonged relationship with Donna, causing her great pain. Donna's friends warned against it and were sympathetic and supportive when finally she cracked up under the strain. They knew, better than Donna, that Mick was thoroughly exploitative and well known for causing heartaches as Liz, Donna's close friend, said angrily after Donna had gone home in tears: 'He only wants one thing and then, when he gets it, he finishes with the girl and gets another. He won't change. He did it to the last one and he'll do it to her.' Liz's response, and that of many of her friends, was an assertion of a woman's right to be more than a sexual object: in their contempt for Mick, they expressed a rage against the imbalance of power between men and women and the consequence of this for women. Romance had its limits, and Mick was definitely at the outer-edge of these.

If you were young enough to stand the pace and had money in your pocket, Friday and Saturday nights were nights spent in town at the pubs and discos, dancing, flirting and getting 'pissed up'.[2] Friends went together to the clubs in town and danced in groups until they were divided by the men who, it was hoped, would finance drinking for the night and not prove too trouble-some at the end when the group would re-form to go home in shared taxis by twos and threes. It was the model for the bride's night out, the 'hen' party which I describe later in this chapter. Meeting new men was part of the fun of being around town. Men, however, were classified: 'yobs' were avoided even for free drinks and a quick dance and my friends were quick to spot them. Getting drunk was part of the fun. Although parents disapproved, on the whole they were fairly indulgent towards their daughters and if Lisa or Tracey were told off it was soon forgotten. Weekends were so important that they were kept alive for most of Monday and Tuesday by recounting events from Friday or Saturday night: how Ena lost her shoes and Frankie the whole evening because she was so drunk she could not remember it. And the way that Lisa rowed with Gary and went home alone and Tracy found a new bloke while Tessa and Julie both quarrelled with their new fiancés because they were drunk and flirting with other women. Stories of wild women and comedy told often against themselves, but which emphasised their adulthood and their freedom to be out late in the city.

A diamond is for ever

The energy and enthusiasm with which Lisa, Tessa and others pursued engagement rings made me wonder if they really did believe that 'a diamond is for ever'. I was reassured by my friends that nothing so simple was at work. The importance of the ring was not so much the diamond, although its design and value were discussed at length, but the way in which becoming engaged marked another point along the road to adult status:

Beth I'm getting engaged tomorrow. We're saving up for a
  house.
Gladys Young people today have got to learn to be
  responsible. You're only a girl yet, but you're all the same –
  so keen to get married.
Beth [*angrily*] I'm as grown up as anyone else and getting
  engaged is being responsible.
Gladys But you're not a woman yet.
Beth Huh.
Sallie When do you become a woman then?

Gladys Well, when you're responsible. When you've got a home and family to look after. They don't know what life's about at their age. They think it's all romantic and easy because they've never tried to run a place of their own. It's fine when you're living at home to pretend to be grown up.

Beth [*furious*] I pay my way at home and we're saving up for a place. What are we supposed to do? Things weren't so expensive in your time.

Gladys Maybe not, but wages were so low we had to scrimp and save for everything. Young people today expect to have everything just like that with HP and credit all over the place.

Beth Huh, well even if it's HP you still have to pay for it. I don't know how it makes you less responsible. People are always telling us we've got it easy, but it doesn't look like that to us. At least you had jobs to go to. A lot of young people don't have that anymore. [*aside to me*] It makes me sick how she goes on . . .

Beth was furious with Gladys and she threw the clothes she was packing up in the air and walked off to the canteen for a cup of coffee. Her rage was not surprising, given her attempts, at 17, to be adult and responsible in a way that would allow her to be a woman. Womanhood was clearly defined in this conversation as being a wife and mother, a view accepted by most of the women and celebrated on the shopfloor through the rituals which surrounded engagements, marriages and motherhood. Gladys was trying to put Beth in her place because, as she confided to me, she felt that becoming engaged was simply an excuse for young people to play at being adult by going to bed together rather than taking on the responsibilities of a home and children. This view was shared by some of the other women, such as Tula who, when I talked to her about the importance of engagements, looked at me quizzically, sighed and said: 'It's tradition, you see. They all want to be *engaged* and to have a *ring*. It doesn't mean, like it used to mean that a woman is promised to a man and is special. Now, they are engaged to one bloke and sleeping with three others. It's just about sex now.'

The comments made by Gladys and Tula are interesting because they emphasise sexuality and the way in which an engagement signals the arrival of a woman's sexuality because she is linked to a man. Being engaged allowed young couples to become lovers, legitimately, in the eyes of parents. Although often engaged couples slept together on family holidays or at each other's homes, this did not mean licensed promiscuity. On the contrary, it was one way in which working-class families and communities regulated the sexual behaviour of their daughters. In principle, an engagement tied a man and woman together. The continuity of life with your mates, holidays with 'girlfriends', away from both families and fiancés, meant that this regulation could be disrupted by the discos of Skeggie and Blackpool.

I was fascinated by the clear passion for engagements exhibited by young women throughout the department so I spent a long time talking to women of all ages about the meanings that they attached to engagement parties, diamond rings and having a fiancé. Despite my persistent questioning, however, none of them clearly articulated the role engagements played in their lives. Most of the fiancées in the department were still in their teens and did not expect to marry for several years unless they were pregnant. They didn't seem to be anxious to rush into marriage and it was this reluctance, amid the general interest in weddings, flowers, confetti, and the like, which initially baffled me. It was only by getting to know the women that I gradually built up a picture of the importance of being engaged and how this changed not only the status of young people, but, most important, the economic relations between them.

The common pattern among engaged couples was to pool their income and to save one wage packet and live on the other, as described by Lisa: 'After we get engaged, we're gonna open a joint account and save his wages and live on mine. Then we'll be able to get a house and the things we need for it. It will take a long time, but it's worth it. I don't want to get married in a rush like the twins.' In fact, this arrangement proved quite flexible and Lisa sometimes saved her wages and lived on Gary's wages: 'I saved nearly all my wages this week because Gary paid my board.' Angie, who was 17, was involved in a similar situation, as she explained one lunch-hour to Marsha and Rosamund:

Marsha When are you getting married, Angie?
Angie Don't know, when I've got enough money I s'pose.
Marsha When's that? You've got loads of money.
Angie Well, I'm not sure if I have. I put my money in the bank
 every week, but I don't count it so I don't know what I've got.

Rosamund How come you put it in the bank? How do you
  live?
Angie My boyfriend pays for me. He uses his money. He pays
  my Mum £10 and then he gives me another £10 for
  spending.
Rosamund What about clothes?
Angie He buys those, as well, and, anyway, I don't have many
  clothes. I manage with what I get at Christmas and
  birthdays. But anything I really like, he buys for me.
Marsha Well, that's all right, sounds like you're onto a good
  thing, Angie, stick with it.
Angie Well, he's on the building, he earns plenty of money so
  we save mine. I s'pose we'll get married in a year or a
  couple of years when he's paid for his bike.

Angie was not unusual. She had left school at 16 and a year later
was locked into a relationship which left her virtually no control
over her own earnings. Angie had few clothes and spent very little
money on anything else. Her boyfriend behaved towards her as he
would when they were married, taking on the role of breadwinner
and providing for her basic needs. This relationship reproduced
the ideal pattern of working-class family life as it was constructed
in the minds of men. In this case, though, the family wage was a
combination of Pete and Angie's wages, the most common economic basis for family life.[3] Angie was waiting for Pete to pay for his
bike before they could marry, but she didn't wait long. By the time
she was 19, Angie was proudly and happily pushing her baby son
through the city market with her mum and told me she didn't
expect to be going back to work in the factory for a long time.
  Engagements, then, allowed young couples to plan a future and
to put money aside for it. Saving was a way of trying to deal with
the material limitations of working-class life; for those involved, it
meant that hedonism gave way to a much more restricted life.
Engaged couples seemed to spend most of their time at home in
front of the telly, at the house of one family or the other. They
carefully rationed nights out in the pub or at the discos in town
and these soon became part of a routine. So the excitement of the
engagement ring very soon gave way to the rigours of saving and
the constraints that this imposed. It was not surprising that this
situation generated resentment and regrets. Beth, for example,
told me later in the year:

My bloke's going to be made redundant. He's on a three-day week now. We can't save up to get married, his money pays for us to go out, and that's that. It plays on my nerves because we're never going to get a house at this rate. I know I shouldn't worry because we've got each other, but I do. I can't see it going anywhere – him out of work and me in this stupid factory.

For Beth, love was not enough. She saw her vision of the future threatened as marriage and a home of her own receded in the face of unemployment and Ted's growing dependence on her. The relationship broke down under the pressure and she returned her ring, she told me tearfully. Poor Beth felt that she had been cheated.

Saving together did not necessarily mean suffering together. It seemed that the men had fewer restrictions on them. They still bought motorbikes and went to the pub for a night out with the blokes while Angie or Beth stayed home to do the ironing. A few years of this and, not surprisingly, marriage began to look more and more like liberation and the opening onto a wider world, as Michelle explained: 'We've been saving for the last five years and now we'd like to go out more while we're young and have lots of new clothes. You know, I haven't bought anything for years while we've been saving.'

Some of Michelle's friends were deterred by the sacrifices involved in a prolonged engagement and simply found a place to live together for a few months before they married. Living together, of course, strengthened rather than weakened the knot that was tied between the couple and placed a woman more firmly within the orbit of a man. But the women on the shopfloor inverted my view of the situation and claimed that an engagement and marriage gave a woman some control over the world of men. Through a boyfriend, a lover or a husband, they said a woman gained access to the resources controlled by men and because of this women were prepared to stay at home and save their money. They had, they believed, effectively improved their bargaining position *vis-à-vis* men, as Lisa told me with her hand on her hip and eyes flashing: 'He's not bloody goin' out if I'm not. If he goes with his mates then I'm goin' to go with mine.'

Lisa fought a constant battle to maintain some kind of equality in her relationship with Gary. When he decided he would go on holiday with his mates, she responded by going away with one of hers. While on holiday, she found a new man and Gary never found out; it was a sweet revenge, she told me, for all his 'bloody muckin' about'. Hers was, in fact, a very brave struggle: quarrels with her stepfather had led to her being kicked out of home, and she therefore lived at her boyfriend's house.

On the occasions that I spent with Lisa, Gary and the other couples, there was little open affection between them. At discos or parties the men drank and talked to one another while the women danced and laughed together. The men never seemed to talk to the women, they barked at them or made off-the-cuff remarks that were intended to be hurtful. Happily, this seemed to have very little impact on my friends (it infuriated me) although the pattern appeared to be set for later life. For the moment, the women shrugged off the power that the men attempted to exert over them; they still had an option, not much of one it was true, but they had their mates, a job and a romantic glow which somehow seemed to carry them through the routine chauvinism of the men and the material confines of their lives.

From girl to woman: the bride's ritual

Engagements were often celebrated with a party which brought friends and relatives together to toast the new couple and possibly the eighteenth birthday of the bride, as well. At work, sweets and cakes were passed around while everyone admired the ring and the wearer became a celebrity for a day, recounting the details surrounding the choice of the ring, its cost and where it was bought. The real event was still to come. The wedding was the centrepiece which brought the women in the department together in the most complex and creative drama in the life of the shopfloor, the event I have called the bride's ritual. The pattern for this event was set way back in history and no one was able to tell me when or why it began in the hosiery industry, whether it was similar or different in other areas of the country or if it was part of shopfloor culture among women in other industries.[4] It was so much a part of life in 'the hosiery' that everyone took it for granted. Though the celebration of the bride corresponded to the passing-out ceremonies and celebrations used to announce the arrival of a new craftsworker, the bride's ritual celebrated neither a craft nor a skilled worker, but womanhood. It was a rite of passage for the move from girl to woman, from daughter to wife; the symbolism used not only celebrated the bride, it also pointed to the subordination of women in marriage.[5]

The bride's ritual, which was staged many times during my year in the factory, is best described in relation to the twins, Tessa and Julie, who married in the summer of 1980. They were the source of special excitement because they were planning a double wedding. By concentrating on young white women, I do not want to give the impression that Indian women were not involved; they were, but in ways which were tempered to suit them. For example, it was well known on the shopfloor that few Indian women drank alcohol and so they were not expected to come to the pub in the lunch-hour. White women also felt that too many bawdy references to sex were not welcomed, by the older Indian women, especially, so they cut this out and concentrated instead on romance and hearts and flowers in an effort to be sensitive to the needs of their Indian friends.

When the date of the twins' wedding was fixed, the women on their respective units set to work to make appropriate costumes for them using company materials and time. This was the first part of the ritual and one which emphasised the creative skills and abilities of the women on the units in making forms of fancy dress. Some of the units were well known for producing very elaborate and inventive costumes, which they tried to relate to the kind of person the bride was. Hence, when Geeta was due to get married, Eve's unit made a charming schoolgirl outfit which emphasised Geeta's lack of experience in matters of sex and marriage – even so, this outfit was more risqué than the one made for Ranjula, a very shy Indian woman. Her outfit closely resembled pink pyjamas and had an 'L' sign on the back; the unit also put up a poster showing Ranjula and her fiancé surrounded by hearts and flowers and ribbons. The twins were not credited with needing such gentle treatment. It was well known that Tessa was pregnant and already living with Carl. Julie, although not pregnant, was also living with Dave – something, it must be said, she was not very happy about. What this meant was that their costumes could be very suggestive without any possibility of offending either of them; it was on this basis that they were created.

On the day of their celebration (a Thursday, the day normally chosen), the twins arrived at work grinning and looking a little wary as they waited for their units to unveil their handiwork. Both units had excelled themselves and, amid roars of laughter, Julie was dressed in a St Trinian's outfit with a short gymslip, black suspenders and stockings, her tie askew; the ensemble was topped off by a large black top-hat made of crêpe paper and cardboard and decked with gaudy pink tinsel that flowed around the brim and trailed down the side. On the back of the gymslip was an 'L' plate with a contraceptive pill stuck to the side of it. The suggestion that Julie might be a Learner was greeted with total disbelief. '"Learner" – that's a joke Julie!' said her friends. Her sister, who also pointed to her suspenders and short skirt and made jokes about Julie's lack of ability in school, prompted another set of innuendoes about Julie's sexual experiences. Julie responded by telling Tessa that she was in for a shock, and we set off to see Tessa dressed in her costume.

Julie's gymslip paled into respectability when it was confronted with Tessa's costume, described by Avril as 'a pornographic Andy Pandy suit'. Hands covered smiles, heads rolled and everyone stared at Tessa almost in disbelief before they burst into raucous laughter which degenerated into a prolonged fit of the giggles. Tessa's dress was outrageous. It was an oversize Babygro, a fairly loose fit on Tessa, with two large pink cloth breasts attached to the front and two hands appliquéd on the seat of the suit across Tessa's bottom. Over one of the hands the words 'It feels good' had been embroidered. To set off this creation – it did look like a piece of soft sculpture from a distance – the women on the unit had made a large black-cloth penis and testicles which Tessa wore around her neck, when she was not pushing them into everyone's faces; 'Nice innit, Sal? I'm gonna give it to you as a memento,' Tessa said wickedly, grinning at her friends and tilting her new acquisition in the direction of the managers. She took on the mantle of the suggestive clown as it was given to her by the costume, and clearly thoroughly enjoyed it. To crown her clothes, she wore a lopsided mobcap with 'the pill' stuck to it and cotton reels dangling from it. As Lisa summed it up: 'Gawd, you look a sight, Tess.'

Dressed in these clothes the twins spent the morning touring the department and organising the collection and distribution of a large number of cakes, sweets, crisps and drinks. After we had been downstairs (to the large factory canteen) for the third time we settled into our canteen and laid out cakes and drinks for all the twins' friends who then came, unit by unit, to eat and chat, laugh and giggle at the way the twins were dressed and to make jokes about sexual adventures. Once in the canteen, they stayed – which prompted Eve or Jessie to make an appearance and order the women back to work. As Gracie pointed out, though, 'It's not worth bothering, there's nothing to do.' (The department's production had reached an all-time low at this point.) It was, in fact, fortunate that there was so little to do on that day because half the department didn't want to do much work, they were much more involved with the events surrounding the twins.

Gifts were an essential part of the proceedings: while the twins donated gooey cakes, their friends brought gifts of a more practical kind which were displayed on a table near where Julie and Tessa were working. Their units had provided collective gifts; friends and well-wishers from other parts of the department added to these. Laid out on a table were a collection of pyrex dishes, bathroom mats, tea-towels, saucepans and tin-openers – all sorts of really useful domestic items. Tessa had a gift which she especially liked and which she showed to everyone. It was a bottle-opener in the shape of a fat little man with a wobbly head. I thought it might have come from a day out in Skeggie, the colours and the rough painting making it look as though it had been won at the fair. Tessa was absolutely delighted with it.

Stuffed with cakes and pop and still giggling at the sight of Tessa, at lunch-time we headed for the nearest pub where the twins' mum, Rita, and one of their older sisters, Gina, were waiting for us. Management had given the twins an extra ten minutes on their lunch-break. Although it was not intended, this extra ten minutes was also taken by a number of the twins' friends. The pub was unimpressive: its tiny bar had scarcely enough room for a dozen people, let alone the factory outing we had become. Nevertheless, we pushed our way towards the bar and ordered drinks for each other. Julie and Tessa were plied with rum and coke, although Tessa protested mildly and tried to drink only coke; instead, others drank vodka and lime, gin and orange, and some, like Sally, drank everything in sight. While Rita laughed and encouraged her daughters to drink, bundles of binding were being passed between hands, unknown to Tessa and Julie, ready for the next stage of the celebration. Rita thought the clothes made for her daughters were wonderful, she laughed loud and long at Tessa's costume, especially the groping hands on the seat which she particularly liked. The pub was thrown into disarray by the arrival of another bride in jeans and a large shirt with a pointed black witch's hat on her head. She was Jane from 'Socks' I was told and this information was followed by some critical comments on her costume and how it compared poorly with the ones that our brides wore.

We were all pretty pleased with things and preparing for the next step although, by now, Julie and Tessa knew what was coming and looked at each one of us and asked us not to tie them to the railings outside the factory. But, tradition demanded that this be done and a few drinks later we were all outside the tiny pub a few steps away from the pedestrian bridge over the dual carriageway next to the factory. It was pouring with rain. Lisa and Marie grabbed Julie, while Tracey and Jo made a dash for Tessa as she tried to run back to the factory. As the twins struggled, Jo tried to wind some binding around them and the support for the pedestrian bridge so they were at least a little sheltered, but the cars threw up spray from the road and the twins struggled harder. Reinforcements managed to make secure the binding: yards and yards of it wound round and round the two women, their legs and arms tied to the concrete bridge. Meanwhile, their mum laughed at their plight. They called to her, pleading with her for help and for her to stay with them, lend them an umbrella, do something to help. But Rita was enjoying the lark as much as everyone else and she wanted to take photos rather than help them out of a fix. Their friends, too, giggled at their problems and taunted them with jibes, asking them to 'get out of that then' – which looked impossible, considering the length and strength of the tape used. The other bride, Jane, was actually chained to the railings alongside the road and was by this time struggling to free herself. Her friends had already disappeared back into the factory. Soon, everyone from John's department had started back to the factory and Tessa began to complain loudly that she felt sick, that it was dangerous in her condition to be tied up, and so on, until her voice was a scream. Julie was beginning to look as though, of the two, she was definitely going to be the one who was sick, her face growing paler and her hair wringing wet. No one paid any attention. Those who stayed a little longer did so to ensure that the binding was tight or to take a few more shots of the twins and Rita and Gina so that they would all have a souvenir. Though Julie began to wail as we left, everyone told her determinedly, 'this happens to all brides'. Her fate was sealed, the knots were tied and checked and she and her sister were left in the pouring rain to struggle free as best they could.

They struggled with the binding, cursing and swearing and promising revenge on their friends. It eventually gave way under their constant pulling and tugging; they were bruised in the effort, their ankles cut and their clothes soaking wet. Tessa and Julie re-emerged in the department a sorry sight, Julie's black stockings were torn and muddy and Tessa's red outfit was soggy with the rain. They were greeted with hoots of laughter and shouts as they staggered in, Julie looking very green and complaining that she was about to throw up. Before Julie could decide whether she was going to be sick, she and Tessa were bundled into one of the large 'wheely baskets' normally used for moving work or scraps around the factory. Michelle, Jo, Lisa and others then pushed the basket at increasing speed around the department between the machines, around the press, up and down the gangways, amid shrieks of delight from the rest of the department who threw scraps and paper into the basket onto the screaming twins who looked terrified. They clung to each other as their basket was hurtled from side to side by their friends, who took it in turns to keep the basket moving through the gaps. It looked as though it had escaped from a fun-fair as it sped across the floor with the twins looking more and more like two rag dolls – limp, white and gasping for breath. The spectacle raised women from their seats to cheer and shout, 'faster, faster,' while Tessa tried to say it was dangerous in 'her condition'. Until they were finally puffed by their efforts, no one heeded her cries. The basket was finally brought to rest near the canteen and, falling over one another, the women tried to help the twins out. Julie insisted she couldn't move, while Tessa just sat staring at everyone, trying to recover her strength and stop the room going around. They were both very unsteady, very dizzy and looked like they were going to be sick – as did some of the runners who, like the twins, had had too much to drink too quickly in the pub.

Crumpled, wet and bruised, they were finally helped to a seat in the canteen and given coffee while they slumped head in hands across the table, exhausted, giddy and almost tearful. The others giggled mercilessly, delighted at the havoc they had wrought and the wrecks that their friends had become. Jo had lost her shoes in the race with the basket and Tracey brought them into the canteen, teasing Jo with them. Everyone was now exhausted and

most sat down heavily with coffee or tea and a fag. Before anyone
had had time to light up, we were faced with a group of visitors –
men in grey suits who looked stunned at the sight of this female
debris littered around the coffee machines. Undaunted, the
managing director, Mr Hallam, who was leading the visiting party,
quickly advanced towards the twins with a flashing white smile
and asked them when they were to be married and where. He
listened attentively to their replies and wished them great happiness
before he rejoined the visitors who were staring over their
shoulders trying to get a glimpse of the twins. Mr Hallam
displayed no surprise at Tessa's pornographic Andy Pandy outfit,
nor Julie's obvious drunkenness and he managed to keep a straight
face throughout his chat with them. I found his ability to do this
quite impressive but, as he disappeared, the others sneered and
Tessa shuddered: 'Ugh . . . I hate him, he's so posh and all that.'
She and Julie mimicked him and then started to fall about
laughing and pushing each other.

By now, it was three o'clock in the afternoon and neither the
twins nor their friends had done any work. They were asked to go
back to their machines, where they slumped forward with heads in
their hands. Julie was looking a greenish shade at this point and
Tessa looked white with fatigue. In ten minutes they were back in
the coffee bar, trying more coffee as an antidote to their developing
hangovers – to little effect. Julie complained: 'My head feels as
though it's goin' to roll off.' Everyone else, though, was beginning
to talk about the 'hen' party, which was to follow that evening – a
night on the town, the last one as unmarried women for the twins.
The twins groaned at the idea and started to pack up their gifts
ready to go home. By four-thirty, they were staggering down the
stairs aided by friends who helped them and their goodies into
their dad's car.

This exhausting ritual was enacted again and again throughout
the summer and in each case the drama was the same, although the
costumes varied. Michelle, too, had an all-in-one outfit modelled
on the Pink Panther complete with tail, while another unit made
two versions of diddy men costumes for Kerry and Linda who
were getting married on the same day. Kerry had 'Mild' and
'Bitter' embroidered across her breasts and 'Sex' on her seat;
Linda was festooned with 'L' plates and 'Sex' from paper cuttings
plus a large notice, 'Keep taking the pill', across her back. Each of
these costumes was fashioned with great care and cherished by the

women who wore them and subsequently kept them for many
years. It was an opportunity for the women on the units to use
their creativity and technical skills for each other and everyone
enjoyed the excitement which surrounded each new creation.

It was also clear from the women who had worked in other local
factories that the ritual was followed in at least some of these.
Elaine described one: 'The last place I worked at they didn't do the
bride's thing but at Barnes they used to cover you with rice. I had
rice in my knickers and they gave you a big carrot and two
potatoes, really rude it was, and then they tied you to a lamp-post.
I'd never go through that again.' Sheila and Myra could also recall
similar events at the factory where they had worked before they
came to StitchCo:

> They dress you up there to look like clowns, put flour in
> your hair, on your face – it gets everywhere. And then
> everyone gets drunk at lunch-time, not like here, no one
> does any work all day. Then they tie her up to the
> roundabout and one time we all got on a bus and tied our
> mate to the bus and she went miles away. She thought we
> were all going on the bus and we hopped off and she was
> stuck there, tied to the bus.

The memory of their mate tied to the bus prompted laughter from
Sheila and Myra and everyone else around the table and it gave
some of the StitchCo women an idea for the next bride who came
along.

All of these versions of the ritual share in the powerful sexual
imagery which saturated the events at StitchCo and which
amplified the jokes, sexual innuendoes and ribaldry of the shopfloor. It was bawdy and everyone enjoyed it. The emphasis upon
sexuality must be viewed in the light of the comments I have
already made on the privileged position of heterosexuality; women
became sexually active as wives following their weddings and this
meant that their sexuality was crucially mediated by men. The pill
found its way onto all the outfits, suggesting a clear change in
status between the sexually unavailable girl and the sexually
experienced woman. Womanhood was defined in the ritual in
relation to becoming a wife and therefore becoming a woman was
located within the context of marriage and being joined to a man.

It was also abundantly clear that marriage was equated with

bondage and the binding of a woman to a man – the notion of capture and plunder lingers on in the ritual. While the young women were bound, they also sought to struggle free – thereby securing for the bride a new freedom. This struggle was enacted in public as though the whole exercise was a shaming experience, a way of showing women as harlots and witches symbolised in the costumes worn by the brides. The scarlet woman, the vamp and the sexually alert schoolgirl were all part of the ritual, just like they are part of the enduring myths which surround women's sexuality. Such myths are not, of course, simply benign. They are part of the subordination of women, clearly expressed in the ritual and cheerfully emphasised by the women involved in the drama. It was, in all its parts, a deeply contradictory event – not because the symbolism was ambiguous, but because it involved women in a celebration of their own oppression in marriage. And it was this oppression that the young brides came, all too quickly, to know and articulate.

While management was clearly tolerant of the whole event, as Mr Hallam showed, concern was expressed by the senior personnel manager following an occasion when the bride was tied up perilously close to the road. The issue was raised at the factory-wide safety reps' meeting. The reps acknowledged the possibility of an accident and, as far as I know, no one else was tied up to the traffic lights or in the middle of the dual carriageway – the binding, however, did not stop. The ritual was too important and too deeply entrenched in shopfloor culture for it to be outlawed. It remained as a comment on youth and adulthood and the institution of marriage. For the brides, the ritual ended their girlhood and they moved across to the world of women and 'real life' in marriage and domestic responsibilities.

The hen party: out on the town

Celebrations for the twins did not end at the factory gate but were carried into the city later in the day when everyone met for the hen party. A hen party made a statement about solidarity and affection between women and how these bonds would remain important to the bride despite her marriage. At one level the hen party reasserted the sisterhood of women although, like the other aspects of the bride's ritual, it had deeply ambiguous elements which the twins' party showed forcefully. Their night on the town followed what was a recognised route around the pubs and clubs which offered free gifts or free entry to hen parties.[6]

Our evening began in a pub in town where everyone arrived wearing more make-up than they did to work and clothes that made them look older and more affluent. Debbie was wearing a fur coat and she looked carefully dressed and made-up, but as Liz quickly pointed out: 'You scrubber, Debbie, where's the tights?' Debbie shrugged, 'No money, it's Thursday night, you know, and I had to have some money for this, didn't I?' she said, sipping lager at the bar while we all waited for Julie. Debbie and Liz looked around the bar and complained of boredom until the arrival of a group of men whom they eyed, 'Look at that one, Liz.' Liz, however, was looking at a group of women who had arrived, one of whom had a large cardboard hat on her head. Liz was scathing about the hat: 'Not much of one is it? She looks a bit old to be getting married, doesn't she?' Our group, which was now quite large, turned around and stared at the woman who was about 30. Before they could comment further, Rita arrived with the twins' older sisters Gina and Marie and joined Tessa. Julie arrived breathless with her prospective mother-in-law and hurriedly bought drinks for everyone while we prepared to leave because Liz and Debbie and some of the others were getting very restless. Gillian arrived last, completing the party, shaking her umbrella because it was raining.

When the rain stopped we were ready to go and 24 women fell out of the pub *en route* to the next. Singing and linking arms, we tried to render a version of 'Viva España', but none of us really knew the words. Debbie shouted, 'C'mon, women,' encouragingly. The terms 'girls' was forgotten, left inside the factory; out on the street in force, we were women. Julie and Tessa still sported their hats which prompted passing cars to hoot and men to whistle as we moved up the High Street with Lisa and others ducking in and out of the pubs asking the men to buy them drinks and laughing loudly as they ran away. We were on our way to the city's 'fun pub', The Rocking Horse, which, as Lisa pointed out, 'used to have a male stripper, but he went over the top, like letting women lick his thing and pushing it into their faces, so they stopped it.' Trish pushed Lisa and giggled at this description, but we were now at the pub.

We squeezed into the already very crowded pub where the music was so deafening that it abruptly ended all conversation.

Some of our group made their way towards a small dance floor where they formed a circle and started to raise their legs high in the air in their own version of a can-can. Fran was wearing a tight skirt which split all the way up the back and which we then tried to pin together amid giggles while the can-can went on around us. We couldn't talk to one another because the music was so loud; occasionally, though, Lisa or Trish or Julie would shout while they went back and forth to the bar buying drinks. Most of us didn't buy drinks in this pub, we were there to dance a bit and to see the current male stripper, as Rita made clear, 'C'mon, we've come to see the stripper.'

She was interrupted by the arrival of a huge gorilla which lunged at the women on the dance floor while they shrieked with horror and delight. The gorilla dashed from one end of the pub to the other, grunting and leaping at any women in its path until it disappeared behind the bar. The gorilla, like the bartenders in clown costumes, was part of the fun at the fun pub. On the small stage next to the dance area, a disc jockey appeared clutching a record and wearing a kilt, bloomers and wellington boots topped off by a blonde wig. Liz ran over to him and explained that we were celebrating a twins' wedding. Rita shouted across, 'Get on with it, will you?' at him, so prompted, he sounded a fanfare which brought a lull to the pub. Julie and Tessa, encouraged by some hefty pushing, went up onto the tiny stage with the disc jockey.

Amid the laughter of their friends Julie and Tessa scowled at the DJ and the audience as he asked them to raise their skirts and show their knees to the sound of the 'Stripper' music. He pushed them forward and suggested they might put their blouses off-shoulder. Poor Julie and Tessa were covered in embarrassment and desperately looked for some way out. Their friends, though, shouted, 'Get 'em off' at them and clapped and laughed as the DJ lay down on the stage and dragged the twins with him. He then showed them how to wave their legs in the air in time to the music. Julie and Tess tried to hold their skirts around their knees and kick at the same time – an impossible combination which caused more peals of laughter from everyone. The music was blaring, but the pub was transfixed by the spectacle. Everyone stared at the stage and the twins while the women shouted and laughed at their friends' acute embarrassment. Tessa and Julie wriggled about and tried to get up again as the music finished and the applause rang out loudly. The compère gave them a bottle of champagne cider and shouted out wedding greetings to them both. But these were nearly drowned by the mounting call of 'Strip, strip', coming from our group who hissed and shouted at the DJ. Above the mêlée the music began again, and the disc jockey leapt high in the air onto the stage.

There was both growing excitement among my friends and loud shouts of 'Strip, strip' as they stood below the stage expectantly grinning and pushing each other. The man on stage made a flourish with his arm and discarded his jacket and threw it into the crowd which had gathered around him; this was followed by his kilt, which Liz deftly caught and threw back at him before he could turn around. The loss of the kilt revealed an enormous pair of bloomers which were greeted with shouts of derision and whistles. There was no doubt that he was an extraordinary sight in his bloomers, tights and gumboots; he looked more like a circus clown than a male stripper. He counted – one, two – and off came the bloomers to reveal another pair; when these were discarded, he produced a cloth replica of a penis and testicles in fawn – a poor imitation of the one Tessa had been given. Standing on stage in tights over pants and wellington boots waving his cloth penis at the crowd, he was a pathetic sight. Debbie shouted loudly, 'He hasn't got anything, no wonder he sewed that together,' which prompted more laughter and a growing number of taunts from our group. Undaunted, he shouted back, 'Well, you came to see the male stripper, here I am. Who wanted the stripper?' which prompted more abuse from Deb and Liz while Tessa and Julie shouted at me, 'C'mon, Sal, we're going.' Fran whispered, 'We only came for the bottle.' All together, we surged towards the door – half-emptying the pub as we went, shouting, complaining about the stripper and his lack of assets.

Outside on the pavement we shook the bottle of cider so hard that when it was opened it gave us a shower and Fran and a few others drank what little was left. We were off again, passing the police station with linked arms and in good voice, we were loud, noisy and abusive, shouting at passing cars, the police and anyone in range and enjoying every minute of this freedom. Debbie continued to shout at all of us 'C'mon, women,' while Chris and Judy tried to confirm their arrangements: 'If you get someone tonight don't go home without me, remember we said we'd share a taxi.' Judy looked annoyed, 'Okay, don't go on. What if you get someone?' Every so often Liz, Trisha, or one of the others would rush at the group and grab their friend's waist and try to lift her off the ground, while others danced up the street, jumping in the air and giving out shouts. We were all high on our friendship and the sense of power it gave us, but also on the excitement surrounding the expectations of the evening, the unknown adventures that lay ahead. As we danced and ran through the city centre everyone seemed to know where we were going; the hen party route was familiar to everyone, and no one asked, 'Where next?' The important thing, it seemed, was to get there in a hurry because we were bound for a club, The Baby Doll, which let groups of women in free if they arrived before ten. We were like a collective Cinderella and we just made it.

Out of breath from our run and laughing at the impracticability of stiletto heels, we arrived at the club entrance which was on a side street and was poorly lit. Though we were all anxious to get inside, the sight of two large and menacing bouncers temporarily subdued the group and we went into the club quietly, meekly almost, a very brief moment of quiet in an otherwise noisy and raucous evening. Inside, disco music blared out from loudspeakers and the place was dark but for the dance floor which had spotlights trained on it. Velvet booths scattered around the area and near the bar were almost empty at this point, although there was another hen party under way and a group of men at the bar. Rita pressed drinks on everyone while Lisa and I and some of the others staked a claim to a couple of booths near the dance floor, across from the small stage. Tessa looked tired and pale by this time, after the events at work. Rita tried to encourage her daughter to cheer up: 'It's your hen party, you know, not your funeral, Tessa.' Julie was already on the dance floor with some of the others who formed a circle and danced with impassive faces around their handbags while the men at the bar made sexist comments on the faces and bodies of the women: 'Well, she's not bad on the body but I don't fancy the face, the blonde one there with the tits.' Tessa, who was sitting next to me, turned to face the man who spoke and told him to 'fuck off' and then said to me: 'They make me sick, that's all they think about. Let's have a drink, Sal.' I agreed with Tessa and felt my anger rising to explosion-point as we made our way to and from the bar amid a sea of such comments. We were in a cattle-market.

From our seats beside the dance floor, Tessa and I watched our friends dance and Debbie came to join us and to survey the men, 'I think he's all right, I like 'im. Do you, Sal?' She pointed to a tall, dark-haired young man. I was non-committal as she dragged me onto the dance floor to join the others. The club began to fill up because the pubs had closed. The men had grown bolder. They started to interrupt the groups of dancing women who still had impassive faces, although Lisa and some of the others were beginning to sway and Julie was bumping into people and lurching from side to side. Lisa announced, 'I'm pissed,' and Fran agreed with her.

As we were dancing our group was approached by three large drunken men who started to make remarks about legs and 'tits' and who lurched towards us, prompting me, my anger now very visible, to tell them loudly to 'piss off' which was applauded and cheered by my friends who could hear me, it seemed, above the disco and the drunken roar. From nowhere a dark-haired man ran onto the dance floor and started to kiss and hug Julie before moving on to Fran and Lisa who enjoyed every minute of the encounter. Julie reeled back to our seats and, laughing, said, 'Did you see that, Mam? Terrible, init?' Rita grinned and disagreed, 'Go on, it's your hen night, have fun and kiss all the boys you want. You're going to be married tomorrow.' Rita sipped her drink and smiled benignly at everyone (Julie's future mother-in-law had already gone home) while she told me about the wedding and her family. Brenda interrupted to say goodnight and explain that she had to leave because her father was very strict. Rita sympathised and Liz explained that Brenda had a stepfather who wouldn't let her out after eleven, 'He could make it different for tonight, poor Brenda. Some people say he beats her up as well, he's a pig.' Liz said this out of Brenda's hearing and then went with her to the door to say goodbye.

At the witching-hour of midnight a seedy, fat man in a white dinner-jacket appeared on stage and announced the names of all the intending brides. When Tessa and Julie were mentioned we all cheered and edged closer to the stage. Each bride was called up on stage in turn, seated on a stool and subjected to the following:

What's your name?
Mary.
Well, you'll soon be a bride so lots of luck to you. Are you
    wearing tights or stockings? ah, it's stockings, look at those
    suspenders.

At which point the seedy fellow in the white jacket raised Mary's leg high in the air and placed a blue and white garter on her thigh. The leg was raised higher and higher with each bride amid cheers that grew louder and louder. As each woman left the stage she was handed a bottle of Asti Spumante and soon corks were popping all around us and the floor was awash with sparkling white wine. The twins were last on stage: 'Well, twins, two of you, well I'm not sure how we're going to manage this. Let's have you one at a time. Who's first?' Julie was pushed forward by our group who were crowded around the stage and the compère tried to get her to sit on the stool, but she pushed him away. Her friends shouted at her to sit down and the seedy man tried again, a little shaken by her resistance. Finally, Julie sat down on the stool and he moved towards her to put the garter on only to be met by her foot kicking out at him. He backed off, gingerly putting the garter around her knee, to the delight of the crowd which was shouting and laughing. Julie fell off the stool and grabbed the bottle of Asti and fell full length into the arms of her friends. Tessa had watched Julie's ordeal and she arrived on stage with a clear warning to the compère 'not to mess around,' which he heeded. He did not try to raise her leg high in the air and asked her most civilly if she would please sit down on the stool where he put a garter around her knee. She started to get off the stool very quickly and to put her hand out for her bottle of Asti when the compère tried to intervene to say that they had had a bottle. Tessa grabbed her bottle and ran back to her seat. We opened both bottles and Rita produced a camera and took pictures of us as a group and of Tessa and Julie with a few friends. We were slipping around in the sticky wine which was now everywhere. Julie was still angry about her encounter with the man on stage: 'Did you see that, Sal? The way that bloke was trying to push me around? I'll punch his face in. I don't like him, dirty ol' man.' Tessa agreed wholeheartedly and also commented on his meanness: 'What about that? He didn't want to give us a bottle each, huh!'

Julie ran off towards the bar and slipped along the way, her friends helped her to sit down while they produced more drinks for her and each other. Tina sat down with us and suddenly threw up all over the dance floor and was helped into the loo by her friends. Julie was now quite drunk and was starting to fall over and cry. She moaned and wailed that she didn't want to go home to the flat she shared with Dave because he would be out all night with another woman: 'They all do that on their stag night, go with another girl.' Rita began to look quite worried about Julie and suggested that she go home with her. Kim intervened and offered to take Julie home and stay with her. While we were deciding this and organising a taxi, other women continued to dance and the men around the floor kept up a steady commentary on the faces and bodies of the women, talking over their heads as though they were absent and discussing parts of the body – legs, breasts, hips – as though they had no relationship to the whole. It reminded me of nothing so much as images in pornographic photographs.[7]

At three, we headed for home having gathered up the remnants of the group and put them into taxis; Tessa and I went home together which made us laugh. 'You and me, we're the sober ones, eh, Sal?' At Tessa's we went up the three flights of stairs to her attic flat; there was no sign of Carl and she looked very sad, but said she was too tired to care where he was.

The following morning in the canteen most of us sat dazed, clutching our heads and complaining of feeling sick and tired. Painful though this was, everyone agreed that the night before had been a really good night, 'a laff' and something to remember. Only Lisa, it seemed, had gone home with the man she had met and she was now worried about her boyfriend's reaction: 'He'll kill me if he finds out.' We all agreed that he had better not find out. All of us sat about through most of the day hardly able to stay awake and rather envious of Julie and Tessa who had the day off to make final preparations for their wedding the next day. Although there were many other hen parties during my year at the factory, it was the twins' night which was most often conjured up as a special memory and 'a really good night out'. In this way, it passed into the folklore of the department.

It is easy to see from my description that the hen party is a deeply contradictory event. Even its label, 'hen' party tells us a lot about how women are viewed when we compare it with the virile symbol of the stag used for the men's night out. Nevertheless, a night on the town does present women with the opportunity to come together outside the confines of home and work and my friends clearly gained strength and support from the occasion. Their loud and aggressive public behaviour, with its dancing and singing, was every bit as exciting as a Reclaim the Night march. The sisterhood generated was, however, undercut by the sexism of the setting and the events to which we were subjected. The local clubs, it seemed to me, saw a ready market in young women who could be exploited to provide free entertainment for the crowds in the clubs, most especially the men. Throughout the evening it was 'woman as sex object' who was promoted and sustained through the strip club music and the routines with legs in the air, garters, the constant references to 'tits' and 'bums' which presented women as commodities, as strippers and prostitutes. The male stripper, it might be said, provided a counterpart to all this, but this was not so; he was a joke, the real action in the 'fun pub' beginning when Julie and Tessa went up on stage.

Men, although physically absent from our group, were the ever-present, all-pervading context which surrounded the hen party and this male world was constructed on stereotypical lines: sexism was rife. One reason for wanting a bloke around was that he would pay for the drinks; this was an important consideration, as my friends made clear. An evening such as this, despite the free entries and free bottles, was an expensive night that fell on a Thursday – a man who paid for the alcohol was an asset. There was, therefore, a lot of talk about who they hoped to meet during the evening and one way to meet men was to chat to them in pubs and to make them aware of you in the clubs by dancing. You danced with your friends because this gave you the support that you might need at any point in the evening. It was quite clear that, throughout the evening, everyone took a keen interest in one another and that they all watched out for drunks who might be dangerous or unpleasant. I want to emphasise this and the fact that no one in the group saw herself simply as a recipient of men's favours and appraisals or at their mercy. Instead, we all tried to stay in control of the evening and what we would and would not do. Despite this, all women in the clubs were treated simply as sex objects, complete only in relation to the approval of the male eye, given value only by male attention.

Unhappily, what appears to be an event which gives power to women through their solidarity is undercut by powerful sexist ideologies which contradict this. Women are placed in a situation of competition for male attention and yet the evening overall emphasised the distance between the world of women and the world of men. It is women who must be drawn into the world of men and this in itself diminishes the culture of women and its strength. Relations between the sexes were characterised and caricatured as sexual relations, relations that are natural and, therefore, immutable. They were not viewed as socially constructed forms of behaviour which brought biology and culture together. It was biology that was emphasised and, with this, the inferiority of women. The events of the hen party - the strippers, garters, legs in the air and sexual innuendoes provided by clubs, and seedy licentious men in white dinner-jackets - all emphasised the subordination of women and the power of men to trivialise and denigrate us all.

Here comes the bride

Tessa and Julie, having survived the bride's ritual and the hen party, had ahead of them the final stages of the process that changed a girl into a woman, the traditional marriage ceremony which, as Michèle Barrett and Mary McIntosh have pointed out, powerfully symbolises 'the whole historical baggage of male power and patriarchal authority'.[8] The wedding publicly tied sex and economics together; the very foundation of marriage which was forcefully acknowledged in the rituals of the shopfloor. This did not change the fact that to be a bride was to be a celebrity, not just for a day in a white gown, but for weeks prior to the event as details of the wedding were discussed in the breaks over and over again. Still, amid the discussions on white or cream dresses, blue or pink flowers, two or six bridesmaids, there was an underlying and enduring theme struggling to invert the notion of patriarchal authority in marriage. It was a theme which Lisa and the twins often brought to the fore and it can be seen in the following canteen discussion:

Julie Well, we've got this flat so we've moved in [*eyes down*].
Sallie If you are living with him, why get married?
Julie Dunno really. It's better to be married. I don't really
   want to live with 'im, it's just that we got this flat so we
   thought we'd better move in. Tess is moving to her place at
   the weekend. When you're married you can tell 'em more
   what to do and you know where they are and if they go
   out, you go as well. He's not goin' out without me. I'm not
   staying at home without him.
Lisa That's right, if he wants to do something and I don't, I tell
   'im. He goes his way and I go mine. If he tried telling me
   what to do I'd smash him. I tell him to go off with his
   mates and I go off with mine.

For Julie and Tessa, Lisa and others, engagements and marriage, as I have pointed out, offered the possibility of power over men and the shopfloor ritual which surrounded marriage starkly illuminated this in the emphasis upon the phallus, symbol of male power which became available to women through marriage. Julie and Lisa raised the issue of their ability to circumscribe male freedoms, but there were no illusions about the power of men: engagements and weddings were strategies for trying to curb it.

The twins' wedding was surrounded by gossip, partly because it was a special occasion but also, because Tessa was pregnant: 'Tessie is getting into debt for this wedding of hers, white dresses, bridesmaids. I don't think it's right, going up the aisle pregnant. They are all sex mad these young ones.' But to show that she, too, could join in, Jess continued: 'Talking of that, let's look at your teeth. We were telling Savitri and Sharmilla that if you had lots of good sex it showed because you had good teeth – it's the calcium from the sperm. Poor Savi was really embarrassed and Sharmilla wouldn't open her mouth!'

Despite the gossip, the shaking of heads and 'tut tuts' the twins went ahead and bought their dresses, arranged for the cars, flowers, photographers and the reception while their mum made bridesmaids' gowns. They did it all on borrowed money.

Those of us from the factory who were invited to the wedding found our way through the maze of roads that made up the drab 1950s Furzedown Estate, where all the houses were grey, to the equally grey church in the middle. It was a modern building and the guests were gathered around a central altar when the music played and the twins arrived one each side of their dad, followed by Gillian from the department and their sisters and tiny cousins in cerise gowns and holding flowers. Julie and Tessa were almost hidden under clouds of white net and flowers. Smiling and looking very embarrassed, they moved somewhat haltingly to the centre of the church and to Dave and Carl who were dressed like twins in grey suits. The service was a modern one and soon over and the guests tumbled out into the cold, dank day. There were very few women in wedding suits and hats, most of the guests wore unremarkable clothes and our group from the factory wore skirts and white jackets, which seemed to be a sort of uniform. Few of the men wore suits except for the grooms, attendants and the father of the brides. This was not an affluent wedding.

When Tessa and Julie emerged from the church, we all cheered and threw pounds of confetti and rice over them. Friends and relatives gave them wooden spoons, mops, horseshoes and black cats for luck; they could barely hold them along with their flowers. Rita hovered around them and warmly welcomed everyone from the factory as well as other friends and relatives, while the photographer tried to move people about like dolls in a doll's house. The male photographer had a female assistant whom everyone agreed was 'worse than a teacher' because she was so bossy. She tried to set up the photos without regard to the feelings of the twins or anyone else and everyone became more and more angry. But the situation was saved by a bit of slapstick when the photographer demanded that Carl and Dave should pick up their brides and be photographed. Carl collapsed under the weight of Tessa and Julie giggled and wriggled so much she fell on her knees revealing, in fact, the blue-and-white garter from the club. Despite the cold and the drizzle, these photos caused lots of laughs and, still giggling, the brides were gently nudged towards the waiting car, a white Rolls which took up the whole road. The brides waved regally and we clapped and cheered. As they stepped into the car their bouquets went in two directions and there was a scramble to catch them. Gillian bashfully emerged with one and Debbie, obviously delighted, with the other. Anxious by now to be out of the cold, we all made a dash for the community centre where the reception was to be held.

The interior of the community centre was as drab as other parts of the estate and was laid out in familiar style with trestle tables covered in white paper cloths and a central table piled high with sandwiches, crisps, sausage rolls, biscuits and chicken legs. Inside we waited for the couples to arrive. They came in glowing, Julie and Tessa flushed with excitement, eyes sparkling, looking very young and very pretty like picture-book brides; the older women wept and the younger ones sighed. But this romantic cameo was soon overturned by a sudden rush towards the table with the food, a noisy scrum developed and the food disappeared in a matter of minutes, leaving the wedding cake amid the debris of crisps and paper plates.

Tessa's new mother-in-law looked around disapprovingly and complained that the wedding party had not eaten, which was true. Apart from complaints and disapproval, she said nothing all afternoon and spoke to no one outside her immediate family. She was considered 'stuck up' and 'lah de dah' by the twins' family and no one was surprised when, later in the day, Rita and Mrs Coburn quarrelled fiercely and the Coburns left the party.

Music played at full blast from the time we arrived and efforts by the twins' brother, Keith, to read out wedding cards and telegrams for the couples were lost in the noise and distortions produced by the PA system. No one seemed to mind. We began our dance routine in a group while small children also clattered around the dance floor and ancient aunts and grannies smiled benignly and shouted encouragement. Finally, Keith did manage to call everyone to order to witness the cutting of the cake and we stood on chairs, whistled, and cheered and threw paper plates in the air which added to the festive atmosphere of the celebration. More and more drink was consumed from the bar in the corner, along with a large quantity of crisps and nuts because we were all hungry. Some of us had completely missed the food and Rita was angry that the caterers should have provided so little for £250. Later, some of our crowd went for fish and chips for themselves and some of the other guests. It added to the informality of the wedding party. While we danced the evening away the men who were attached, in one way or another, to my friends sat around talking to each other consuming a great deal of beer and occasionally trying to police 'their' women. Sally was in trouble because she was already high and her boyfriend kept shouting at her, which meant that she shouted back and fell into the lap of another man. Exhausted, with sore feet, we retreated to some chairs where Linda was musing on the wedding: 'I'm not going to get married, it's such a waste of money, look at all this. If I do it will be in a registry office in my jeans. My sister always lived with her bloke, but now they've got kids they think they might get married.'

Kris agreed with her: 'I'm saving up for a car so I can go places, not get married to some bloke.'

The others disagreed. For them, a white wedding was magic like nothing else could ever be. As Sally said: 'Married in a registry office, no thanks. It's not right. I want a white dress like Julie's and lots of bridesmaids.'

Some of the guests had arrived with gifts for the couples, unwrapped household items like plastic bowls, tea-towels, sheets and saucepans, most of them cheap and cheerful practical things which were at the limits of what people could afford. They were welcome gifts, graciously received, and both couples thanked people profusely – but they were then stacked up in a corner so that they did not get in the way of the party, the dancers and revellers who were becoming wilder as the night wore on. Julie and Tessa joined in once they had discarded their bridal dresses for more ordinary skirts and dresses. Julie had a shiny black 'boob tube' which invited comments from everyone who thought it 'very sexy', which pleased Julie enormously. She was transformed from the demure bride in white lace and ribbons back into the high-heeled vamp, in a shiny top, black skirt slit to her thighs and a cigarette in her hand. Tessa had a new dress which hid her expanding waistline and both of them looked as though they had thoroughly enjoyed their wedding and intended to party late into the night, which they did. Tessa and Carl were spending a night in a local hotel, but Julie and Dave were going home and then away during the regular holiday fortnight.

Everyone enjoyed the twins' wedding, from their great-grand-mother who insisted on calling Tessa her 'chickie' to the women from the factory. It was a wonderful party, a relaxed noisy get-together totally removed from the stuffiness of formal weddings and a wonderful climax to the celebrations at work. Rita, the twins' mum, told me with tears in her eyes that since they had been born she had always hoped they would have a double wedding and 'it's like a dream come true, for me.' She glowed throughout the celebrations and nothing marred the day for her – not even the unfriendliness of Carl's mother.

The twins' wedding, from the moment of its inception, had a special magic which everyone at the factory revelled in. There were, however, other weddings throughout the summer which followed the same rituals and involved lots of women. Everyone was aware of the enormous costs of a white wedding. The twins' wedding probably cost about £800 and at least £600 of this was borrowed money. By the end of their wedding the twins and their mum were in debt – so much so that, months later, Tessa and Carl had still not collected their wedding photos because they could not raise the money to pay for them.

Michelle and Pat who both married during that summer also had elaborate white weddings and they could cost every detail from the calling of the banns to the church flowers. Most wedding dresses cost £100–£200 and all brides wanted to buy one, whereas they were keen to make their bridesmaids' gowns. A reception started at £250 and took off depending upon the number of guests, the place, the wine. Michelle had her wedding reception at the company social club and everyone who went acknowledged that there was plenty of good food and enough to drink. Even though she, too, thought it was good value, she pointed out: 'That's only the start, on top you've got cars, flowers, photographers, it's coming up to £1,000 easy. It cost such a lot of money in the end you begin to wonder if it's worth it.'

Given the costs of white weddings and average earnings among young working-class people it is not surprising that they spend some time saving for the big day. They do not, because they cannot, rely upon their parents to foot the bill and they are all very anxious to get the day right. This is especially interesting in the light of Diana Leonard's study of courtship and marriage.[9] As she points out, there are wedding manuals written to ensure that tradition is upheld and that people will spend their money on getting it right. The firms that service weddings have a trump card: they can appeal to the 'once in a life-time' nature of a white wedding. Using this as a form of emotional blackmail, they gently but persuasively cajole parents and brides into buying expensive flowers, cars, printed invitations, photo albums and so on. The wedding becomes, in fact, a commercialised event which requires large amounts of money and months of painstaking work on the part of the women involved. On the day, though, it is all forgotten in the glow that surrounds the bride and the opportunity a wedding affords for the reassertion of family ties and the bonds of kin.

Kris suggested that she would rather buy a car than spend money on an elaborate wedding. She was in a very small minority. Most of my friends wanted a white wedding, a day when they could be beautiful and the centre of attention. This was the day when Pat and Michelle, Tessa and Julie were admitted to the world of women; in stepping into this world, or falling into his arms, they soon realised that the party was quickly over. All too soon, the wedding dress was packed in polythene and the bride realised that weddings are one moment, marriage something else: as the saying has it, 'you sink into his arms only to wake up with your arms in the sink.'

7

You sink into his arms
. . . by arrangement

The last chapter emphasised the way in which shopfloor culture among women celebrated the bride as a symbol of womanhood. Despite its specific history and cultural setting within the white working class, the potential power of the shopfloor celebration lay in the way it could abstract the bride from her cultural context and, thereby, offer the experience as a unifying one for all women. That there were common themes surrounding the bride was not in doubt; these were captured in the delight with which women shared their wedding photographs. This does not mean that all brides are the same. In this chapter I want to discuss the cultural context in which Indian women become brides, and the way in which this is subject to changes and conflicts which are crucially played out within marriage. My concern is not so much with the ritual and ceremony of weddings (although these are fascinating), but with the way that Indian women understand and act upon the contradictions of their lives.

Most of the Indian women I knew at StitchCo were Gujarati Hindus who had arrived in Britain following the exodus from East Africa. This had taken them initially to India and their relatives in Gujarat, but, when it proved difficult to earn a living without land or capital to sustain them, they moved on to the cities of Britain. For many of the second generation this meant that they had been educated in Needletown and that, because of this, they had been introduced to Western notions of sex and romance in the school playground. They spoke English easily and fluently although they often felt uncomfortable if they were asked to read and write in English. For some, there was the added problem that they were not literate in Gujarati either.

Despite having moved once to East Africa, and again to Britain, Gujaratis (and especially certain groups among them) held fast to the life of the village, including its caste distinctions and the

importance of reproducing these through marriage. Caste, as
M.N. Srinivas has written, 'is popularly understood as the division
of society into a fivefold hierarchy with the Brahmins (priests) at
the head, followed in order by Kshatriyas (warriors), Vaishyas or
traders, Shudras or servants and labourers, and, lastly, the
Untouchables.' This last group was renamed the Harijan, or
'Children of God', by Mahatma Gandhi. But, as Srinivas has also
pointed out:

> The idea of caste as the fivefold division of society
> represents a gross oversimplification of facts. The real unit
> of the caste system is not one of the five *varnas* but *jati*,
> which is a very small endogamous group practising a
> traditional occupation and enjoying a certain amount of
> cultural, ritual and juridical autonomy.[1]

Caste relations are regulated by notions of purity and pollution
which allow or forbid interactions and which prescribe specific
roles for certain castes. Midwives, for example, come from the
Harijan because they deal with the polluting aspects of birth.

'Gujarat', wrote H.S. Morris in his book on the Indians of
Uganda, 'is pre-eminently a land of castes, and in no other part of
India are the sub-divisions so minute.'[2] Given this, it is hardly
surprising that arranged marriages should be so important in the
Gujarati communities. Although caste distinctions must be
maintained, in certain communities – such as the Patel community
– generations of status may be overcome by marriage if families
with daughters can marry them upwards. In order to do this they
must compensate the groom's family by the provision of a large
dowry. Amrit Wilson suggests that the move to East Africa
generated new wealth which inflated the size of dowries and the
importance of gold among the Patels.[3] That dowries were already
large can be seen from D.F. Pocock's study of the Patidar in the
mid-1950s. He wrote that when he arrived in Gujarat the local
press of the time was highlighting the case of a man who had
offered a dowry of £100,000 for his daughter.[4]

Money, gold and marriage are inextricably linked together
despite the outlawing of dowry in India, as the following
description by Richard Lannoy makes clear:

> At one temple ceremony at which I was present, the bride was
> ignored while the heads of the two families sat in ceremonial

> attire with their accountants and their bulky ledgers to discuss the financial transactions associated with the marriage. Heaps of banknotes were piled in front of them on the marble floor at the feet of the deity.[5]

Lannoy also wrote that, although this emphasises the economic value of the bride, it does little to enhance her sense of self-worth.

In order to find a suitable bride or groom the Gujaratis in East Africa looked back to India and the Patels continued to support the marriage circles, composed of certain villages who exchanged brides. The move further from India to Britain did not initially halt the exchange of brides and would not necessarily have done so had the immigration rules not changed. But the problems surrounding the marriages of urban and Western educated men and women to village women and men had grown and with this a certain resistance from young people in the Asian communities here.

There are other issues as well; large dowries present increasingly difficult problems for the impoverished sections of the Indian communities. East African Asians have, too readily, been characterised as a wealthy people who left East Africa with the fruits of businesses and merchant ventures. For the most part, this is simply not true. Very few brought capital with them (and these had left earlier or sent their money ahead of them) because many were shopkeepers existing at the margins – as they now do in Britain – or artisans earning wages not profits from business enterprises.[6] The poverty of the East African Asians is, in part, marked by the proportion of women who are now employed in factories, shops and other industries and who, like white working-class women, contribute essential income to the family. It is important to lay the ghost of this mistaken stereotype of the wealthy East African Asian merchant or shopkeeper. Most of those involved in the exodus, especially from Uganda, are now (if they are lucky) working in manual jobs earning wages. This is the economic reality and it has been confused with the importance of an ideology which emphasises commercial enterprise, trade and entrepreneurship, a concomitant of the trading background of Gujarat and the fact that in East Africa Asians could have trading licences, but not land.

None of this affects the desire for caste exclusivity and the reproduction of the traditional ways by the older generation. One of my friend's fathers told me categorically: 'Patels only marry with Patels, but there are differences of caste and region. Our family only marries with certain other families.' An arranged marriage means that women can be vitally important in promoting alliances that are avantageous to a family, or in bringing goods and cash into a household in the form of dowry (lately a source of considerable concern among women in India where the numbers of deaths among young brides is increasing, and the circumstances surrounding their deaths is suspicious).[7] In the British context they not only set up alliances or raise the status of a family, nor do they simply bring gold and cash with them; they are also workers in the labour market. In addition to the domestic services they provide for the receiving household, they bring earned income into the household which was previously part of their own family income. It may not, therefore, be quite so easy to part with a daughter who is essential to the economic well-being of a family unit, especially in a situation where elderly relatives are dependent upon the younger members of the family or younger brothers and sisters upon an older sister. Suraya was an example of this situation. Set against this is the problem of maintaining the status of a family that does not seek to marry its daughters well.

Parents are under an obligation to ensure the marriage of their children. They conscientiously seek a good match for each child because they will be held responsible for the success of the marriage. It is an anxious time for the parents of a daughter because they know that they are sending her into another family, probably at some distance, and that they must try to secure her future happiness, but that this can only be achieved by marrying within the right caste among families with sound histories and good prospects. In the British context caste is the most easily discernible feature of the match, the other factors are less easy to control and are not now surrounded by the familiar world of Gujarat or Kampala. The young people in Britain understand this and see the possibility of exercising more control over their choice of bride or groom. Such a suggestion is a direct assault on parental rights and duties and on a patriarchal hierarchy in which fathers are synonymous with power and authority in the family. Although the pain caused by the attempt to make a decision for themselves was enormous, there was no doubt that some of the young women in the factory wanted to make that decision and to exercise a choice – not wilfully and outside parental advice, but as adults who had grown up as Indians in a British, urban environment. The debate surrounding marriage became part of a wider discussion on the independence and autonomy of Indian women. It is this, set against the traditions of the arranged marriage, which is at issue in this chapter.

Two generations

My friends usually lived at home until they married when they said a traumatic farewell to their parents and siblings. While at home, as daughters, they were subject to the authority of their fathers and brothers who circumscribed their freedom of movement, and whom they could meet. All women are subject to the restrictions imposed by the notion that they hold within them the family honour, their actions reacting upon the whole family not just on themselves. Women are seen as the keepers of culture and tradition, the upholders of moral values, and this burden weighs heavily upon the younger members of the family. This notion is internalised and thus there was an effective self-policing system among women who used gossip, shaming and ridicule as effective sanctions against themselves.[8] Older women are often the fiercest and loudest critics of the younger women. It gives them a degree of power; it is also a measure of their powerlessness in a patriarchal situation that they can only exercise control over other, younger women, usually at the bottom of the hierarchy in the household. Nevertheless, it means that women I met were divided and placed in antagonistic relations; for those who were subject to gossip and derision, it was a painful and effective sanction which others bore in mind.

Women like Shanta were acutely aware of the mechanisms through which the older generation sought to control the younger. Her situation and views on marriage presented the opposition between generations. On one occasion when I was having tea with Shanta's family, her father told me that he was planning to take her to India 'to find a nice boy' for her to marry. Shanta was out of the room at the time and her father, at this point, knew nothing of her plans to marry her boyfriend. When I told Shanta what her father was planning, she sighed and shook her head while she explained that this was not the first time he had made such plans:

My father is very traditional and he took me to India last time and tried to marry me. I was there for four months and I met this nice man, very good-looking and all, going to be a doctor, and he liked me. He said he wanted to get engaged and my dad was really keen. A doctor, you know! But I didn't want to marry him. He came to London and found out where I was and he was supposed to get married and he's stopped it because he found out I wasn't married. But I don't want him. You can't marry *a doctor*, you marry a person, and I like my boyfriend. If I can't marry him, I won't marry anyone. You see, when you are my age people start to talk, to gossip all the time, that's why I like to stay away from here. Indians are always gossiping, they talk behind your back.

Shanta's version of a marriage based upon mutual attraction broke all the rules surrounding arranged marriages which were based upon factors outside the likes and dislikes of the individuals involved. Her conception was a 'love-match', for which there were certainly precedents. It was bound to mean gossip, though, and if it should fail then Shanta alone would be held responsible. She showed remarkable courage in resisting the force of tradition, the power of gossip, and the emotional bonds of her affection for her father, which were very real. Shanta was single-minded in pursuing her version of marriage, which was much more closely aligned with the Western view of romantic love and a companionate relationship between a man and a woman that confused the separate spheres of men and women characteristic of Indian cultures.

Shanta's friends knew just how difficult it was to choose the path she had chosen because they, too, were wrestling with the contradictions of their lives. Their parents, like Shanta's father, did their best to pretend that life would carry on as before. Sushila, especially, was aware of this and the problems it was generating for her and how these would be amplified for her younger sister:

Our parents don't understand the younger people at all. They think we are going to be just like them, but our lives are different, in a different country. Those girls who have grown up here want more freedom. I have a little sister who was two when we came and is now 12 and she doesn't understand half of what my mother says. She has gone to school here, she has English friends and she wants to do what they want to do. It's going to be very hard for her when she is 16 or 17 because my parents don't understand her, and, like the older people, they don't try very hard. They are too bothered by gossip. Our

> community is full of gossip and if a girl does something wrong
> they blame the parents. Our parents always try their best for
> us, but they don't understand our life here.

Sushila's sensitivity to the problem was all too apparent as was her
desire for her parents to be more aware of the situation that their
daughters faced. She, like Shanta and the other women, was
annoyed by the importance of gossip in Indian communities and
the power that it exercised over their lives because their parents so
willingly granted it credibility. Gossip was one area of social
control, the other was the differential treatment of brothers and
sisters which Sushila and others saw as unfair and in need of radical
change:

> I wouldn't like my parents to be upset by what I did, so I do as
> they say. But, you know, my brothers can go out any time and
> come back next day and no one asks them where they are
> going, where they have been. It's very unfair to the girls in our
> community and they talk about the girls who go out a lot.
> And it's not very nice, some of the things they say.

The issue was fraught with difficulties: Sushila and others wanted
more freedom to go to places alone, but this carried the danger of a
bad reputation and no woman wanted to risk that. Instead, they
tried to live within the constraints, while they made persistent
efforts to move the boundaries of their lives further out, to shift
their field of vision and of action. Many felt that without the
power of gossip in their local communities their parents might
have been encouraged to be more liberal. Such an idea was a
measure of the loyalty that daughters felt towards their parents,
and the generosity with which they tried to understand them, in
relation to the irksome restrictions of their lives.

Sushila, like Shanta or Rekha, Suraya or Lata, was clearly aware
of the momentum of social change surrounding her and how these
changes were affecting the way that Indian women thought about
their sexuality, marriage and relations between husbands and
wives. Sushila, at 19, was aware of the decisions that some of her
other friends had made in relation to sex and their own virginity.
Her views, shared by her friends at the factory, were quite clear: 'I
don't think you should go to bed with a man when you are not
married to him. I wouldn't do that, but Indian girls do now, they
do, as well as drinking and smoking. They are mainly the girls who
grew up here.'

Taruna agreed with Sushila, and, like many of her friends, she made the comparison with English women: 'English girls go too far. It's not nice. When Indian boys and girls go out they will go to a film or a café, perhaps they will hold hands – even kiss, but no more. I don't think it's right until you get married.'

What, in fact, Sushila wanted was a boyfriend and marriage, not a series of sexual adventures: 'I would like to choose my husband and get to know him before I got married, just to have a boyfriend, not lots and then get married.'

Sushila had no intention of becoming a wayward woman, a 'modern' woman and of flaunting her sexuality. Instead, she wanted more control over her marriage and the possibility of a relationship with her husband which was more equal than the traditional one. She was not unusual in wanting this or its concomitant, a house where she and her husband could live independently of parents-in-law and other relatives. Sushila and her friends tried to innovate, but in ways which would not be considered outlandish and reprehensible within their own communities. They knew that there were going to be limits; in trying to set these, they often related their own actions and desires to the situation of one of their friends – Sharmila – who found herself at the centre of gossip in the department. While we were at lunch, and generally discussing the issue of arranged marriages, Rekha mischievously announced to the group around the table: 'Everyone says Sharmila is pregnant, she's been acting so funny. Yesterday she was in tears and shouting at everyone, and before that she was fainting and bumping into things – sounds like she's pregnant.'

Sushila contested this as another piece of departmental gossip: 'Well, she's very stupid if she is, people here always say that when anything is wrong. I don't think she is, but she is having trouble with her boyfriend.'

Leaving the rest of the group to decide one way or the other, Sushila turned to me to explain Sharmila's situation. It was clear from the tale as she told it that Sushila did not want to judge Sharmila harshly, but that she trembled as she put herself in her friend's shoes:

> You see, Sallie, Sharmila was married – an arranged marriage – and she has a child. But she didn't like the man, or they quarrelled or something, and she got divorced. After that her

parents gave her the freedom to meet anyone and go with any boy. I think they thought, well, the boy we chose was no good for her so it's better if she chooses her own next time. So she started going out with all kinds of boys and then this one who is married and she wants to marry him. But he has discovered that if he divorces his wife she will keep half the house and the furniture and things so he doesn't want to divorce her, and Sharmila doesn't know what to do because his wife says she wants him to come back, so he is going to end with Sharmila and she is very unhappy. But, you know, she is partly to blame, going with all these different boys. I wouldn't be surprised if she was pregnant because they say she went to bed with him, and some of the others. I wouldn't like that. I don't want to go like Sharmila with one boy, then another boy, I don't like it. My parents don't let me do that. I would hate to go like Sharmila, married, then with other boys.

Sharmila's path was a daring and lonely one and the strain showed often in her face and in her frequent illnesses which meant time off work. At one level, she was a romantic figure – young, beautiful and, literally, reviled by some of the older women who were not willing to accept that a divorced woman could be a full member of the community. The younger women sympathised with her as much as they dared because they knew she was an outsider and the subject of vicious gossip – which was unromantically painful. Shanta did not agree with Sharmila's behaviour, but did sympathise with her because she was, herself, the subject of gossip and fiercely resented its power in the community:

Indians are always gossiping, they talk behind your back, it's the same at work. You know, these older Indian ladies are always talking behind my back. They do it to all the younger ones, Hansa and Usha are the worst. They prattle about you all the time. How we should do this, and not this. I hate them. Asha is just as bad; they creep around people. She is always giving sweets and things to Gillian and Lisa in a creepy sort of way – secretly, so that other people won't know about it.

Shanta not only had a boyfriend she hoped to marry, but she also had a sister who had divorced her husband because she was ill-treated by him. Shanta was keenly aware of the courage that was required even though divorce was not, now, unknown in her community. Like Sushila, she wanted the older generation to try to come to terms with the new situation of women's lives in Britain:

> My sister's husband was horrible to her. Finally, she decided to divorce him. She is very brave. More Indian women do have divorces now. It's the same with boyfriends, more Indian girls know the boy they will marry. We younger ones prefer it like that, the older ones don't like it, but we have to change. We are not in India now and we want more freedom, not like running about with boys, but to make up our own minds.

Shanta was quite determined to 'make up her own mind'. In order to smooth the path to her marriage, though, she tried to involve one of her brothers-in-law as a go-between, hoping he would suggest her boyfriend as a possible husband for her. Her plans were pre-empted by her father's insistence that she should go to India to marry. His insistence meant, finally, that the news of her relationship with Vijay became public and her father resolutely set his face against the marriage, although her boyfriend's parents were willing and her mother gave tacit approval (although she chose not to rebel openly against her husband). Shanta was torn between her love for her boyfriend and her loyalty to her father, and, very courageously, she resolved the situation by insisting upon her right to marry – whether her father approved or not. He did not, and she married in a registry office with some friends and her boyfriend's family to support her. Her father cut her off completely, yet Shanta hoped that they would be reconciled after a year when the community would have registered his disapproval.

All her friends supported her in any way that they could: Rekha provided legitimate excuses for her absence from home and other friends gave her sympathetic support. They judged her father to be very intolerant because Vijay was from the same community, although not from one of the families in Shanta's marriage circle. In fact, he had a higher status than Shanta which in normal circumstances would have been welcomed. The problem was that this was a relationship that had been formed outside the control of fathers and brothers and the older generation; it reversed the hierarchy and could not, therefore, be accepted.

The conflict between generations is a very real one and it is born as much out of misunderstandings and an unwillingness to listen to daughters as out of the issues involved. Had Sushila's parents heard our discussions they would have discovered that the issues were autonomy and adulthood, much as they are for any young person, and not sex and sexual license. Sushila and Shanta were as reluctant to develop a reputation for being promiscuous as were their parents who sought clumsily to protect them from this charge. The codes that they were trying to develop did not stop them laughing at sexual innuendoes or developing a few themselves. Still, there was always a shyness surrounding the discussion of sexuality because it was a taboo subject in Indian homes.

The restrictions surrounding women did not mean lives based only on domesticity. Suraya, for example, was a member of a local Indian drama group that performed in Needletown and elsewhere. Lata and others belonged to dance groups which meant that at festival times they were away from fathers and husbands late at night. In addition, there was the local temple, visits to friends, and weddings which provided entertainment and fun and an opportunity to meet both men and women. Rass Garba (a traditional dance) nights were also popular, and while women and men arrived separately they didn't stay that way. Whatever the constraints and the power of gossip, Gujarati boys and girls met at school and in the city; it was in these encounters that relationships were often started which became serious and led to marriage. Among some families there was a growing tolerance for this as a legitimate means to marriage – provided that the boy and the girl were compatible on religious, caste and other grounds.

As I have said, for Indian women, marriage was the issue which brought into sharp focus their subordination and the way in which they were subject to the power of parents and older brothers. There was, as this discussion has shown, a growing resentment of the manner in which women were denied the opportunity to have a part in what was the most important decision of their lives. There is an argument that arranged marriages mean no competition on the marriage-market among women, because they are not in competition for men's favours, and thus sisterhood is more easily generated and sustained. This view had no support from my friends. It was also quite clear that if women were not divided against themselves on this issue they were so divided in other ways. The structural constraints of the system made daughters into daughters-in-law and thereby subject to the power of older women who, within the hidden world of household, exercised and extended their authority over younger women. It is important, therefore, to view the desire for romantic love and companionate marriage as only part of the issue. The fundamental claim that was being staked was that women should be given greater freedom and control over their lives as individuals in their own rights.

The point for women like Shanta was that her new-found freedoms through work and the money she earned, in combination with her ability to look at Indian cultures and communities anew, meant that she wanted something different. She was quite clear about this, and spoke for many younger women when she told me, adamantly:

> I mean younger women now don't want to have a mother-in-law and a big family because you get all the work. It's not so much living with a mother-in-law, if they were free-minded it wouldn't matter, but most of them are not. They are just like those women at work, ordering you about, telling you you must wear a sari and cover your head. Well, I'm not like that and I don't like to be in the kitchen all the time.

There were contradictions, too, in the brave stance that Shanta took. Her generation of women would live with, and work through, the difficulties inherent in Western styles of marriage and nuclear-family situations. They were all quite clear that English marriages were unstable and not to be emulated, but they regarded this more as a product of cultural than structural factors. They knew, because they had friends and sisters who had experienced it, that divorce was now on the agenda and that it was important as an option for women in situations that were intolerable. They also hoped that they would be the lucky ones.

A marriage is arranged

For many of Sushila's and Shanta's friends, the decision had been made and they were now married like Amita who was expecting her first baby. Unlike her friends, she supported arranged marriages:

> Arranged marriage is better because parents always want to do the best for their children and so they find you a good wife or husband. I had never seen my husband until he came from India, but I am very happy. If you have an arranged marriage and it doesn't go well you can blame your parents and they will take you back. But if you have a love-match then they

don't have to. It's only your choice and no one else is involved. My husband thinks differently. He says he doesn't mind cross-caste marriage for his children. Say, we have a daughter – he says people should be free to choose, but I disagree. I would want my daughter to have an arranged marriage with a boy from the same caste. My husband is very modern because he lived so long in the city. He studied in Ahmadabad and he has this modern view.

Greater disquiet was expressed by Rekha, Lata and Taruna, who all supported Shanta in her difficulties. They had all had arranged marriages, but Taruna's marriage was contracted without her being consulted until the final stages when her husband had already arrived in England. She and I talked about this in her kitchen, while she made chapatis for her husband and her brothers-in-law as she explained the circumstances surrounding her marriage and her feelings about it. She was bright and cheerful as she told me, a different woman from the one who became a bride.

I am the youngest in my family. My mum and I were the last to come to England. I was born in Uganda, but I don't remember it much and then we went to India, then we came here. I'm 23 now. My sisters got married at 16, but because I was the youngest of all they kept me at home longer. I got married at 21, in the September break. I didn't know I was going to get married. When I found out I was terrified. I went to meet my husband and I had to decide, just like that, and it's the biggest decision of your life! I cried, but my parents said he was from a good family, he's the right caste, this and that – so I was married to him. I went to this place somewhere near Wolverhampton, I think it was – I didn't know where I was. I was so frightened, I cried and cried and I lost half a stone. Rekha said she was worried because I was so shy that I would just sink in a corner and not come out. I nearly did!

Taruna grinned as she concluded the story of her first encounter with her husband. When she said she was terrified, she meant it, and her friends were genuinely concerned for her. For them, Taruna's marriage highlighted the problems of a system which offered such little control to women and which required a snap decision that could not, in effect, be made. It meant that the parents of the bride decided without reference to the wishes of their daughter. This was Shanta's view of Taruna's wedding, while she recognised that there were modifications which allowed more possibilities to the couple:

> Rekha married in the traditional way and she is very happy, but she knew him already. Taruna just had to get married. It was all arranged for her and no one asked her anything. She is so quiet she doesn't like to go against her parents, so she married him. But, she has so much work to do because of all his brothers, and they don't help her. She has to do all the cooking and all the shopping for them all. Her husband makes her wear saris and tells her where she can go and who she can go with. I wouldn't be able to stand that.

Taruna was married, without consultation, to a man from India who clearly took seriously the notion that for an Indian woman, her husband was her lord. He expected Taruna to behave like a woman who had been brought up in India, not one who had been at school in England and who, until her marriage, had rarely worn a sari or cooked a chapati.

> I came here and went to school, so I always wore English clothes, now I wear saris much more. I used to think they were not nice because you couldn't walk about in them, but my husband likes them. He says it's not nice if someone comes to the house and I am in these clothes [her working clothes]. There was another thing, too. I couldn't cook. I used to help my mum, but I didn't know how to cook curries and other things, but now I cook it, somehow. Sometimes, I forget the salt or put too much pepper, but I manage, somehow.

Again, Taruna grinned as she told me this and laughed at her own incompetence. As she made curry and washed rice, I thought of her eating bacon sandwiches in the factory canteen, a secret unknown to her husband who insisted upon a strict vegetarian diet.

Taruna may have been subject to the authority of her husband, but, because he had come from India, she did not have to cope with her mother-in-law. In this, she recognised a bonus:

> Life in India is very different, more strict, my mother-in-law is there so I don't know her. She may be very nice, but I hear she is very strict so I like to stay here with my husband and his

brothers. We do more what we like because his parents are in India.

Taruna's views were echoed by Geeta, who was leaving Needletown for London after her marriage. She was also leaving her mother-in-law in Needletown: 'Most young Indian women like to be just with their husbands. Our parents and the older ladies are more traditional, but we prefer to live on our own.'

Modern marriage, as it was viewed by the women I knew, did not include living with a mother-in-law. This meant that a woman could exercise greater control in her home and that she did not need to compete with her husband's mother for his time or affection. It also meant, for young women like Taruna, that the burden of housework fell on her. Fortunately, she was assisted by her new sister-in-law, the bride of one of her husband's younger brothers. The two women, who had been strangers a couple of months previously, had quickly developed a warm and supportive relationship which allowed them to make light of the housework, cooking and shopping – although these tasks were, in fact, very onerous.

An arranged marriage, as it was experienced by Taruna and other young women, was a traumatic event over which they had no control. Given this situation, it was hardly surprising that Taruna could remember very little of her wedding day. She was, she said, 'terrified' and this paralysed her mentally and emotionally. But, she had a memento in her wedding photographs which showed a stunningly beautiful Taruna swathed in silk and gold sitting, head down, eyes turned away demurely, a diminutive startled figure who later reported, 'I kept thinking I would wake up and it would all go away.' Instead, her life radically altered, catapulting her from daughter to wife with all that that entailed. Many brides reported that they could remember little of their wedding days and this was a product of fear and exhaustion, plus the dizziness promoted by fasting and incense, the priest's incantations and the noise and liveliness of the guests at the wedding party itself.

Geeta's wedding

An Indian girl is encouraged to dream of becoming a bride, seeing in her mind's eye a glittering sari, gold earrings and bangles, flowers and henna-painted hands and feet. It is a romantic picture which everyone knows leaves out the terrible sadness of separation when the bride leaves her family to live among strangers, as a person who has virtually no status in the hierarchy of the new family group. Also omitted is the sense of the bride as an object described by Richard Lannoy: 'The new bride is an object of prying and pawing curiosity, every detail of her costume, ornaments and behaviour loudly commented on, the colour of her skin the source of discussion among the men.'[9]

In order to lighten her skin, in fact, a bride may spend several days with her face encased in a paste made from turmeric and gram flour which, it is said, will give her a fair and flawless complexion. Indian weddings in Britain hold out the same excitement and terror for women as they do for young brides in India, but the street processions and minstrels have been replaced by cars festooned with tinsel and ribbons and the time spent on ceremonials has diminished. Nevertheless, Indian weddings in Britain offer a glimpse of the festivities, the colours and sounds of weddings in Gujarat or other parts of India. The lavishness of wealthy Patel weddings is well known, both in Britain and in India, because their weddings are major events involving hundreds of people at enormous expense.

A Hindu wedding is a complex event involving a series of stages which require elaborate plans made by the fathers and other senior members of the two families who may use a go-between for the initial approaches. A bride or groom must be found, the dowry negotiated and the individuals involved must be informed. Meanwhile, an astrologer is consulted about the bride and groom, and a possibly auspicious date for the wedding. The rituals and ceremonies surrounding these events are beyond my scope here, so I will dwell only briefly on the final stages of the wedding, using Geeta's experience as a way of dramatising this.

Happily for Geeta, she was marrying a man she already knew and both families approved of the match. She was looking forward to her wedding. In fact, like other Indian brides, Geeta married twice because Gujaratis, no less than other migrants, are conscious of the necessity to have a marriage which is sanctioned by the state. This meant that some weeks prior to her 'real' wedding Geeta was married to Anil in a registry office with a celebration afterwards involving only the immediate family. Some families join this civil wedding with the traditional engagement and hold a small party, exchange gifts and receive the blessings of the priest. Although by the end of the day Geeta and Anil were legally married they were not married in the eyes of their community and they parted, returning to their separate homes, until the wedding day which would mark the change in their status.

Geeta was popular and well known in the department; because of this, she wanted to invite as many of her workmates as possible to her wedding, which prompted the following advice:

Eve You'd better send out your invitations to the girls, otherwise they won't think you're serious about it.

Geeta I will, I will. I am serious about it. We are going to do some English food. I've been talking to my mum about it, just small things like sandwiches and that.

Eve [*slyly*] And what's to drink?

Geeta [*perturbed*] It's a Hindu wedding, we don't drink.

Eve [*loudly*] Bloody Norah, Geeta. You can't expect us to bring our own. You'd better get some drink in for us. I expect to get ploughed at a wedding. I've been to other Indian weddings and there's plenty of booze. Maybe the women don't drink, but the men certainly do. A *dry* wedding! Well, there's always a first time, I suppose.

Eve turned around towards the other women in the coffee bar and, to Geeta's acute embarrassment, shouted cheerfully: 'Do you hear that girls? A dry wedding!' She turned back to Geeta and concluded: 'I'll bring me own and sup it in a corner.' Both of them laughed at the suggestion because Geeta knew Eve well enough to trust her not to turn up at her wedding clutching a bottle – which she didn't.

Although Geeta cheerfully joined in the celebrations of the shopfloor and allowed herself to be dressed up in a gymslip with black stockings and suspenders she, like her other Indian friends who joined in at work, did not have a hen party. Instead, according to custom, she went home and in the days prior to her wedding she welcomed visitors to her parents' home and smiled while they sat and talked, and the women painted their hands and feet with henna, and sang songs praising Geeta's beauty and telling her what the duties of a wife involved. Although there were romantic phrases in some of these songs, sex was not mentioned. The bride was celebrated as a virgin who would come to her husband on her wedding night, chaste and demure.

Arrangements for a traditional wedding are very taxing because the family of the bride has to organise the preparation of food, drink and accommodation for several hundred people. Geeta's family, like Lata's and others, relied on relatives and friends to assist. I had no cooking skills to offer, but I did have a car so I helped by ferrying women, food, dishes and bedding from one side of the city to the other. The network of women involved in the preparations was very wide and spread across all age groups. It was a remarkable demonstration of co-operation and the culture of women because all knew the rules and rituals surrounding the event. Relatives came from other cities too, crowding into the tiny terraced house, laughing and smiling and complimenting the bride on her beauty and her talents, and asking about future plans. Lata's sister, who also married during that summer, enjoyed the same demonstration of affection and support. Because she, too, was going to London, she showed the same sadness at leaving her mother and her sisters.

The ritual and ceremony surrounding an Indian wedding are complex and drawn out and involve different members of the family group in different processes. Geeta's father and the father of the groom had met weeks before to agree the dowry which must include household items and, traditionally, a bed. Now, dowries include radios and money sufficient for a deposit on a house. The men from each family will come together to greet one another during the wedding celebrations which spread over many days, and in Gujarat involved the groom's kin arriving in the bride's village and staying as guests of her family. It is still important for the bride's family to do everything in its power to ensure that the groom's family is fêted and given the appropriate hospitality. They are the prized guests at the wedding and they must leave with the sense that they have been well treated. If they do not, it may have serious repercussions for the way in which the bride is treated in her new home and it will become part of her history in that household. The bride goes to her new home with her jewellery, which is part of the dowry her mother has saved for over many years, and the gifts she has received from her husband and his family. Saris and gold travel with her and stay with her, for they are her wealth because she will have no share in her father's land or other property.

Amid the drama and festivity of an Indian wedding the bride has a very specifically scripted role to play and Geeta was no exception. Normally energetic and impish, the tiny Geeta played her part beautifully from the moment she arrived swathed in green, red and gold silk, weighed down by the number of bangles, anklets and earrings she wore. Her head was bowed deeply – and not just by the weight of gold and the heavy silk sari. The weight of custom and tradition demanded this attitude of submission as appropriate to the demure virginal bride who would look at no one until she gazed upon her husband's face. Her demeanour must be one of acute pain and sadness because she is leaving her family and going to a new life. For many brides there is no need to strike a pose; they are frightened and sad just like Taruna had been. But, as Geeta pointed out to me, she was sad to be leaving her family. She did, nevertheless, want to marry Anil and she was both pensive and excited because she feared that at any point she might let a smile cross her lips – which would be completely inappropriate.

According to custom the bride and groom must feed each other from silver talis. Although neither Geeta nor Anil seemed anxious to eat, they offered sweets to each other and nibbled on them with their eyes averted from each other, while the guests enjoyed the food. It is said that those who come and eat from the same plate as the bride and groom will marry soon after them so both made sure that there was food for their friends – especially Geeta, who knew that among her friends and cousins were those who wanted to marry and, indeed, knew whom they wanted to marry.

The priest, who presided over the wedding, recited passages from the *Vedas* in Sanskrit next to the fire (it is the god of fire that is *the* witness at a Hindu wedding). The fire smelled of sandalwood smoke and was encouraged to burn by the addition of pure ghee which raised the flame. The Sanskrit verses are as much of a mystery to the guests in this setting as the Latin of the Roman Catholic church; like that, it adds mystery and piety to the ritual. The bride and groom must travel around the fire seven times, four times the groom leads and three times the bride, while the priest blesses the couple and offers advice to them. To Geeta for example he suggested that the bride should always stand on the left of her husband so that she might be closer to his heart. Although Anil and Geeta had to remain pious and demure, there were times during the ceremony when physical contact between them was essential; exchanging garlands, feeding each other, putting their hands together, meant that they did have a sense of physical contact prior to their wedding night.

Although for the bride and groom the wedding was a very

serious affair, the guests were joining in a great celebration. There were times at Geeta's wedding, amid the shimmering saris and the smell of incense and rose-water mingled with curry, that I caught a glimpse of another continent, another time and place: it seemed almost possible that the groom's horse, or, better, elephant, waited under the trees outside. In fact, there was a white Cortina in readiness for the couple and this was steered towards the coconut – symbol of good luck – that waited near the entrance to the community centre; it was broken by the wheel of the car. For Geeta's mother, aunts, female cousins and sisters, the day must have been an exhausting one. Still, everyone managed to find time to welcome Geeta's friends from the factory and to try and show us what to do next, and what meanings were attached to the ceremonies. It was a happy wedding, the whole place seeming to be bathed in a warm glow which matched the approval surrounding the couple.

Everyone from the factory enjoyed Geeta's wedding although, of course, they didn't manage to get drunk: young Indian people at the wedding used the space as an opportunity to flirt and tease one another, with the women making coy gestures in groups, supposedly rejecting the advances of the men – especially if parents or older brothers were watching. Out of sight, they carried on much as they did at school or at work, using their cousins as 'safe' men and women and introducing each other. Just as the twins' wedding was a glorious family party so, too, was Geeta's wedding: it brought friends and relatives together to celebrate the bride. Geeta was given good-luck charms, just like the twins, and her bangles held silver and gold threads which were part of this. Her sister told me that it was important not to be too complimentary about the bride because she may be subject to the evil eye which would cloud her future. Geeta, the bride, was at the centre of the wedding and she received a never-ending supply of advice from her parents, friends, relatives and the priest. She was reminded, for example, that when she stepped into her new home she must not go in left foot first because this is inauspicious.

Though the bride has the lead role in the drama, it is a play that she has not necessarily chosen to be part of. It is not surprising that even Geeta said that half-way through her wedding she began to feel it was all happening to someone else because she was part of a process over which she had exercised no control. The bride may feel like a package and not a woman, although she has been told that it is this process which makes her a woman. She sits surrounded by her family and friends, feeling isolated and alone, frightened and more like a beautifully wrapped doll than a person. The ceremony is exhausting, but before the wedding is completed the bride will have had her veil lifted by her husband and she will have experienced the mysteries of the flower-bed night.

The flower-bed night

Those who remembered weddings in India or Uganda often commented sadly on the fact that the practice of decorating the bridal chamber of the new couple was so difficult to reproduce in Britain. In a gloriously romantic gesture to the new couple the room where they will spend their first night in the groom's house is lavishly decorated with frangipani, jasmin and other exotic and sweet-smelling flowers in garlands and patterns across the bed. This provides a setting in which the bride loses her virginity as gently and delightfully as possible. Supposedly, it is amid the fragrant and romantic flowers that a bride's sexuality is awakened by her husband who is pictured, god-like, as Krishna the great lover.[10] Like all romances, the picture of harmonious beauty amid the flowers hides the real terror experienced by women in their initial encounters with the strangers who become their husbands.

Taruna was probably the closest to the traditional Indian bride because she had seen her husband only once, briefly, before she married. Her wedding was traumatic enough, but her wedding night found her terrified because she had had no advice on what to expect from her mother, or her sisters. She and her sister-in-law, Leela, talked about this at home while their husbands were out and after we had talked about the changes taking place in the lives of Indian women.

Sallie Did anyone talk to you about your wedding night, about sex or birth control?
Taruna [*shaking her head*] No, never, Indian families don't talk about it, no one ever mentions it. But you get to know a bit from school, and being in the factory you can't miss it. But you still don't know how it happens and what it's going to be like.
Sallie Didn't your older sisters tell you anything, give you a few hints?

Taruna No, they talked about cooking, but not about the other
– no one ever talks about it.
Leela It wouldn't have helped me anyway. I'm the eldest.
Taruna When you get married, it's terrible, you don't know
what's going to happen to you and you've never been near a
man before [*chuckle*]. I can laugh now, it seems funny to think
of it, but at the time I thought I might die, really.
Leela [*on the edge of her seat*] That's true, you think you might
not survive the first week. You just want to go home, but then
you get used to it and a new life. We are all right here because
our mother-in-law is in India. We haven't even met her. Their
parents write to us to go there, but I don't know if we will ever
do that.
Sallie You had no advice on birth control, either?
Taruna No, nothing [*hands in the air*].
Leela No, not really. There was something about it at school,
but we were all too embarrassed to look, or take it in. The
younger ones will know more and I think that's good if you
don't want to have a baby too soon.
Taruna It's very frightening, really it is. We all get frightened
when we think of marriage.

It is hardly surprising that Taruna speaks of fear in relation to
marriage, an emotion prompted by a marriage system which gives
women no control over their future and which makes of men wife-
givers and receivers. The system is located in a society which the
older generation have tried hard to reproduce in Britain, but
Shanta and her friends know very well that the cities of Britain are
not Rajkot or the villages of Gujarat. They want to marry whom
they choose and in emphasising this they are elaborating the need
for Indian women, who are now wage earners and who participate
in the public sphere, to have greater autonomy in their lives. Their
struggle is not a new one; despite the emphasis in Indian cultures
upon the submissive, subordinate wife devoted to the wishes and
needs of her husband, her lord, Indian women have fought against
this, against child marriage, against *sati* (the practice of widows
throwing themselves upon the funeral pyres of their husbands)
and currently they fight against a dowry system which, it is
suggested, costs the life of a young Indian bride in Delhi every
day.[11] They have come together to protest, as they have done in
the factories of Britain, and as women did on the shopfloor against

unfair rates and production targets. They are, and will continue to be, fighting women, fighting against racism and sexism in the public sphere and their position in the family and household, which is all the more insidious for the way it binds women to men through duty and affection. It is to the sphere of domesticity that I now turn, bringing together again the lives of Indian and English women who share in the double shift.

8
And end up with your arms in the sink

> Most of the young women here are really keen on engagements and marriage – it's a way out, as they see it, from home, boredom, something new to try. So, they try it, and marry at 19 and they are in a trap.
>
> —Clare, the personnel manager

In the last two chapters I have tried to illuminate the over-whelming desire for marriage among the women at StitchCo and the path to understanding has required us to make sense of an exuberant celebration of romance and womanhood. But the party does come to an end: the flowers fade and the bride finds that she is 'in a trap'. The nature of this trap is explored in this chapter, which moves from the bride to the wife, and the way in which women's lives are bounded by that nebulous and complex construction, the family. This chapter concentrates on how young women cope with the new roles that are thrust upon them by marriage, and the way that more experienced women set models of wifely duties for them to follow. It is a story of disillusionment, of 'arms in the sink', and of time spent labouring for men and children. On the other hand, it is important not to underestimate the way in which women themselves reconstruct family life. For many women (and this is true of men as well) home and family appear as the only area of freedom in a routinised life – a haven of warmth and affection in an alienated and aggressive world. This is the rosy glow that surrounds *the* family: a glow that feminists have challenged for many years. In their efforts to demystify the family as a benign cosy world with women at the centre, they have put in its place an analysis of the family which has alerted us to exploitation and inequalities, brutality and fear in family life, to the way that heterosexuality is privileged, and to the over-whelming importance of the family in reproducing the subordination and oppression of women.[1] These issues are concretised in the lives of the women at StitchCo and explored in this chapter.

Before I become immersed in the world of domestic labour, budgets and home management, it is relevant to consider, very briefly, the distinction and interrelationship between household and family recently explored by Rayna Rapp.[2] She points out that people live in households, which she defines as 'units within which people pool resources and perform certain tasks', and, following Jack Goody, she emphasises that households may be analysed as 'units of production, reproduction and consumption'.[3] Although she is crucially aware that households have different relations to the pool of wealth and resources in society, and so belong to different classes, she is less concerned with gender differentials in access to resources, both in society generally and in individual households. Her conception of a household is essentially an economic one, in which the reproduction of capitalism is secured through the wage form and the way in which women labour to transform wages into goods and services in the home. The notion of the family, on the other hand, 'carries a heavy load of ideology' and provides a set of meanings, motivations and illusions which ensure that women perform necessary domestic tasks, and that they do so without experiencing them as oppressive and exploitative.[4]

The lives of the women at StitchCo provide an illumination of the relationship between household and family as lived experience. It is possible to see, all too clearly, the way in which familial ideologies impinge upon economic relations in the household so that patriarchal relations may be seen to have real, material effects upon the lives of women in the family, just as they do in the workplace. As the preceding chapters have graphically illustrated, the world of work and the world of the home are not two separate spheres, each with an independent existence. They are, as I have consistently stressed, one and the same world brought together not only in the persons of women who are daughters, wives, mothers and workers, and men who are workers, husbands, fathers and sons, but in the coincidence of the relations of production with those of the relations of reproduction, a point grasped by the women on the shopfloor and expressed in a variety of ways.

In the budgie cage

Young women married, in part, because they wanted to be recognised as adults and women, and also because they had to find a way to gain access to resources controlled by men. These reasons were not always uppermost in their minds when the excitement and glamour of a wedding day beckoned and in an atmosphere where romance was so celebrated. Eventually, though, the bride returned to the everyday routine of the factory and, in addition, to the new responsibilities associated with becoming a wife; the disappointment and the anti-climax with her new life was quickly evident. When I asked the twins how it felt to be married women, their response was withering rather than enthusiastic:

Julie It's no different, it feels the same [*shrug*].

Tessa Well, you do the same things, don't you? So it doesn't seem very different. If you weren't living with 'im before I s'pect it would be different, but with us it's the same.

Avril echoed their disappointment when she explained: 'Married life is all right, but it was a real comedown, coming back to the flat. It's just the same and you expect it to be different, and it isn't.'

Getting married was supposed to be an antidote to the boredom of home and factory, but very soon after their wedding the twins complained of precisely this in their new lives: Julie, talking to me about her life with Dave, sighed as she thought of going home at the end of the day: 'It's boring, really. We make the tea and then we sit around looking at each other; we don't talk or nothin'.' Julie's picture of married life was echoed by some of the other young brides who were also discovering that boredom was only part of the problem. In a break from counting the production record for the week, Michelle and Pat confided their difficulties to one another:

Michelle Sometimes he drives me mad. He comes in and he does the crossword. I just go to the kitchen, and if he's had a bad day he doesn't speak – he just wants his tea.

Sallie What if you've had a bad day?

Michelle I don't have them, according to him. I don't really work anyway, I just walk around all day. He does the hard work. If I feel bad I just go into the kitchen to get away from him. But he works from 7.30 to 4 and I work from 8 to 4.45 and I'm the one who gets up first and I'm the one who's last to bed. I get up and get his breakfast before he goes to work, and I go to work at 7.30. I'm really tired by today. I'm not sleeping either . . .

Pat [*with a grin*] Well . . .

Michelle [*irritably*] No, really, I just don't like this bed we've got

– not that it matters to him. If he wants a bit he gets on with it and I play dead.

Pat [*sadly*] Yeah, I know.

The rapidity with which the hearts and flowers surrounding men and marriage disappeared suggested that the women recognised all along it was a partial view, founded on illusions. But there was the problem of how women coped with the understanding that domestic bliss was a romantic fiction. From Michelle's account, it was clear that her husband held stereotypical views of what counted as work. Women's work was not *real* work which was, of course, a convenient way of suggesting that women had sufficient time and energy to organise home life as well as earning wages. Michelle's response, two months after her wedding, was to withdraw emotionally from her husband and spend her time in the kitchen, which she felt was her own space in the house – a comment on how soon the pattern of domestic life on the traditional model began. The glamour surrounding marriage quickly disappeared in the realisation that marriage was far from the partnership it was supposed to be. The new brides discovered that the burden of work fell upon them, and that they had much less power over the men they lived with than they had imagined they would have.

Indian women had a workload in the home which was, if anything, greater than that of white working-class women. It was the older women who complained most about this, not the younger women like Taruna – who, everyone reckoned, had a greater workload than they did. Taruna responded to her new duties with tremendous energy, and without complaint, taking on the responsibility of caring for her new house, husband, his brothers and their cousins who came often to visit. She approached her new life as an adventure and explored this, and her new roles, with spirit and zest. Neither she, nor Lata or Rekha, expressed the same feelings of isolation and emptiness in their domestic lives as the twins and other brides did.

Michelle and Pat missed their mums and their dads, their old rooms and Sunday lunch. It was left to Julie, who had a sense of humour everyone enjoyed, to sum up her situation and, with this, the feelings of her sister and some of their friends. Sitting in the coffee bar having another illicit break and her third cigarette in ten minutes, puffing loudly and moving restlessly in her seat, she turned to us and shouted:

Dave, Christ, he makes me sick! I'm not joking. Every night he comes in the door of the flat, straight over to the budgie cage, 'Pretty boy, budgie, budgie,' he says, and he *ignores* me. One night I'm gonna climb in the budgie cage just so I get a 'Hello' – I'm not joking.

At this point Julie's audience started to rock with laughter, but she shook her head and said again, 'I'm not joking', and continued:

Then he says 'Mek us a cup-a-tea.' Last night I made him one and he had his tea and wanted another one so I made him another one, five minutes later he wanted another cuppa. So I went into the kitchen and made a flask.

Julie grinned at the memory of this, but her anger returned:

He thinks all I'm good for is to mek the tea and I'm really tired when I get home.

They're all the same, Sal, Tess is really fed up with Carl. He's never in. Last time I went there she wouldn't let me go, she kept sayin', sit down, 'ave another cup-a-tea.

Julie's wit was an attempt to hide her pain and frustration, but it did little to mask her disappointment and the realisation, within six weeks of her wedding, that marriage meant the tedium of getting through everyday with the same person, and a burden of unpaid work which fell upon her shoulders. She and Tessa, like their friends, discovered very quickly that marriage was about work of a very specific kind. They found themselves, within the home, servicing the needs of their husbands and treated not as co-partners, but as servants with a subordinate status. Though it was a blow, it was still cushioned because they could still come to the factory and talk to their mates who were sympathetic and interested in their new lives. Soon this would end when they gave up waged work for motherhood, thereby tying themselves more securely to the home and the male wage.

Beyond the budgie cage

There were women in the department who were able to stand at a distance from the romantic view of weddings and marriage; having demystified this world, they decided that they wanted something else. Carol, for example, shook her head in despair at the enthusiasm surrounding weddings and marriage:

It's ridiculous to get married at 17. They really think
everything will be different when they get married. But how
can it be? Then what happens? They have a baby and they're
stuck. I'm not going to do that; all their young lives gone and
nothing's changed. They are washing, cooking and all that.
It's a bad idea to get married too young, but some of them
here are just marriage-crazy.

Laura agreed with Carol and also sought an alternative. She, too,
saw through the confetti and the wedding bells, to the power
struggle between men and women which, Laura believed, women
always lost:

I don't think I'll ever get married because I never seem to be
able to fall about for a bloke. I've never been engaged. The
young ones here get really upset if they haven't got a
boyfriend, but I'm not bothered by it. You know Trish came
in last week and she had weals all over her neck and I asked her
why she let this bloke do it. Do you know what she said? He
put the lovebites on so that the other blokes would know she
was already taken . . . like she belonged to him, or something.

Laura's feminism was a powerful example of the way in which
some women were able to cut through the ideology of femininity
and reach out towards a different vision, one which provided much
greater power and autonomy for women. She desperately wanted
to forge a life of her own, distinct from the normally accepted
pattern among the women she knew: 'What I'd really like to do
would be to travel a lot and see places, and have lots of different
experiences.' The problem for Laura was: How? Given that she
had no qualifications and no one to open doors for her, she opted
at one moment for the role of nanny, seduced by the notion that
she would be able to travel. Instead, she found that she saw no
more of the world than any other housewife or mother and that
the isolation and boredom of women at home was reproduced,
alongside the burden of domestic work. Laura later abandoned her
job as a nanny and returned to the factory. Her dreams, however,
remained and she had not given up the idea that life held out
alternatives to marriage and motherhood. She managed to acquire
a council flat of her own during my year at the factory.

The other women recognised the tension in Laura and they
admired her courage in trying to find alternatives. This was

reflected in the way that they talked about her: Laura was very popular and she was always referred to as 'a person', never as 'a girl'. Her friends said she was a restless person; a person who wanted more out of life. The other women respected her for having aspirations beyond the factory and a boyfriend. Laura's strength consisted in her ability to seek a different path, but not one that cut her off from other women; she was very conscious of the solidarity of women and their ability to hold life together.

Domestic labourers, or stand by your man – while he sits down and has a cup of tea

The notion that women were the foundation upon which the whole edifice of social and familial life was based was a common view among the women of StitchCo, and they expressed this in the sentence, 'Men, ah, they don't know they're born, they've got no idea,' which was, of course, very convenient for the men generally. Women, we know, are engaged in the double shift; they work outside the home for wages and within the home for 'love'. It is women who carry the responsibility of organising, managing and executing the work of reproduction in all its aspects. Much has been written on the contribution that this unpaid, and until recently, hidden labour makes to capitalism.[5] Christine Delphy's work also presented us with an analysis of the way in which women's labour is appropriated by husbands in the home and, therefore, how women are economically exploited by the men they live with.[6]

The material oppression to which women are subject is carried on in the hidden world of the family and in isolated households. Yet it was made public in the department at StitchCo because the women who came to work brought these concerns with them, into an environment where the definition of woman as wife and mother was elaborated upon by the culture of the shopfloor, thereby reinforcing the view the women held of themselves as wives and mothers first. Thus, many women expressed considerable anxiety over the whole area of housework. It was fraught with difficulties because, it seemed, women never had enough time to cook and clean and polish to a standard that they considered acceptable. The emphasis upon cleanliness and order has a long history among large sections of working-class women who tied this to respectability and created a distance between themselves and those families who were poorer, less well organised and labelled 'rough'.[7] The enormous burden of domestic work which this involved has long been recognised as a serious constraint on women's ability to get involved in workplace and other struggles.[8] The women at the factory were a more recent manifestation of an old and continuous story which was well known to them. Dol, for example, who worked on the portable iron, told me when we were discussing her workload:

> Most women spend all their time working. They work at the factory, then they do the shopping and cook and clean. I was hanging out washing before I came to work today. Mind you, I wouldn't be at home all the time; it's too lonely. When you come out to work it's more social, you meet other women and seem more alive, somehow.

Dol was quite clear that housework was not only irksome and never-ending, but was also carried on in isolation. She, like many women, welcomed the opportunity to work outside the home because it put her in touch with a larger world, with other women, and herself.[9]

The amount of time women spent on housework was apparent from the discussions that they had in their breaks. Not only did this work consume so many of their waking hours, but housework also became a major subject of conversation. Some of the women from the examining and packing sections were celebrating Mave's birthday by eating cream cakes mid-morning, while poor Mave was sitting with her right leg heavily bandaged and supported by another chair. There was great concern for her leg, which had been injured when she fell down the stairs the day before. Mave insisted she was fine and that on no account did she want to go home, 'I'd be on me own there.' Instead, as a measure of how little her injury was going to interfere with her normal working life she said, 'I'm lucky, at least I've done the ironing this week.'

Sallie How long do you think you spend on housework?
Chorus Hours and hours, at least as long as we spend here, and more . . .
Flo We do two jobs, one here and one in the house. We'd earn a fortune if we ever got paid for both.

The rest of the group agreed and Bridie added: 'I mean house-keeping's for the food and the house, not to pay for washing and cleaning.' Everyone in the group accepted the view that they worked at home unpaid, and that the work that they did had a cash value which they never realised because they were servicing the needs of their families. There was no romance surrounding housework and no illusions about the time and effort involved. Yet this knowledge and understanding never seemed to dim the enthusiasm of the younger generation of brides. It seemed to pass over them until they became wives when, in fact, they looked to the models around them and followed them.

Flo [continued] Housework is a full-time job, let alone coming
here all week. There's so much to do and you don't do half of
it when you're working. You've got to have a routine
otherwise if you don't do it one day you've got two jobs the
next.

Everyone murmured their agreement and nodded as they started to tell me about the routines they followed.[10] What this meant, in effect, was that the discipline and routinisation of factory production was brought into the household as a way, the women said, of getting through the week. This is an interesting and important amendment to our emphasis upon the way in which women workers bring the world of the home into the workplace. It is a two-way process: women not only domesticate production, but take production imperatives away from the factory into the home, recreating aspects of the capitalist labour process in their housework. What some women have learned from this is that there must be time off and so they build into their routine a space for themselves. Consequently, when Flo described her week it included a night off. Flo was a married woman of about 50; she had no children and lived in a flat that she and her husband were buying. Her week went like this:

I always do my washing on Sunday and then Monday it's
ironing. Tuesday is my night off and I won't touch a thing.
Thursday I do the bathroom and if it's 3a.m. I won't go to bed
until it's done. I hoover the bedrooms on Wednesday and all
the other rooms Friday. Friday I go up town and pay the bills,
do the shopping and get the 4.40 bus home. I get in and make
a cup of tea and, while Les sits and has his, I unpack the
shopping. Then I hoover the hall, lounge (we're in a flat so it's
a bit easier) while I put the dinner in the oven. Every morning

> I make the bed and do what's needed for dinner, like cut the potatoes, make the gravy, whatever . . .

Before I had time to interject and marvel at Flo's energy, or ask what was wrong with Les, the other women came in and supported Flo's account of the week. Kath intervened quickly with her own routine. She was a woman who looked older than her 40 years; she was frail and had had pleurisy the previous year. This had not stopped her working 20 hours a day for her husband and her children, who were all living at home; one son was working and another son and her daughter were still at school.

> I'm the same as you, Flo, 'cept we've got a dog so I hoover downstairs everyday. I get up first, but not until 8.30 on a Sunday now. I get the tea on for the first lad and give him his breakfast because he has to go at 6.30 then, it's me hubby. I make the lad's bed while the tea's brewing, then it's the other two and then I get meself ready while I make our bed, cut the sandwiches and I'm off out the door. I wash about three times a week because me hubby and the lad have overalls. You have to soak them, they can't go straight in the machine, then I put them in. I do all my pressing for the whole week on Sunday afternoon and pick up all the washing for Monday. The whole house gets a clean at the weekend.

Kath lived in a council house, a 'semi' with three bedrooms which she was definitely not interested in buying because, as she put it, 'It's rubbish, I don't want the worry of all the damp, no one wants 'em along our street.' The discussion of housework continued with Flo saying to Kath: 'But you know, Kath, with all that, you don't do half what you should. Take my curtains, they get washed twice a year, but it should be more and the cupboards are never cleaned until the holidays. I just open and shut them quickly.'

Flo, perhaps, had time to worry more about the inside of cupboards and how many times to wash the curtains. For Kath, Mave, Norah and Bridie, it was a question of how to get through the pressing workload each week. I asked them if they had any help with the housework, or shopping, or things around the house. Kath jumped in defensively to reply:

Kath My kids have always helped me, me daughter will hoover and they make their own breakfast on Sundays; they are good kids.

Sallie What about washing, ironing, shopping, those things?

Bridie, Kath, Flo and Mave agreed in unison that 'No, no they don't do much of that.' And Flo added, 'But Les does the garden when he can.'

The domestic lives of Flo and Kath and the others in this group were part of a general pattern on the shopfloor. Women spent all their waking hours working; they carried the responsibility for managing home life and the manual work it involved. The only assistance they seemed to receive came, predictably, from their daughters; this often meant friction between sons and daughters at home. There were, though, single women in the department who were treated just like Kath's sons. Mam made breakfast, cut sandwiches, washed clothes, shopped, cooked, cleaned and generally set the world in order for the other members of the household. It was this pattern that young men and women brought to their own marriages and, on this basis, it was not surprising that Dave expected Julie to make the tea, wash, cook and shop for him.

During another lunch-hour Jean and Mo were musing on just these problems and their conversation highlighted the issues raised above, and the way in which their homes were organised for the benefit of men. Jean commented:

> I've been cleaning the house out because our lad's bringing his girlfriend; she's not snobby or nothing, but you like to have it nice. I've left them a bunch of notes on what they've got to do, but I know Gary won't lift a finger. He's real lazy and the girl complains. I don't know what you do with lads, the girl does her share, but not the other two. Then she gets fed up – well, it's not surprising. With girls you expect it, you don't have to tell them all the time, but the lads are real lazy.

Jean was a single parent who had brought up three children on her own. They were now older and one son was at university, while her daughter and Gary were working in the hosiery industry at the time of this conversation; later, they both lost their jobs when their firms collapsed. Jean's comments on her children were interesting because they demonstrated the effect of gender stereotyping: girls were expected to do housework, boys were not, and although this was not considered entirely legitimate, Jean appeared to have no sanctions she could apply to Gary and her other son. Mo, a married woman with two children, a boy and girl, who had recently left school agreed: 'It's the same in our house. When the lad was working and Kerry was at home she had to do more, he said, because he was paying into the family. But when she started work she was still doing more than him and she complained. Lads expect you to look after them.'

They expected to be 'looked after' irrespective of the pressures on the women in the family. Mo's son was an interesting case of a young man anticipating his role as breadwinner. He had already imbibed the notion of himself as a male wage earner, a status that meant his wages were traded against time and effort in the home – the time and effort of women who were viewed as available for domestic work. He clearly took no account of the fact that his mother was also a wage earner.

Jean started to leave the table and, as a passing shot, she said: 'Yes, and, you know, they'll get the girls to do it for them when they get older.' This did, indeed, seem to be the case when I talked to Julie, Tessa, Michelle and Pat:

Sallie How are you managing as a working wife Michelle?
Michelle It's great, it really is, if you've got a helper. We go and do all the shopping on a Friday night because he finishes at four. We drive down to Asda and I have a list [*giggle*]. I have to have a list otherwise I don't get the right things. He always wants to buy beer and I won't let him and he gets fed up. We do that and then we drive home again. Sunday is our day for cleaning and all the washing. He hoovers while I do the washing, put it through the spinner and hang it out. We get through so many clothes. He wants clean socks everyday, and at the weekends he changes his tee-shirt three times a day, and I'm left with a pile of clothes, and I wash by hand. By the time I get back he's got the tea mashing and we sit down.
Sallie What about cooking?
Michelle I do it mostly. He makes such a mess and then I have to wash up. I can't bear to leave washing up overnight and then come down to it. [*Michelle's friends agreed with this*] But he doesn't care. I tell you, he uses three pots to make a Vesta curry. I came in the other night and there he was with his curry, all the pots dirty, but none for me. I shouted at him and he told *me* to clean the saucepans.
Pat I do the same as Michelle, he helps with the shopping but I do the washing and cooking.

The burden of work in this very unequal division of domestic labour was enormous because wives also packed sandwiches, decided what was for dinner and what was in the cupboard. Any contribution young men made was at the edges; they expected their new wives to do the housework, shop, cook, etc., but women like Tessa were already protesting their lot:

> Carl's bein' really 'orrible to me. I tell him to help and he does nothing. I keep saying we've got to go and do the washing and he won't bother. He doesn't clean up, wash up, nothing. I told him I'm not doin' owt for him. I didn't pack his lunch for 'im today. He should do more, he lives here as well. He just goes out with his mates, comes in, and flops into bed. Well, it's not good enough, is it?

Tessa was very unhappy and often alone in the evenings when I went to visit her. I would find her ironing or washing, trying to cook and clean in her small flat. I agreed with her that Carl could do more, but with many of the other women I often had the greatest difficulty in raising questions about their workload at home. Any faint suggestion that I was critical of what they did sent them springing to the defence of husbands and children. Husbands were 'good' men because they brought their money home regularly, and they didn't get drunk and beat up their wives and children on Friday nights. 'Good' kids were prone to fits of sentimentality on birthdays and at Christmas which meant they bought huge cards with poems celebrating 'Mum' for her unselfishness, and her heart of gold. It was a poor trade for the work the women gave to their husbands and children. The problem for the women was that they had internalised the notion that womanhood was bound to the care of others, especially husbands and children. This was pointed out to Beth by Gladys when Beth was insisting upon her right to decide to get married. It was a matter of pride to the women at StitchCo that they cared for their children and their homes as they might have done if they were full-time homemakers. Any criticism seemed cruelly out of place and was interpreted as a criticism of them, not of the men and children in their households and the way that domestic labour was organised.

It was all perfectly understandable, but it meant that women colluded in their own oppression by insisting upon their rights to manage the home and their duty in working for their family. To them, this was women's work, their *proper* work which offered them a place at the centre of family life, and, through that, status and power – which work outside the home did not offer. The women were conscious that domestic work was isolated and lonely and few wanted to be on their own all day. It was this that they complained about, not the physical effort involved in washing and cooking and cleaning, nor the fact that it was routine manual labour, as boring as sewing side-seams all day. Instead, it was invested with a special status because it was done for love and was part of the way that women cared for their families. Boring, manual work was, therefore, transformed into satisfying, caring work which required both an emotional and an intellectual commitment; that commitment could only be made because the context for this work was the family, with its attendant ideological load.

It all came together for me in the institution of Sunday lunch which everyone said they enjoyed and planned for during the rest of the week. Sunday lunch brought the family together in a celebration of itself. Young couples went back to their mums and dads on a rotating basis to reassert old ties and demonstrate continuity over generations, and they would do this until they had children of their own. At the centre of Sunday lunch is the cook who labours through the decision of what to buy, does the shopping and finally prepares and cooks the meal. The man of the house carves the meat, a symbol of his role as provider and his status in that he decides how the meat will be cut and apportioned. He decides on the division of the spoils while his wife – mum – labours in the kitchen to produce the goods. This is the picture of the English family we are used to, and reared on; women working, men reaping the rewards. Sunday lunch brings together this division of labour and the ideologies that allow it to appear natural and immutable.

Housework, family work, domestic labour, whatever it is to be called, is surrounded by a powerful mystique which each generation of wives creates anew, making it their own. As some of the new brides will show, however, there is an underground movement that wants to shake off some of the myths surrounding women's work in the home.

When discussing their domestic loads, some of the white women in the factory would tell me that they were lucky compared with the Indian women, whom they described as working 'round the clock' – a description which applied equally well to many of them. In fact, it was Indian women who were most vocal in their complaints about the amount of work they had to do. While the white women turned their domestic labours into labours of love, some Indian women looked back to a situation where minions and servants had done the cleaning and washing, shopping and, in some cases, the cooking. Housework carried no mystique for Asha or Pritty who already knew that there were less arduous, more interesting and pleasant ways to spend their time. They regarded the situation they found themselves in, where they were involved in wage work and housework, as the worst of all worlds. Whenever I went to visit them at home they were working in the kitchen, preparing food for that evening, or the next day for other members of the household to take to work. No concessions were made to the fact that they worked all day at the factory; they were still expected to prepare food and serve their husbands as though they were at home full-time. This meant that their days started early, before everyone else's, and finished late, after the rest of the family had gone to bed. Like all the other women on the double shift, they paid a heavy price in terms of their health and well-being.

Usha, for example, always seemed to be run down and unwell, complaining of leg-aches, back-aches and period pain. She had three children – two daughters who were studying at the local polytechnic and a younger son who was still at school. She and Pritty were waiting for some work to arrive when Usha said to me:

> I get so tired because I work here all day and then I go home and cook for all the family. Work, work, it's always the same in England. In Uganda we had servants to do the washing and cleaning and ladies didn't work.

Usha smiled as she remembered what were clearly the good old days.

> My husband had a shop there, now he works in an engineering factory. I have leg pains and back pains a lot so I don't like to stand, and, you know, in Indian cooking you have to make so many things. Sometimes I make this many chapatis. [*Usha demonstrated a pile about 18 inches high*]

Pritty joined in:

It's the same for all the Indian ladies; we have so much work in the house. If you are a young wife you have to cook for his family, his parents and brothers. It is like that in my house. All weekend I am doing the washing and cleaning and everyday I must cook curry, dal, chapatis for all of them. Indian men don't work in the house.

Sallie Do you have any help with shopping?

Pritty Yes, but you still have to go because if you say get this and this, they don't know what size to get or what is fresh and good.

Usha Sometimes my husband comes with me on Saturdays.

Pritty, like some of her friends, didn't look as though she was strong enough to carry the burden of work that fell on her, and on top of her workload there was the worry associated with her husband's unemployment which she kept largely to herself. She confided in me:

My husband tries and tries to find a job, two years he has been trying but when he phones they say the job has gone. It is so hard for us here, I would like to go back to India. I went to visit two years ago for my marriage and it was so nice. The weather is nice and the people are friendly. Maybe we will go back there, but there's no work in India, either. It's very hard for us wherever we are. Ladies in India don't go to the factory; they are at home, they work in the house, but they have some help from one another and they have time to relax as well. We ladies here, we don't have any time for ourselves. We work at the factory all day and at home all night. I get up very early and make some of the food before I go to work and then I start again when I come home at night.[11]

Pritty's situation was not unusual. She was among the growing number of women who not only carried the burden of domestic work, but also the responsibility for earning the money necessary for the family. Like many other Indian women, she lived in an old terraced house that was badly in need of modernisation; this meant that housework was even more difficult. She, like Taruna and Lata, was trying her best to be a dutiful wife in a house without an inside bathroom, running hot water, or a long-handled broom to help her sweep up. Taruna and Lata polished their old houses and their meagre furniture until it shone and, unlike Pritty who was tired and unwell, Taruna scrubbed and cleaned, shopped and cooked with tremendous energy and enthusiasm. She redefined the disadvantages in the house into charming, old-fashioned quirks that gave the house character – like the front door that had to be pulled to open, and the kitchen shelves that were far too high for her to reach. The materials with which they built their lives were unpromising; nevertheless, as Taruna has already shown, she regarded it all as a part of the adventure of marriage in a situation where she was in charge. This sharply differentiated her from Pritty, who had her parents-in-law to cope with in addition to the lack of money, security and decent housing.

Money, money, money

From what the women said, it was quite clear that men as fathers, husbands and sons exploited their labour. More than just energy and the ability to work was at issue: it was also a question of money and the way in which resources in the household were controlled and allocated. Households, as Rayna Rapp has reminded us, are concerned with the pooling of resources and effort as part of the general process of reproduction.[12] This work turns consumption decisions into a specific standard of living through cooking and cleaning. As I suggested earlier, reproduction is made possible under capitalism through the wage form: wages are turned into goods and services through the efforts of wives and mothers. Generally, it is women who have control over the domestic economy and the household's resources on a day-to-day basis, while men may control the public world of mortgages and bills – a division which reasserts the traditional view of women in the home, the private sphere, and men in the public sphere. In effect, it means that men do not have to worry about the day-to-day details of life which sap the energies and fill the minds of women.

It was often at tea-time on Fridays before they went home, but after they had been paid, that the women discussed the ways in which they managed their money. I joined in with the groups, rotating between them, asking for advice and information. One Friday I asked Pat and Michelle how they managed their money, and the latter replied:

> I do it. We bring in £130 a week between us and he gives it all to me, and I look after the shopping and the bills. On a Friday we go shopping so he can carry all the heavy stuff and we go and fill up with petrol. I buy me fags for the week. He doesn't

need much money because I make his sandwiches, he's got petrol and he doesn't smoke, so it's just me. I have some spending money for here, just a few quid which includes fares. I budget for the bills by putting a bit away every week for each one, then we put the rest in the bank. Where we are going it's really cheap so I reckon we can easily live on £50 a week and go out one night a week. So we can save the other £80 and we'll soon have £1,000, it won't take long.

In this case, Michelle controlled the household income and joint decisions were made in relation to major purchases and savings. She was very frugal; a model, she said, that had come from her mum who always controlled the money at home. This has been a common pattern among sections of the working class and it was reproduced by some of the other women in the factory. A common alternative was expressed in Pat's life:

Well, Bob gets paid on Wednesday which helps so his money goes in the bank to draw on for bills and things we want to buy. Every week I put some of mine in the building society to add up for the mortgage. I have another account for savings and I try to put some in there. Then I spend my money on shopping or whatever Bob and I need through the week. We just budget it out, like.

Gracie and Tula, who were also at the table, joined in at this point:

Gracie Well, you've got to [budget], otherwise you never keep it straight, do you?

Tula That's right, you get in a mess if you don't plan it out right.

Sallie So, Pat, do you share the expenses or do you look after everything?

Pat No, Bob pays the bills from our account, that's what we do. I keep an eye on the food.

Tula That's like me, 'cept I really see to it all. His money goes in the bank from work so it's there. I buy the food and things we need and he draws out what more we want and pays the bills, when I remind him! Ha ha!

Gracie You've got to pool it, you can't manage on one wage these days.

Maria That's what we've always done. We put our money together and put bits away for the bills every week.

Gracie Well, you've got to plan it out, it's the only way
everything gets paid and you can save a bit.
Tula Yes, I have my savings taken out here so that's one lot and
then we try to save some more on the side, out of his money in
the bank.
Michelle I know what happens to every penny and I keep
accounts. He can look at them, but he doesn't seem bothered.
But it's for my peace of mind. I have to know what's
happening. It took me a while to get straight, but I never
borrowed off me Mam. She said I would, but because she said
that, I said I never would and I haven't needed to.

The income that the women had available to them varied according
to the age and skill of their husbands and children. Gracie's
husband was a toolmaker earning £130, close to the average male
wage for the area in 1980. Tula's husband was a bus driver and he
earned less than this. Most of the women lived on the council
estates which ringed the city, and a few were already involved in
buying the houses they had lived in for a while, from the council.
Even those women who were married to knitters – the aristocrats
of the hosiery industry who were earning £150 a week – were not
living in households where there was much spare cash. Because of
this, all the women took great pride in their ability to manage the
resources they had as well as possible. They operated with strict
budgets which allowed them to save some of their income every
week. A week in which there was no saving was considered a
disaster and everyone would be very upset. Most women spent
their wages on food and cleaning materials, and not on goods for
themselves. They took care of the day-to-day matters and most of
their money was, in fact, eaten because it bought food which they
transformed into meals.

The women were in no doubt that two wage packets were
necessary for a minimum standard of living; this recognition
reinforces my earlier conclusions on the economic importance of
marriage to working-class people. It is a way in which they can
generate sufficient income for a reasonable, but definitely not
extravagant or elaborate standard of living. But there was more to
it than just pooling resources, these had to be managed and they
were managed by women who tried to stretch the household
income as far as possible. The current generation of home
managers showed a remarkable continuity with the women studied

by the Fabian group in Lambeth in the early part of the twentieth century.[13] The women in Maud Pember Reeve's study also emphasised budgets and tried to save; they also endeavoured to provide the best possible food and clothing for the man of the house, the breadwinner.

The situation of Indian women varied according to the type of household they lived within. If it was a joint household, then money was pooled and traditionally controlled by the father of the family. In changed circumstances, many fathers had lost this role and economic affairs were controlled by brothers. Parents often had little say in decisions, except in relation to their daughters-in-law, and because their power had waned in other areas they have tried to exercise it more virulently in relation to the women of the household – not always with success. Some women lived with their husbands and children, like Lata and Amina, or with their husband, brothers-in-law and sisters-in-law, like Taruna. In these cases, there was often more pooling of resources and discussion surrounding the way in which money was to be used. Some women were the main wage earners, but they handed their money over to their husbands who gave them housekeeping and pocket money in return.

There was no doubt that for some women the money they were allocated was insufficient, and the union reps and the welfare officer commented on this. Annie said:

> You know, Sallie, these Indian women are so malnourished and mostly it's because they haven't got money to buy a meal at lunch-time. Their husbands or their mothers-in-law take their money and give them five bob a day to eat and have drinks. We have men in here boasting about the fact that they give their wives £5 a week for housekeeping. I'm not kidding.

Annie's indignation was fired by what she saw as a major injustice. Indian women did not seem to have any access to their own earnings because they were handed over to the male members of the family and became part of the 'family pot'. But this was not so far removed from the situation of English women who spent their earnings on the well-being of everyone else. However, there were Indian women I knew who would have liked more control over their own earnings. One of the great bonuses of a Western-style marriage commented upon by women like Lata, Shanta and Geeta, was that they could control more of their earnings in the home. Money became even more important when the women had children, who, in a joint family, would have to compete with other members for resources; whereas in a nuclear family, resources, if available, could be used by them. Young women controlled resources in a way that their mothers did, but they did not have to wait until their sons were grown and they became mothers-in-law to do this. It added to their status and sense of power in much the same way as it did among the young brides like Michelle and Pat.

Indian men could, and sometimes did, appropriate the earnings of their wives. But they were not alone in this. There were plenty of non-Indian examples on the shopfloor, including Tessa and Julie. However, the difference was that the twins were less likely to accept this as legitimate or normal because, of course, it conflicted with the ideologies surrounding the notion of the male breadwinner and the family wage.

Julie was scrounging a fag from a friend and, as she took it, she waved it at me and said angrily:

> We've got no bloody money because Dave hasn't been paying the HP on his car and they sent the law around. He's got to go to court over it. Huh! He thought he'd pay up some of the instalments, and it means no money from him and he's living off me! I'm payin' the rent and buying all the food. Well, I'm not doin' it this weekend. I'm not going through another week where I have no fags again. Men are stupid; they never grow up. Well, he and Carl are gonna have to grow up real quick because soon he's going to have me at home and a baby. It makes me sick!

Julie's twin sister was no less sanguine about her own financial affairs, which seemed to deteriorate week by week. Carl had been sacked and because of this he faced problems getting his dole money.

Tessa At the moment I've got to pay for most things and we've got an electricity bill that I can't pay. Normally we share the price of the shopping and we go together to get it and that's about it. He won't cook anything and he won't clean. Still, he'll have to learn when the baby comes.
Sallie What will happen when you aren't earning, Tess?
Tessa Well, he'll have to cough up for housekeeping and expenses, won't he? Then he'll find out what it's like to have a

family. I hope he goes back to work soon, I'm fed up with paying for him.

One response to this reversal of the notion of the male bread-winner which both Julie and Tessa made, was to insist upon male responsibilities in relation to them as wives and future mothers. They did not regard it as legitimate that their wages should be keeping their husbands, but it was a growing pattern among the women as their husbands lost their jobs in the engineering and hosiery industries locally. At the same time, women with youngsters ready to leave school looked pessimistically at their job opportunities, and resigned themselves to the ongoing burden of young adults. Previously, they would have expected them to be working and contributing to the family income.

The older women emphasised budgets and savings because they had grown up with the insecurities surrounding manual work under capitalism, while their daughters took these models from them into the current recession. Indian women, as part of an immigrant community, knew the importance of savings against hardships, to send money to poorer relatives or help new arrivals, or, as they became more settled, for the education and future of their children, for the chance to go back to India or to renovate the terraced houses they had bought. Savings, in all these cases, were being used as the year wore on for the shortfalls created in the homes where unemployment had struck.

More generally, the lives of the women at StitchCo demonstrated the deep contradictions apparent in the situation of women wage earners who were also wives and mothers. As wage earners, women have the possibility of greater economic independence and, therefore, of autonomy in their own lives – but they do not earn living wages. Their subordination in the labour market encourages women to marry and join hands with higher male wages; it also means that their wages are conceived of as secondary wages, adding to the main wage supplied by the male breadwinner which, in turn, means that their status in the family unit will not be greatly enhanced by their economic contribution. The equation 'money equals power' is a gross oversimplification in relation to the lives of women.

As a wife and a mother, a woman might have a great deal of control over the management of the household's budget and this could give her power in the domestic unit. But it may be that a woman controls nothing more than her own wages because what used to be housekeeping money paid from male wages has been replaced by money from women's wages – which again poses problems for the notion of the family wage and the male bread-winner. It suggests that women are subject to even greater levels of exploitation: not only do they carry the burden of domestic labour and home management, but also pay for the immediate reproduction needs of family members. While a man's wages are transformed into cars and housing through mortgage repayments or rents, a woman's wages are used to buy food which she transforms into meals that are eaten. I do not want to suggest that housing and food are not equally necessary. The important point is that men have access to both; women have to fight for rights to housing if they separate themselves from men.

Resistance

It was impossible to believe that the lively, clever and irreverent women I knew on the shopfloor did not find ways of resisting the level of exploitation that they suffered in their homes. As this chapter makes clear, however, the intricacies of family life are not easily fought and the fight may be hazardous. In relation to their wages, one way in which women asserted their rights to spend part of their earnings on themselves was to buy into clubs and receive goods from mail order companies. Certainly, younger women bought clothes and shoes; some of the other women, though, bought kitchen equipment and household goods because, they said, it made life easier, or more pleasant for them. For the women who ran the catalogues there was, of course, the bonus of some extra cash. Amita, who was an Avon representative, kept the money she earned from this to buy things for the baby she was expecting. Sometimes women asked for special arrangements to be made in relation to bonus payments, or increased wages and the welfare officer did arrange this for special cases, such as the Indian woman who wanted to save her rise to buy things for her baby. This money was put into a separate pay packet. Her family did not know about the rise and, apparently, never found out after she left the factory. The company savings plan also allowed women to save for themselves if they chose to. Nevertheless, on the whole, savings were part of the household economy I have described.

Publicly, women were loyal to the private world of the family, keeping up appearances and not admitting to the privations they suffered. Indian women, of course, had the models of Savitri and Sita from the Hindu scriptures, who showed great loyalty to their husbands, to remind them of their duties. It was because of this, and fear of gossip in the communities to which they belonged, that they maintained certain fictions about their husbands. Sackings or redundancies were kept quiet, and only privately at home did they ask me about their legal rights and the course of action they should follow if they believed there were cases of unfair dismissal to answer. It was a matter of pride that they maintained their husband's position and that of the family in the community.[14] Only when we were alone would they speak of the hardships and the difficulties of making ends meet. They acknowledged that Indian men did not take their share of responsibilities in the home: 'Our Indian men do not cook or work in the house,' a situation often pointed out to me.

Indian women, like their white counterparts, were tied to a model of domestic life which had the dutiful wife at the centre, in service and servitude to her husband. If an Indian woman was lucky, she would have supportive female relatives who would help her. They would come together to share the burden of work and overcome the isolation imposed by housework in Britain. Taruna and Leela, for example, were a great team in which, as Leela acknowledged, Taruna acted as manager. In addition, Taruna had a very supportive aunt who made pickle for them, showed them how to cook, found the best price for rice and lentils and popped in regularly to see that they were well and happy. She was a charming, lively woman with masses of energy and good humour and we spent wonderful evenings laughing at her stories and jokes. This was one example of the way in which the separation of male and female spheres allowed women to come together and draw support from one another. The women felt very relaxed with each other and this sisterhood was one way in which women resisted the imposition of patriarchal power in the home. It did not overturn the situation, but it tempered it and worked against the distances among women created by a marriage system which separated a woman from her own mother and her sisters – the major sources of support among white working-class women.

The support networks among women at the factory were one way in which they resisted the isolation of their homes and the power of men to decide how they would spend their time. It is clear from the earlier chapters in this book that these networks were a vital source of sisterhood for women and that they were guarded against male intrusions. Women wanted to spend some of their time with other women. They valued their 'mates' and they tried to maintain their links with them after marriage and when they had become mothers. But the younger women were not willing to use their friends as a repair and maintenance system, unwilling to exploit their friends' energies in the same way as they were exploited by family members.

The older women commented often on the way that men 'have it made', 'expect to be looked after', and are spoilt by women who spend all their time working to make life comfortable for men. Women like Tessa and Julie or Pat and Michelle were more vitriolic about men generally. They angrily struggled within their new marriages for more power and greater credibility and a more equal division of labour in the home. Their criticisms were couched in a new language, one that had come from the women's movement, and which allowed them to express some of their oppression in novel ways. After Christmas, Pat and Michelle returned to work and it transpired that they had both had rows with their husbands during the holiday, which they talked about on their first day back:

Michelle Men, they're all chauvinist pigs!
Pat Yeah, all men are male chauvinists, they are!

Michelle then went on to explain that she and Jim had had a major fight because he had taken money she was saving for bills and used it to build a garden wall. It was a direct attack on her power over the budget in the house and Michelle resented it very much:

He had no bloody right, I told him he couldn't have the money. I swore at him, I shouted, 'Fuck you'. He always gets his own way in everything. It's always what he wants to do. We can't live in the bloody garden, the house needs doin' up first, but he won't listen. Then, he comes down from having a bath trying to creep around me, thinkin' I'll want a bit because he's just got a towel on. Well, I looked at him and his body made me sick! They always think they can get around you that way. It's come up to bed, or kiss, kiss . . . well, not bloody likely. Anyway, he'd used all the hot water. They always get their own way. Then he's complaining there's no bread for his

pack-up. I just shrugged my shoulders, but I was so fed up I
hit him, I really did and he threatened to send me to work
with a black eye. I'm not kiddin', he got right mad – but there
I am packin' his lunch and then he borrows me money. We
each have £9 a week for spending. He's finished his by
Wednesday and I've still got mine so he wants that as well.
Sod that – I told him I s'posed he'd go into my purse next. He
says he never would, but I don't trust him, I don't trust any of
them, men they're all the bloody same, chauvinist pigs.

Michelle was enraged by the way that Jim reasserted his power
in the relationship over both resources and her. She responded
with verbal and physical assaults which were met with similar
threats from her husband. Both she and her husband tried to use
their sexuality as a bargaining counter, with Michelle anxious to
withdraw her services (a strategy she said she used quite often)
while Jim tried to manipulate her via her sexuality and insist upon
his control of her body. Behind these tactics are a complex set of
assumptions about the nature of male and female sexuality which
keep alive stereotypes like the submissive, dormant woman
waiting to have her sexuality triggered by the active, aggressive
male, who then claims her as his own. These powerful myths,
supported by marriage and the family, have ramifications throughout family and social life which encourage the subordination of
women and distort both women's and men's sexuality.

Pat, too, had a fight with Bob:

Bob and I had a fight one night because he kept joggin' my
arm while I was trying to do my hair. It nearly came to blows,
but in the end I left the house and walked around a bit and
then, I thought, what am I doin' out here? So I went back but
he had gone. When he came back I was sitting, all calm,
drinking me vodka. I never asked him where he went.

Michelle saw this as part of the problems that Pat was having in her
marriage. She was convinced that 'Pat's marriage isn't going very
well you know. Last night she told me she fell asleep and Bob said
she was boring – bugger that – if you're tired, you're tired. We
work hard all day here. These men should try it sometime.'

Michelle and Pat resisted the imposition of the work and
patriarchal authority that marriage implied, and there was no
doubt that the language in which they chose to express their
disaffection was different from that chosen by their mothers'

generation. But both generations have had to deal with an added factor which hovers on the underside of family life – male violence, which I will explore in the pages that follow. It was an ever-present threat to the women in the factory although, as feminists have insisted, it is something that *all* women must live with.

There were other ways in which women resisted the power of men in marriage. One way was to call the bluff of the male breadwinner and demand from men material support: 'I'll be at home with the baby and Carl can forget about me working or owt. He's goin' to find out what it means to be a family man. He'll have to cough up for expenses and housekeeping.'

Julie, too, echoed Tessa in her determination to give up the factory after the birth of her baby. Dave was working: 'but he'll have to grow up quick because soon he's goin' to have me at home and a baby to support.'

For Tessa and Julie (and they were not alone), this was one way in which they thought the unequal relation between men and women could be turned on its head. Women would be supported by the men who claimed the family wage and the role of breadwinner: it was a form of passive resistance, but it sent women back into the home. As a strategy it also contained a fatal flaw: it was not economically viable because the family wage was always a con. As the women on the shopfloor knew, it had always required their labour to transform wages into goods that could be consumed by the household and now it also required that they should earn wages as well. The family wage, whatever reality it might have had in the past, had become the joint wage of husband and wife.

Battered women: Frankie's tale

It was quite clear from the way the women talked openly about their domestic rows that the threat and reality of physical violence from men was commonplace.[15] Both Indian and white women talked in hushed voices about the women they knew, or suspected, were battered at home. Anjum had taken the courageous step of leaving her husband because he beat her up. She was fortunate in having an elder brother who recognised her problem and helped her to find a place to live, away from her husband. Other women were less lucky. Nirmala was downgraded one week and arrived at work on Monday morning with a black eye and unable to walk without pain. Her husband had beaten her up because her wage packet was lower than the previous week and he thought she was keeping the money from him. She responded by asking Annie or Bill to tell him the truth, which they tried to do. They were both concerned at the number of women they feared were beaten:

Bill We have so many cases of women being beaten.

Annie The women are terrified of being downgraded because the men think women are keeping the money from them, and they aren't, but that's why they burst into tears when they are downgraded. I don't know what we can do about it.

Younger white women also complained that their fathers and step-fathers beat them up when they came home drunk on Fridays. Brenda was living in fear and dread of her step-father and desperate to leave home as Lisa had been; so far, Brenda had nowhere to go. Her friends sympathised with her and invited her to spend weekends with them, but this seemed to cause more problems. Although I came across cases of battered women throughout my year on the shopfloor, I touched only the surface of the problem. Of the women who were beaten, Frankie was the woman I knew best and, though she didn't advertise the reason for her black eyes, fractured nose and ashen face, it was easy to guess the origins of the bruises. Some of her friends were told and tried to help and support her while she was at work. Frankie's tale was horrific.

Frankie was such a contradictory woman. She could so often analyse the situation of women and their vulnerability with lightning precision; she was not naive and demonstrated a formidable understanding of the problems faced by single parents, including herself. Frankie had one daughter and she had quarrelled with the child's father soon after the child was born and had never lived with him. When I first met Frankie she had just managed to get herself housed by the council in a small but pleasant council flat. She was spending her weekends with a man called Vin, whom she liked a lot. Even at this early stage of the relationship, however, she expressed concern over his drinking and the fact that it led to quarrels between them. Nevertheless, after coaxing from him, she moved with her daughter to Vin's house; her wise old mum had told her to stay where she was. There was no doubt that she needed the support that Vin seemed to offer. After five years of struggling with childminders, nurseries and lack of money, she wanted, she said, to settle down. Frankie set about reorganising

Vin's house and his life, and was lively and funny as she reported this to us at work. She seemed very happy and said her daughter, Vicky, had settled in well. So no one paid a great deal of attention to the morning that Frankie appeared with a stiff leg, or the day she could not move her shoulder. She confided in me that she was frightened when Vin was drunk and that she was trying to stop him drinking. One way she hoped to do this was by getting pregnant, which she did, and this encouraged Vin to work longer hours and to spend his weekends decorating the house rather than going out with his mates. Frankie seemed pleased until one day when she arrived at work and told me she had spent the night at her sister's house because Vin was drinking again, and she was terrified he was going to beat her. He promised to reform and she returned to the house. Their quarrels, however, became more frequent and she left again. The situation reached an impasse during one weekend.

On Monday morning Frankie came to work, shaking and crying, white-faced with her eyes badly bruised, her nose fractured and cuts on her head. The normally sparky, quick-witted Frankie looked terrorised, traumatised and defeated by what had happened to her. She told me what had occurred while she and I folded dresses for the waiting van, in a quiet corner of the department where Frankie could be away from (as she viewed them) the prying eyes of the other women.

> I was going to meet Vin at his place and stay the weekend, on Friday, but I went with Chris [her sister] for a drink because he was going out with his mates. I said I would go to the house at eleven, after the pub. When I got there he was already there and I said, 'Hello, me duck,' and he turned on me and said, 'Don't me duck me. I've been waiting for you.' It seems that he hadn't been out for a drink but was drinking at home on his own. He went mad, started to hit me. He broke a bottle over my head and punched me in the face – my nose is broken. It all happened so fast. There was blood everywhere and I staggered to the settee and started clutching my belly so he'd think he'd hurt the baby and he sobered up suddenly and started saying he didn't mean to hurt me, and he rushed to get a cloth – and when he disappeared I bolted out the door and up onto the Frinton Road. I was really frightened. I didn't know if I'd lost my eye, and I was covered in blood. I ran straight into two

people who stopped me and sat me down, and one went for an ambulance and the police because they thought I'd been attacked on the street. I went to the Royal and was in for the night.

Frankie shook as she told me this and on her way down to the canteen for lunch she looked broken and depressed and yet she had not finished her relationship with Vin. She phoned him from work because she did not dare phone him from her sister's house; her mum and her sister Chris had both promised to break his neck if they encountered him.

Marsha, too, who was quite close to Frankie, was mystified by her behaviour: 'I wouldn't phone him, I'd just leave him alone and hope he leaves me alone.'

But Jenny was aware that Frankie's emotions were torn in different directions, and she tried to be supportive: 'Yeah, you're right Marsha, but I know how she feels. There is something there for her and she doesn't want to let it go.'

Marsha still looked very puzzled, and said sadly: 'But she's so different now to what she used to be. She's lost her fight, somehow.'

Marsha was quite right. Frankie had changed and she never seemed to recover from this weekend. She went to live with her sister while she waited again for a council house of her own and the birth of her child in a state of dread in case the baby would be damaged. Fortunately, it was a healthy baby boy and her sisters gave her plenty of support after she left work. Still, she missed Vin and a few months later started seeing him again.

Frankie was the most visibly dramatic case of a battered woman that I encountered during my year and she was a woman I knew quite well. But how many other women were subjected to physical abuse and lived in fear, I could only guess. Certainly, with all we now know about the level of domestic violence, Frankie was not alone among a department of 300 women, and the local refuge was testament to the level of domestic violence in the city. This violence sits uneasily with the cosy, warm picture of family life we are offered through the newspapers and television, the adverts and calls to family loyalty. To a battered woman the family looks like a network of terror, not a warm safe island outside the aggressiveness of the market. For her, it is the context in which patriarchal power is fully extended.

Family women

The lives of the women at StitchCo elaborate the point made by Michèle Barrett and Mary McIntosh, 'We cannot overestimate the popularity of the family!'[16] Both women and men are encouraged to believe in the family as 'natural' and, therefore, desirable. The concomitants of this view are that heterosexuality, the gender division of labour within the family and the power of men in the home are all part of a natural world which cannot, therefore, be challenged. Women invest heavily in the family on all counts, from the economic to the emotional and it is a measure of the importance of this world that they worry about housework and shopping, budgets and cooking, taking these areas on as their own and gaining from them, they believe, power and prestige. A situation has been generated in relation to domestic labour, where 'Men have deskilled themselves in order to get out of it and women have colluded in order to gain some pride in compensation for a disadvantaged situation.'[17] The issue is quite clear: 'Nobody should have a housewife.'[18] Instead, we should press for more socialised means of housework and whatever would release women from the burden of work they carry.

There was no doubt, though, that the family was important to all the women on the shopfloor: it provided them with an area of life that they believed was beyond production and the market-place and the arm of the state. Neither, of course, is strictly true, but that was how the women understood family life. It was valuable and important and must be protected and nurtured *by women* who alone had the abilities to create an emotionally supportive environment for others. The family the women spent their time and energy creating and sustaining was a patriarchal family in which men had a privileged position, just as they do in the workplace. At home, women were isolated; they had no mates on the line with whom to generate a protest. As wives and mothers, in the current situation, women can rarely walk off the job in protest without such actions having serious legal and other consequences. Women in the home are on a 24-hour shift and the family, as we know it, is constructed around this exploitation.

The women of StitchCo, although committed to the idea of the family, were not uncritical of the form it has taken and were, themselves, involved in a form of demystification through the support and solidarity that they generated on the shopfloor and in their neighbourhoods. Women were crucially aware that without each other's support they could not cope with the double shift and the demands of family life. While many women at StitchCo were involved in joint financial arrangements and were co-partners in decisions about major purchases, this did not mean that husbands and wives did equal amounts of housework, shopping or managing domestic affairs, that women no longer served their husbands, or that they spent more time together as couples.[19] It is a measure of the power of the ideologies relating to men and women that economics did not overturn the power relations in the family, a point made earlier in this chapter and elaborated in relation to the role of women's wages in the domestic unit.

Women on the shopfloor seemed to express lives bounded by an earlier pattern of support among working-class women which centred upon the importance of 'Mam', the mother–woman who held it all together. Mum, or Mam was, and is, crucial to the continuity of working-class culture – especially as it is lived among women. Mothers cross the division between household and family, bringing both together in one person, joining the economics of work to the power of reproduction. Jamaican, British and Indian women were all committed to their own mothers, and despite distance or marriage, they all endeavoured to keep in close contact with them.

Indian women also drew support from other women, just like other black women did, because all of them were facing unprecedented demands upon their time and energy in an increasingly hostile environment. Earlier chapters have already shown that family life for Indian women was a complex and contradictory experience, at one and the same time supportive and nurturing but also claustrophobic and weakening. Indian women drew on the strengths of family life and tried to counteract the way in which families were controlled by men and organised around their needs. As Amrit Wilson has clarified, women's labour and emotions massaged the egos of husbands, brothers and fathers; women did this, without complaint, in what were often difficult circumstances.[20] For a young Indian woman, this made the nuclear family look very attractive; the burden of work would be less, her power would be greater, and she could bring up her children without the interference of the older generation. The price she might pay could be the isolation of the single household. Indian women needed the support of the extended family, just as white working-class women did. It is crucial, though, that we understand who offers what support. Services exchanged within family groups – childminding, cooking, cleaning, care of the elderly or the sick, shopping and counselling – are all services usually given by women. Consequently, when we celebrate the family as a supportive network in relation to these services, let us be clear that the structure of support is a woman's network and that this could exist without nuclear or extended families. Indeed, in some places it does.[21]

At the centre of the family, as the warm and supportive nexus of relationships and events that are conjured up when family is mentioned, is one person, the mother. The mother was a central character for shopfloor culture which celebrated motherhood as the final, defining, characteristic of woman. Becoming a mother was part of the work of reproduction carried on by women, in which they made anew the lives that they had left in their own families. Most did not wait long to do this. In the next chapter, I move on to the final stages in the drama which turns a girl into a woman, both in the factory and in the family.

9

Women's business:
the politics of reproduction

> The family is Nature's first group . . . but the mother is the
> human anchor which holds it fast.

Although these words were written by Margery Spring Rice over
40 years ago, they would find a deep resonance among the women
at StitchCo today.[1] The last chapter showed women who were
deeply committed to their families, and who laboured long and
hard in the service of an ideal of family life. This ideal is
constructed around a complex set of assumptions, including the
notion that the family is natural. But nature, it seems, takes very
specific forms: the identikit picture of the family, beloved of the
state and the advertising agencies, is a white middle-class family
with two children, a boy and a girl. By the very fact that it is an
ideological construction it takes no account of racial and ethnic
variations and that the lived experience of family life may be very
different; fathers may be absent, for example. While the forms of
the family may be diverse, there is one vital ingredient: children,
who are produced by mothers, 'the anchors' of family life.

Like the family and children, motherhood is believed to be
natural, but this wild oversimplification ignores the distinction
between the biological basis of reproduction in pregnancy and
birth, on the one hand, and mothering, comprising nurture and
care, on the other. The latter is not bound to be the province of
women. The emphasis upon nature ignores the complexities of
motherhood and reduces it to an unambiguous biological fact
which writes off the point made by Adrienne Rich that 'Motherhood . . . has a history, it has an ideology.'[2] Both of these have
been explored by recent writers, such as Elisabeth Badinter and
Barbie Antonis, who show that notions like the maternal instinct
have very little to do with nature, but very much more to do with
ideologies that place women at the mercy of their own biology.[3]

Adrienne Rich sums this up: 'Patriarchy could not survive without motherhood and heterosexuality in their institutional forms; therefore they have to be treated as axioms, as nature "itself".'[4]

Adrienne Rich's powerful condemnation of the experience of motherhood under patriarchal constraints would also find recognition among the women in the department. This chapter explores the contradictions expressed in the way that women celebrate, protest at and collude in the institution of motherhood, and the ideologies which surround it.

'In the club'

As soon as Pauline whispered to Heather that she was pregnant, and Heather announced it to the women nearby, Pauline's machine was surrounded by well-wishers who continued to come throughout the day. The news of a pregnancy added zest and excitement to the working day which would be carried forward as the pregnancy progressed. Everyone wanted to know when Pauline discovered her pregnancy, when her baby was due, when she would leave and, ultimately, how she was feeling. There were 27 pregnancies during my year on the shopfloor, but because they were so celebrated their importance far outweighed their numbers (which were considered high compared to previous years). Management and machinists alike discussed the number of pregnancies, the individual women and their welfare; it seemed such an integral part of the women's world of the department.

Given the constraints of a patriarchal society alluded to by Adrienne Rich, pregnancy had been chosen by the women in the department. Though the pregnancy may not have been planned, the decision to go ahead had been taken in relation to available options. On Eve's line, for example, Sharon, Kamla and Kelly were all leaving at the same time and Sharon told me this proudly as she pointed out that they sat one in front of the other on the unit. Kamla was older than Sharon and Kelly and delighted that she was pregnant for the second time: 'I have a daughter who is seven so I am very happy that this one has come along.'

Sharon and Kelly were unmarried and 17. I asked them, individually, how they felt about having a baby. Sharon replied cheerfully: 'Oh, I'm pleased about it, I'm really looking forward to having the baby.' When I asked her if she had thought about not having the baby at any point, she again replied very cheerfully:

Funny, me Mam said did I want it or did I want to get rid of it.
I said I wanted it and she said she'd help me. My boyfriend
works at a place where they make banners and signs – if we get
short of money, I can do some work from home. I don't mind.
I just want to have my baby and look after it. Shelley, over
there, had a baby and she's come back to work. Her mother
looks after it, but I'd like to look after my own.

Sharon was very positive about what she was doing while Kelly
seemed less certain:

Well, it happens. I want to have it I s'pose, nothing I can do to
change it. I don't believe in abortion. I expect I will stay at
home and look after it, but I will miss my friends at work.
Work is all right really.

Kelly, too, had the support of her mother and after her daughter
was born it was Mum who stayed at home to look after the baby
while Kelly returned to work. Sharon continued to see her
boyfriend and they made plans to marry; Kelly saw the father of
her child less and less.

Kelly was one of the youngest mothers on the shopfloor (12 of
the mothers-to-be were women below the age of 21), and there
were women who did not regard this as a happy situation. Ginny,
for example, was also pregnant and her baby was no more planned
than Kelly's or Sharon's, but she was older (21) and when she
thought about this she said:

I'm glad I didn't have a baby too young, like some of them
here. They are 16 and 17. They think it's romantic to have a
boy's baby and then the boys leave them and there they are
with a baby to bring up on their own.

Satwant was also wary of the magic of motherhood:

Alma will be leaving to have a baby soon. They are really
happy about it because Alma has been married for nine years,
but the ones on Eve's line are so young. Sharon is getting
married, that's what I heard, but I think it's too young, you
haven't had any life of your own and you are really only from
school when you have to settle down and look after a baby. I
think it's a shame, really.

These views echoed Laura's and her understanding of the politics
of motherhood, of the way in which the fertility and sexuality of

women is subject to the control of men. Laura was describing patriarchy in action when she told me:

> You know the young ones fall all over these blokes trying to please them and for what – they end up pregnant and I wouldn't like that. Then the blokes just go out, same as before. It's the women who suffer. My cousin came around to visit and her nextdoor neighbour is a young girl of 17 who has one baby of eight months and is now having another one. She said they've got nothing in the house and the bloke just goes up the pub the whole time. Well, she's not going to have anything, is she? It's all right for the men, isn't it? They want the kids to show off their virility, I suppose, but we have to have them. We have to suffer, the men don't.

Laura's words are an important reminder amid the euphoria surrounding motherhood, that not all women are compliant – some women genuinely want to lead different lives.

There was an alternative understanding that promoted the idea of motherhood not only as the apex of a woman's life, but as a means to obtain resources from men and the state. Tessa and Julie, who were brides and mothers within a year, as we saw, took this view. For them, motherhood was the signal to leave the factory and to depend upon their husbands for support. In doing this they called the bluff of the family wage and insisted they would be dependent upon the male breadwinner. For most couples, this proved a non-viable strategy although it was generally approved of in relation to the first five years of a child's life. For a single parent, it was even more difficult because state benefits did not provide adequately for mothers and children (or fathers, if they were placed in the same situation) as a later section of this chapter will show. Motherhood did give women access to these benefits from the state and, locally, to housing – the local council tried to house single parents as well as couples with a child. This was a key factor in the speed with which brides became mothers. They knew that 'You have to have a baby to get housed,' and they acted on this. It was a powerful incentive to reproduce and it made motherhood a rational strategy in relation to available resources. It was realistic rather than romantic.

The romance surrounding motherhood was an essential ingredient of the shopfloor celebration and it began with the mother-to-be. Pauline's announcement that she was pregnant made her a celebrity. As a mother-to-be she was rewarded for becoming pregnant by a level of attention which demonstrated overwhelming approval. Probably for the first time in her life, she felt that she had done the right thing and that she had done this by exercising a natural capacity. Pauline, and the other women, were showered with attention and gifts for tying themselves securely to their 'feminine' destiny in motherhood. Given this, it is hardly surprising that so many young women opted for motherhood. This scenario is not one that is confined to the shopfloor. Adrienne Rich's writing makes clear that she, too, was subject to this kind of approval which made her feel that she had finally grasped her part in womanhood and that she had, at last, become a woman.[5] Exactly the same feelings surrounded the young mothers in the department.

The interest shown in the twins, Pauline, Amita and Kamla, was sustained week by week as they relayed the latest in their careers as mothers, and as the units where they worked saved to buy gifts for their babies when the women left the factory. On her final day, each woman would have a display of gifts, cards and posters over her machine. Gina, a supervisor and a popular woman, arrived for work on her last day and was greeted by a large banner hanging over her unit which wished Gina and baby well, and which showed a baby smiling at her mother. The unit had collected enough money to buy a highchair and baby clothes and these were laid out on a table alongside tiny bootees, little baby dresses, handknitted jackets and tops, talc and nappies and all manner of gifts surrounded by pink and blue tissue and with flowers and sweet cards. The gifts were for the baby and they were all tiny, pretty things of use in the very early months of a baby's life (except for the highchair, which the practical Gina had chosen). The romance that surrounded weddings was reproduced in the little things which overflowed on the table.

By 11 o'clock in the morning Gina was in the canteen cutting a huge cake and putting out plates of biscuits and paper cups full of orange squash while she encouraged the women to gather round. Very soon the canteen was crowded and Gina's unit, at least, was empty. Everyone wished Gina well and talked about the shape of her body and how it showed that she was going to have a boy or girl – opinions were equally divided. Gina was a large woman and she laughed suggesting she might be having 'a football team, I'm that large', but she also looked majestic and very healthy. She was, she said, pleased to be having the baby. Still, as she looked at her friends and they gathered around her, she said, 'I'm not sure I want to go now and be at home on my own. It'll be all right when the baby comes.' Alma, who was leaving one week later agreed, 'Yeah I will miss everyone. I bet it really drags until the baby comes.'

Neither Gina, who was 23, nor Alma, who was 27, expected to be back at work. Nevertheless, they were both conscious of their rights as workers and of the possibility that something might go wrong. As Gina said: 'I don't expect to be back at work, but I've said I will because you have to in case anything goes wrong, then at least you've got your job to come back to.' Both Gina and Alma thought their lives would have new dimensions 'once the baby arrives'; this was, however, coupled with a realistic view that sometimes things go wrong and that that eventuality had to be faced.

There was nothing in the celebration of motherhood that suggested anything might go wrong; the celebration was an act of faith and confirmation of the joys of motherhood. Indian women were more open about the dangers of childbirth because the lives of women in India and Africa were a more present part of their experience. On the other hand, the hardships suffered by working-class women (and recorded, for example, by the Women's Co-operative Guild early in the century, and later in the account already mentioned of the health of working-class women by Margery Spring Rice) were glossed over, in an account of birth and mothering which emphasised the pleasures and not the emotional and psychological turmoil of mothering.[6] Nothing was said about the possibility of post-natal depression which is, after all, such a common occurrence.[7] The physical pain of birth was given more attention and many women admitted to me that they were frightened of childbirth, but little was said in the groups who came together to talk about babies and mothering. Instead, they concentrated on the names for their babies – and essentially on babies, not on children.

This romantic picture was the final part in a long process which encouraged and cajoled women towards motherhood, all in the name of Nature. By taking over this view, shopfloor culture might have precluded major areas of discussion which were vitally important to the health and well-being of the mother. Behind the romance, however, lurked a suspicion that although staying at home was the most important thing a woman could do, and that it was a much more worth-while job than sewing on buttons, leaving the factory meant leaving behind the social life of the shopfloor, the support and solidarity of women together. Leaving the shopfloor meant exchanging sociability and sisterhood for the isolation of home and much greater dependence upon a man. Alma voiced the fears of many when she said: 'I'm not looking forward to being at home. It will be all right when I've got the baby, but the next couple of months will drag. You miss all your friends when you're at home. I expect I'll be really bored.'

These sentiments were so common and repeated so often that it was obvious the women were aware of the problems of being a woman at home with a small baby. Nevertheless, they were committed to the idea of motherhood as a period of time when a woman gave her energies and emotions to her children because she had come fully into the world of women – into the club. There were other aspects of women's lives beyond the family and mothering which were a source of great importance to them, and which gave them an understanding of themselves as women who were part of a sisterhood – but the setting which provided the basis for this also deterred. Just as they were conscious of the value of women together at work, they were also conscious of the fact that the work they did was boring and underpaid: it was this that made motherhood and life at home look attractive and important. In the home, women felt they organised for real needs and their labour went to support and sustain children and men – real people, not factory owners and profits.

On the re-production line

The power that women feel in relation to their ability to conceive and bear a child is soon curtailed by the intrusion of the medical profession and medical definitions of the state of pregnancy. Ann Oakley's work has charted the management of childbirth as it was experienced by a group of white, predominantly middle-class women who were all having their first babies.[8] The difficulties, misunderstandings and general sense of disquiet expressed by the women in her book are part of the growing level of discontent with the transformation of childbirth into a medical process, offering women a production-line experience they find deeply alienating. It is part of a general pattern commented upon by Ann Oakley:

> The colonisation of birth by medicine is a thread in the fabric of cultural dependence on professional health care. People are not responsible for their own health, their own illness, their own births and deaths; doctors are saviours, miracle-workers, mechanics and culture-heroes.[9]

While this may be generally true, there is resistance to the power of the medical profession and the link between pregnancy and illness, shown in the growth of interest in natural childbirth, home deliveries and organisations like the Active Birth Movement. The women of StitchCo also expressed a deep resentment to the medicalisation of childbirth and the attempt by doctors and hospitals to take control of their bodies.

The resistance exhibited by white working-class women to the intervention of professionals in what they considered to be women's business, which could be managed from their own cultural resources, matched working-class resistance to schooling, the state and the factory manager. Instead, the women emphasised self-help and the use of practical knowledge that was held by experts in their own communities and families: mothers, who were best equipped to offer advice and assistance. Pregnancy was viewed as the outcome of a choice, as cause for celebration and a natural state for women, not as an illness requiring hospitalisation, doctors, prescriptions and paramedicals. Frankie, for example, had this to say about her sister, Ellie: 'Our Ellie is drippin' around at me Mam's clutching her stomach. I keep tellin' 'er, she's pregnant, not ill. She needs to get out and about and get some exercise and that, not to be sitting about getting fat like she is.'

Women complained to one another about the treatment they received at the city hospitals, comparing their experiences over coffee, as the following conversation between Tessa and Heather, who was 19 and expecting her first baby, showed:

Tessa [angrily] You have to wait for hours and they are so nasty to you, 'Come here, go there. Bring your water, take it here and wait there.' Huh!

Heather Yeah, I know. They make you sit and wait and wait.

Tessa They gave me a scan and then I was examined. They took a blood test and then they said wait for something else. I said, 'I've got to go back to work, I'm losing money being here, I can't afford it.' This nurse says, all huffy like, 'Well, your baby comes first.' I'd like to see her waiting two or three hours to be looked at. Me Mam goes with me and it's her time as well. There she is trying to calm me down. Now they think my date is later than they thought. They're as bad as this place. They don't know what's happening. I got really fed up with it all and

me Mam was trying to be nice to the nurses. But why should
she?
Heather Yeah, it's just the same for me, me Mam comes with me.
I hate it being poked about like that.

Heather and Tessa spoke for most of the women. Most objected
to the long waits, the conveyor-belt style of their care and the way
in which they were treated as non-persons and non-workers by a
system of care that was geared to organisational imperatives,
rather than the needs of babies and their mothers.

The problem that Tessa and Heather and some of the other
women seemed to have in getting a date for the birth was picked up
by Eve who saw in this the same cultural dependence referred to by
Ann Oakley. Eve had this to say:

What I really don't understand is how these girls don't know
when the baby is due. You must know when you had your
period and you count seven days from that and nine months
on, and it will be within seven days. These girls keep saying
they don't know, the doctor will tell them. Blow the bloody
doctor, you need to know for yourself.

Eve's view that women should be in control of their own bodies
was shared by the other women and expressed in their resistance to
the professionals who tried to envelope them. Tessa's sister, Julie,
had a fight with the first doctor she saw because 'He asked really
personal questions about sex and periods and that – I'm not telling
him, he can forget it.' Instead, Julie and the others relied upon
their mothers to give them support and guidance through their
pregnancies and this included visits to the hospital. More
importantly, however, they relied upon their mother's version of a
healthy pregnancy. The mainstay of a healthy pregnancy was to eat
plenty and they were encouraged to do this. Little attention was
given to warnings about the negative affects of smoking and
drinking during pregnancy, or the need for exercise and careful
preparation for the process of birth. Young white women smoked
and drank cheerfully throughout their pregnancies and, because
they were young and strong at this point in their lives, they and
their babies showed few signs of ill effects. They dismissed the
evidence on smoking and drinking with cavalier gestures and
cheerful quips like, 'Come on, I'm pregnant, not going into a

nunnery.' Indeed, most of them were enjoying their pregnancies, blooming amid the concern and interest in the department and delighted by the approval they received.

Hospital visits continued to be fraught throughout their pregnancies and, as these progressed, they encountered health visitors and paramedicals who advised them on diets and care of their babies. These encounters were met with the same resistance that marked the encounters between women and doctors; they, too, were discussed by Tessa, Julie and their friends during their breaks, when they would come together to exchange the latest episode in their careers as mothers.

Tessa said: 'This snooty woman at the hospital was telling me how to feed the baby. She wants me to breastfeed. She makes a real fuss about it. She wants to know why I don't want to. Well, I just don't fancy it, that's all. It's not nice, somehow.'

Heather, Ginny and the others agreed and Julie added: 'I'm not goin' to do that, I don't care what they say, it's not nice. How you goin' to take it out at someone's place. No, I'm not havin' that. I don't want to do it.'

Julie grimaced as she spoke and made fun of the idea of breastfeeding; her response, though, was a complex one. While pregnancy was natural, breastfeeding was not given the same natural/neutral status because breasts raised the issue of women's sexuality. The twins' curious coyness was explained by the fact that they had imbibed the notion of themselves as sex objects; consequently, breastfeeding meant that their sexuality would be on show, made public, and in some way debased by this association with babies and birth. It was vitally important to Tessa and others to maintain that sexual attractiveness which they saw as one of their major bargaining cards in their relations with men. They were caught in the contradiction between wife and mother. As mothers, they were going to be more dependent upon men. Consequently their sexuality must be available to men, and their sexual attractiveness maintained because, as they understood their relationships with their husbands or lovers, too much was at stake. Ann Oakley has reached similar conclusions:

Patriarchy defines female biology in special ways; women's sexual availability and response to men is important; reproduction within marriage is necessary; breastfeeding is medically desirable but sexually disturbing, for a woman's breasts belong to men not to babies, and exposing a breast to a baby seems like indecent exposure.[10]

Sexuality was a key issue in the response from the twins. There was also the rejection of professional advice, which sought to label them incompetent and which did so from a position of ignorance. In part, working-class women have to assert their right not to breastfeed their babies because they have pressing demands upon them which force them back to work in the factories and shops of Britain. The rejection of breastfeeding is another aspect of their insistence that they must decide what their needs are and how these are to be met. The twins' response was a deeply contradictory one, operating at a variety of levels which simultaneously asserted the rights of women to control their own bodies and colluded in a patriarchal definition of women's sexuality.

Similar sets of contradictions surrounded the vexed question of the presence of men at the birth of their babies. Julie's views were common among the women:

This is my hospital card, see. They want me to go to classes, but I can't go. And they say Dave can be with me, but I don't know about that. I don't want him seeing me like that, not down there. He could hold me hand or sommat. I don't think a bloke would fancy you again after he's seen that.

Set against this, with its familiar patriarchal assumptions about women's sexuality and women's bodies in the service of men, was the alternative view posed.

Jessie I think it's women's business meself. I wouldn't have wanted Colin there.
Tessa Yeah, I int havin' Carl there, useless he'd be . . . I'd rather have me Mam.

Tessa spoke for many of her friends who were expecting their first babies. It was their mothers whom they would have chosen to have had alongside them for the birth, just like they had been with them through their pregnancies. The bonds between mothers and daughters were a powerful expression of the women's world in which they were all immersed. Their own mothers would take them through pregnancy and into motherhood, thereby strengthening those bonds. Mothers helped daughters with practical matters and by giving reassurance and advice, which was heeded; the advice and instructions emanating from the hospitals were not. The women responded to the white-coated professionals by ignoring them, treating them sullenly just like they had treated teachers in school when they were girls. They felt judged by the paramedics and the doctors, misunderstood and forced into dependence because the cultural competence they possessed was ignored, by-passed in the interests of medical efficiency and hospital rules.

The social relations of health care that Tessa and others encountered were such that they could not possibly assist them; class relations and the patriarchal basis of the medical profession came together and ensured distance between mothers and doctors and rejection by working-class women (and they are not alone in this – women, generally, are involved in protesting at their treatment). The question this rejection posed for me was how far their protest meant that they colluded in the reproduction of disadvantage in their own lives. Modern obstetrics has contributed to the development of safer childbirth and healthier babies. It cannot, however, take all the credit: higher standards of living have encouraged better health and hygiene and thus lowered the risks to mothers and babies. The factors involved in areas of high infant mortality and perinatal rates are invariably poverty and poor housing. Nevertheless, hospitals and doctors and other professionals do have an important contribution to make – by alienating women, their contribution is less than it might be. Working-class women are health conscious and they want good care for themselves and their babies; they also want to exercise some control over this process, and to be recognised as women with valuable knowledge of their own. Health-education projects and programmes which ignore this and the role of working-class women in disseminating and collecting knowledge on health issues are doomed to failure. For all this, I would like to join with Ann Oakley in presenting a caution: 'Woman-controlled childbirth is a fresh vision of an old social arrangement. But there was no golden age in which women gave birth both safely and effortlessly, and it would be a backward step to condemn the whole of modern obstetrics.'[11]

This is an important corrective to any romantic view of the past. Working-class women, and women generally, have consistently fought for better maternity care, for benefits and safe childbirth. The painful pages of the Women's Co-operative Guild document, *Maternity: Letters from Working Women*, demonstrate the continuity in this struggle and the attention that working-class women have given to the health and well-being of their families. Now, the struggle is multi-faceted – to maintain services and to change them so that they are more responsive to the people they serve. Women in the workplace provide an important starting-point because they are together and can offer their views on the changes that they see are necessary. The point is to ask them, and then to listen to what they have to say.

For black women, the struggle was magnified. Despite the attention to the unifying experience of motherhood for all women, they were subject to racism at work. One day, Flo was counting the number of pregnancies and she reported to Norah, 'Twenty-seven on the last count. It's all these coloureds, they breed like rabbits.' Norah, parrot-like, repeated, 'Yes, breed like rabbits.' Statistically, Flo was wrong. Indian women accounted for one-third of all pregnancies; racism, though, has never taken much account of information which does not support its major premises. Overtly racist remarks like Flo's were uncommon, but they were part of the context in which black women worked. Outside they, too, were subject to the sexism of the hospital which enforced dependence and insisted that they were incompetent. For them, this insistence on their dependence and incompetence was further reinforced by racism. As Marsha understood all too well: 'Because I'm an unmarried *black* mother, they give me shit.' She was adamant that she would have her next baby 'in a field' rather than have to deal with 'all that shit' again.

Indian women were quieter in their protests, but just as disturbed by what happened to them. Like Julie, they objected to the personal nature of the questions they were asked and the way in which the specific constraints which surround the female body in Hindu culture were flouted. This was only one part of the general level of misunderstanding which permeated the care that Indian women received. It is a hopeful sign that some training in sensitivities to cultural diversity, which will support an anti-racist stance, is now being offered in the health service.

Some concern has been expressed about the health of Asian mothers and their babies by medical practitioners. There is very little research which illuminates the issues involved. Perinatal mortality rates, it is suggested, are high and birth weights of Asian babies are low compared with average white babies. As a result, efforts have concentrated upon encouraging a higher rate of take-up for antenatal care, especially among Asian women who do not speak English. Maternity care is one among a number of areas of concern associated with ethnic minority health, but there is always the danger that in concentrating upon ethnicity, poverty and bad housing will be overlooked as major causes of poor health. Poor Moslem women living in a deprived inner-city area share the same privations as poor white women; in both cases there is the danger that they will be blamed and that they will become the problem, rather than the social conditions and the institutionalised racism and professional ideologies which affect the delivery of care to those who need it. In a survey of the little work that has been done in this area, Maggie Pearson makes this point and emphasises the need to look closely at the assumptions which surround the provision of facilities for women.[12] She is anxious to stress the need to combat racism in the health services, an oppression that all non-whites are subject to. At the same time, she underlines the importance of recognising the cultural specificity of different ethnic groups and warns against treating them as a simple unity with one problem – which has often mistakenly been viewed as the inability to speak English.

Trying to assess the research in this area is fraught with difficulties because I am never sure if like is being compared with like. When birth weights were compared, were Moslem women in Bradford compared with their poor white neighbours? If they were, would we see a similar profile for both groups? This does not mean that ethnic minorities should not have special consideration, but we need to consider what this should be. They need material resources desperately in some places, as do other inner-city dwellers, but they also need the chance to make sense of the experience of pregnancy and motherhood in an alien environment. In order for this to happen, racism must be confronted in the health sector and, just like other women, they must be given a voice in the care that they want.

The Indian women in the factory were, on the whole, better-off than their sisters in the small hosiery factories locally. They worked for a company which supported women by allowing them to attend regularly at the antenatal clinics attached to one of the city hospitals which took a special interest in Asian women and their babies. The women I knew were not slow to take up services, but some of the experiences they had might well have deterred those who were less forceful, or did not have someone to support them on hospital visits and in general.[13]

In all the discussions of ethnic minority health, little is said of the role of folk wisdom and herbal medicine as it is practised by healers in the Asian communities. Just like their white counterparts, the Indian women at StitchCo were offered a range of advice and experiences based upon folk knowledge which they could draw upon if they chose. In addition, there were the strictures surrounding pregnant women which varied according to caste, but which emphasised that childbirth, like menstruation, was polluting and measures had to be taken to guard against the polluting and dangerous process of birth. In India this is handled by the midwives (dai) who learn their craft through an apprenticeship within their own caste (they are Harijans).[14] Washerwomen and women from the barber caste, another low caste, also assist. Pregnancy and childbirth are managed by women and the process is in their control. The Indian women I talked to were also mindful of the dangers of the old system of midwives in the villages and the rather unhelpful nature of some of the folk knowledge. On the whole, they preferred to follow medical advice – but not blindly. Individuals would compare their treatment, ask each other about the tablets they had been given, consult on the stages of their pregnancy with each other and with the young white women on the shopfloor. Amita was a good example of the way that most women treated their pregnancy: 'Indian women say so many things when you are pregnant, not to eat rice, not to wash your hair. I don't follow it and not many do now. I follow the doctors and the hospital, not silly stories.'

Women like Amita no longer believed that pregnancy was a woman's destiny and that she could not exercise some control over her own fertility. She, like the other younger married women, wanted only two or three children compared to her mother who had had nine. Amita and Rajni and other women were talking about this and Rajni was adamant:

I have two children. It is quite enough, we don't want to have more than that. Indian families like to have boys, but I don't mind. Girls are the same now. In England people don't worry about such things, do they? [I assured her, they did!] Our

mothers had many children, but now it is too expensive and it
wears the woman out. We are having two, maybe three –
that's all. It's much better.

Economic factors have long been known to affect fertility rates.
While children may be an asset in some contexts, in others they are
a responsibility and drain on resources and their numbers need to
be small. Indian women were not, on the whole, looking at
children as a source of access to council housing or welfare
benefits, as some of the young white women were. More
importantly, Rajni's comments also asserted the rights of women
to control their own bodies and to have their health needs
considered, rather than have their bodies used in the service of
male pride in sons.

Rajni continued: 'You know, our mothers were very strong.
They had babies at 16 and they went on having babies – nine or ten,
they had. Some died then. It's different now.' The memory of the
times when mothers and babies died in childbirth were fresh (and
still present) because links with India were maintained by the
women's relatives or their husbands. Just like Gina or Heather,
Amita and Indira expressed fear at the idea of childbirth.
Although the hospital monitored their blood pressure, poked and
probed their bodies, it did not pay any attention to this fear,
leaving it instead to midwives or to relaxation classes run by the
National Childbirth Trust, which the women did not necessarily
attend. There was never any time to ask questions at the hospital
and most women were anxious to be 'good' patients and not
'waste' the doctor's time; their anxieties remained and were,
perhaps, fed by the more lurid tales of birth and pain which
travelled around the shopfloor.

Amita did not need to be told to give up smoking and drinking.
Like most Indian women, she did neither, nor did she gain pounds
and pounds of weight during her pregnancy. She was, in fact, very
fit because she lived in a flat with her husband and so she did not
carry an enormous burden of domestic work. Some of the other
women, though, continued to cook and clean throughout their
pregnancies – in a joint family setting they would have been
relieved of some of these duties. Thus, some of the women were
frail and tired and more likely to be anaemic.

Kamla and Indira, and the other women, took it for granted that
they were going to breastfeed their babies; they planned their

return to work in relation to this. Most of them expected to be on leave from the factory for six months at the end of which they would return to work and their children would be cared for by relatives: Kamla's mother-in-law was going to look after the new baby, but neither Indira nor Amita had mothers-in-law to hand, so they were contemplating other arrangements which included childminders.

As far as the presence of men at the birth of the child was concerned, most agreed with the other women in the department: birth was the business of women and men should stay at a distance from it. The birth was managed by the women as best they could, given the constraints of the hospital setting which made each woman a patient rather than a mother. Indian women, like any other group of women, wanted more control over the process of their pregnancies and the birth event. They asked for more information because they wanted to understand the processes they were involved in, not just be passive recipients of expert advice.

To be a woman is to be a mother; cultures throughout the world set this prescription upon women's lives and in so doing tie womanhood firmly to biology. Indian cultures are no exception to this and women without children are derided or feared as 'unnatural' or cursed. Consequently, if she does not become a mother a woman forfeits the possibility of power and prestige in her family and the community. Most of all, an Indian woman hopes that she will give birth to a son quickly. A son provides continuity and performs the final rites at the husband's funeral, thereby ensuring a safe passage from this world to the next. (Surrogates can, of course, be found but are considered a poor second to a first son.) A woman also needs to have a son who will provide some security for her old age. Once she has a son, it means that she can begin to relax a little in her relations with her husband and her parents-in-law. She has completed her side of the bargain and she becomes a person, an adult who must now be respected.[15] Amita expressed this when she said, 'I want a boy so much, but I bet I don't get it.' Kamla too hoped for a boy because, quite simply, 'It will make my husband very happy,' and this meant that she would feel more secure. Personally, many women may wish for a daughter, especially in the context of their lives in urban Britain, because a daughter will provide support and assistance for her mother. This was expressed to me in a discussion about the arrival of Amita's baby:

Asha Amita has had a son, she is very happy. Indian families like
to have a son, but I like to have a daughter first; it is higher,
you know, to have a girl first.
Sallie Higher?
Asha Like, more spiritual to have a girl. All Indian women want
a girl first, but the men want sons.

Asha's defence of daughters was couched in the language of
spirituality, but this did not make her words any less combative.
They were a defiant gesture against the power of men to decide
who was more important.

The excitement generated by the fact that the sex of the baby
was an unknown did not wane while there were pregnant women in
the department. Everyone had their own way of knowing who was
expecting a boy or a girl. As Trisha wisely said: 'Tess is goin' to
have a boy because she's carryin' on the front. If you're big at the
front it's a boy, if you get big in the bum and round the back, it's a
girl.'

Gina laughed when she heard this and joked: 'What happens if
you're big all the way round?'

Trisha was wrong in most cases, but not in Tessa's. Both she and
Julie had sons, even though Tessa, wanting a girl, had determinedly
collected baby clothes in all shades of pink. The arrival of a boy
troubled her initially, but she recovered quickly and announced
that the next one would be a girl. She and Heather and Gina would
spend long breaks musing on the names they would choose:
Rebecca was growing in popularity; Jason and Ben for boys. Tessa
arrived one day and told everyone: 'Carl says it's gonna be Rocky,
Rocky! What kind of a name is that. I told 'im I int havin' it
because it's me who has to take the baby around and what am I
gonna say when people ask what it's called?' Like Pauline, she
settled instead for Lee or Gareth, Duane or Wayne.

After the women had actually left work, these discussions
continued because they would come back to the department to
collect their pay on Fridays and would stop to have coffee and chat
and see old friends, which generally disrupted production on the
units. It was a wonderful sight to see so many healthy pregnant
women in the factory generating a feeling of support and solidarity
between themselves and the women still at work in the department. They lingered in the coffee bar most of Friday afternoon
and generally added to the euphoria of Friday afternoons. Gracie

shook her head at this and, with her hands on her hips, said:
'Everywhere I look there are pregnant women. John says he's
going to turn the place into a maternity home, move in a few beds
and employ some nurses in case anything happens. I don't know – I
think it's the water!'

Management tolerated the disruption for a few weeks and then
determined that the climb up the stairs to the department was
dangerous to pregnant women, and that, in future, they would
collect their money from the downstairs office. It was a blow
to the dozen or so women who were all pregnant at the same
time, and who openly complained of being bored and lonely at
home:

Amita I'm so bored at home, all I do is sit and eat. Come and see
me.
Heather I'm the same, I just sit about, or, if me Mam's not
working, we go up town together.

Boredom, in fact, drove Heather towards the relaxation classes –
they at least gave her some company, she said.

I took a special delight in the coffee bar full of pregnant women
because it made a statement about the power of women in relation
to production, and, despite the romance of motherhood, when the
women came together they did so as a self-help group in which a
wealth of information about pregnancy and childbirth was
exchanged. They distilled from friends and relatives the experiences that they had had at the city hospitals and they
commented upon the doctors and midwives they had encountered.
Beyond this group of women were all the other women in the
department, who came into the discussion to offer advice,
reassurance so badly needed, and positive encouragement to the
younger women. This was another example of the poverty of a
conceptual framework which separates home and work and treats
them as two distinct spheres. It is usually assumed that pregnancy,
childbirth and motherhood are matters related to family life and
to women at home, rather than in the factory or the workplace.
This assumption has allowed trade unions to ignore issues
connected with maternity rights and benefits. The StitchCo
women's union supported this view in the way that it ignored
the rights of its members. Women found out about their
maternity benefits and entitlements from each other or from
Clare, the personnel manager, and thus knew their rights. Changes

in the law under the Employment Act of 1980 were not clearly understood, however. One of the important changes was that women should make their intention to return to work known in writing. This insistence upon a written commitment was especially onerous for some of the Indian women who spoke English very fluently, but did not write in English. The company was considering producing a standard letter that could be given to everyone and posted back to the department. Consequently, while management took up the issue and employers' organisations sent out information on the law and its benefits – or problems – for employers, the union was much slower to respond. It did so only because there were women like Annie to push it into action:

> The district committee, with us couple of women on it, takes women much more seriously now. For example, we had a long debate over the maternity leave arrangements. All firms must give time off for the first antenatal appointment and then the women must have a card for the others, but not all the clinics give appointment cards. We are much better-off here than some of the firms because pretty much they let you go. But leaving it to management doesn't help in some of the smaller firms. We didn't make a decision, but at least we had it discussed. Then, recently, I went to a day school on the new employment act because that has new rules on maternity leave and how you get your job back. You would think that with all these women workers the union would have organised some leaflets or information for us. But there isn't any, you know.

Instead, it seemed, the union relied upon some hidden process whereby women would come to know their rights in relation to the new law – certainly not the most effective way to maintain members' rights and to promote the idea that 'knowledge is power'. One wonders what the response would have been if the issue was other than maternity rights, a 'women's issue'. The sexism of the union showed very clearly in this lack of attention to a crucial area of members' rights. These issues were viewed as located in areas beyond the workplace – in the home, with mothers not workers. Annie and the women on the shopfloor understood very clearly that mothers were workers, one and the same. Any insistence upon the division between home and work also means that the workplace is ignored as a potential space in which self-help groups can grow and develop and women's issues can be voiced. It is a great loss to working-class women, black and white, that so little has been made of their support for one another as women, in the workplace. Momentous changes like the birth of a child are central experiences for women and form part of the work and home life of women. They are not neatly divided in half as the male-oriented world would like to believe.

A woman's right to choose

Given the status that surrounded pregnant women on the shopfloor and the celebration of motherhood and babies, it was a brave woman who opened up the discussion of abortion. Information on abortion facilities was part of the subterranean world of the department, ready and available to those who needed it; at the same time, it was given little publicity. Despite this, one abortion became a very public affair and, in the discussions which surrounded it, all the tensions associated with women's fertility and their role in reproduction were given an airing. The debates are reproduced in some detail here because they show both solidarity and division among the women, and, in some cases, a clearly developed feminist consciousness.

Ros was 18 and worked in the finishing section of the department with Marsha and Jenny, Frankie and Angie, and others. She was a very warm and friendly woman and we would spend time talking while we worked. Ros had been the subject of speculation as soon as she complained of nausea and loss of appetite; then, she started to expand. The gossips gossiped; more helpful women put the telephone number of the British Pregnancy Advisory Service in her hand and advised her on a course of action, explaining that local facilities for abortion were dismal and that she would have to go elsewhere. If she acted quickly, they added, it could be arranged quite cheaply. Ros refused offers of help, insisting to me, 'They all think I'm pregnant and I keep telling them that I'm not.' But she was, and an abortion had to be arranged at a late stage. I arrived in the department to be greeted by a breathless Flo who spilled the beans: 'Well, I expect you know anyway. They all know. Ros has gone off to Brighton to get an abortion – if they can do it for her. I don't approve of it myself. If you play with fire you've got to take the consequences and she should have known better.'

Flo's punitive condemnation of Ros's actions was shared by some of the other women who made a moral judgement about her behaviour. Fortunately for Ros, there were other women, like Frankie, for whom abortion was a political issue, centrally concerned with the control that women should exercise over their own fertility, and, more, their own sexuality. It was a position completely denied by Flo and the moralists. Frankie, though, quickly and effectively dismissed their case:

> Flo and them others have been gabbing on about how she ought to be made to have the baby. I don't believe that; it's rubbish! I don't think any woman should be made to have a baby if she doesn't want it. Flo was goin' on about how she should have had it and someone could adopt it, who couldn't have a baby. But that's not the point: it's the woman who has to go through the pregnancy and birth and she should only do that when *she* wants to, not because she can supply someone else with a baby. It's her choice, no one else's. And I think women should be able to have abortions when they want them, not because some doctor says so. Look what you have to go through! Instead of asking all those barbaric questions they should ask the woman: 'What do you want to do?' I'm not kiddin'. I think it's terrible how they turn it into an inquisition. It's your body and you have to decide. I tell you, if there were more women gynaecologists it would help, you know. At least they would be sympathetic to a woman's point of view, not like these bloody men.

And Frankie went on, connecting the issue of men's control over women's fertility to the issue of man-made rules for the control of women's sexuality:

> Men are all the same, there's one rule for them and another for us. Well, it's not good enough. Vin's [the man she lived with] like that – spent all his time gettin' his leg over, but God help you if you are his daughter, or if it's me, he goes spare and they are all like it. They screw around but they divide women into two neat categories – those 'bad' women you screw with and those 'good' women you marry. Well, they can stuff that – it's women who get pregnant, women who carry the can.

Frankie's powerful and articulate demystification of the patriarchal basis of women's lives led, as she said, to only one conclusion: the necessity for women to exercise control over their own bodies; a fundamental feminist demand which, in Frankie's case, had grown out of her own experiences and the lives of those around her. She had been able to reinterpret her own experience and that of other women she knew well in ways which cut through common sense, to uncover the real conditions that constrained the lives of women. She went on to relate her sister's experience:

> It's like my sister Chris when she got pregnant for the third time. She was leaving her husband anyway and she didn't want another kid. She also had this funny feeling about this baby, that it wasn't right. So she goes to the bleedin' doctor who tells her she's out of her mind and she's goin' to have a baby. She ends up screaming at them she's not, but they wouldn't give her an abortion. Well, it's all wrong. She's the one who's carryin', she's the one who should decide. Finally, she had the baby early because she had toxaemia and it died. It was all a stupid waste and it put her in danger. She told them she had two kids to look out for already and she just didn't want another one, she couldn't cope with it. Do you know what they said to her? 'Nonsense' – like she was an idiot who didn't know her own mind. She was carryin' the baby wasn't she? I tell you, women, *not* doctors have to make the decision because women know the situation, and they have to live with the decision they make, the bloody doctor just calls the next patient in, doesn't he?

The unequivocal support that Frankie expressed for a woman's right to choose was rooted in her knowledge of situations like the one her sister had suffered. For her, only women could decide what was to be done. She also recognised that women were not all in the same situation and that for each woman the decision was a momentous one surrounded by different pressures.

Frankie would willingly have offered support to Ros. Ultimately, it was Ros's mum who was the key person in arranging the abortion because Ros hesitated and hovered, unable to decide what to do. Just as mothers watched over their daughters in pregnancy, so, too, they watched over their daughters when they decided to have an abortion – in this case, encouraging the decision. Frankie understood Ros's dilemma and her reluctance and she was consistently sympathetic.

The debate surrounding Ros's abortion continued and it

divided the women into factions: the moralists, the uncertains and the feminists. Frankie, taking on all arguments against a woman's right to choose with tremendous strength, was able to cut a clear path through the moral indignation and the emotional confusions. Jenny, too, consistently supported Frankie and showed great sympathy and warmth to Ros as her part in the following discussion shows. The women were gathered at tea-time and the issue was on everyone's lips. Their discussion, produced here in full, shows the divisions between the factions and the way in which Frankie and Jenny argued a strong feminist position, one recognisable to all who have been involved with the women's movement, and the struggles surrounding abortion.

Marsha She let it go too long and then, Sal, it was twins, they told her. And she's really upset about that.

Glenda Well, I think it's wrong, it's murder, abortion, it's just not right. She should have had the baby and given it away to someone who couldn't have a baby. Abortion is immoral.

Frankie Rubbish. It's up to her. That moral stuff is just mumbo jumbo from the doctors and it's not up to them or us, or you, Glenda. It's up to Ros. Each woman must make her own decision. She's got to have the baby, it's her body.

Marsha I could never give my baby away, but just 'cos you get pregnant doesn't mean you can get out of it like that. She knew what she was doin' she came off the pill months ago.

Jenny But it's up to her. People do make mistakes and it's not right not to try and help them. Ros needs some sympathy, not all these wagging tongues about what she's done.

Frankie Quite right. Factories are like that, people always poking their noses into other people's business.

Jenny Yes, there are always people who want to throw stones. They are so quick to pick them up they don't wait to see how they are going to land. She's really upset and I think people should stop judging her so much. She's made the decision and had the abortion. I think she's entitled to do that and everyone should stop gossiping about it.

Glenda But I still say it's not right. No one will ever convince me it is.

Frankie The problem was she tried to pretend she wasn't pregnant and she told half the press room and not the other half.

Jenny Well, really that was up to her. In the end, it's not their business.

Frankie Yes, but people talk and they've upset Ros, especially Norah because she was knitting a baby jacket and told Ros she could have been knitting for her. She said to Ros, 'You've spoiled it all now, haven't you,' and poor Ros was so upset she went to pieces and told Dorothy, and Dorothy got Norah in the office to say she was sorry. You wouldn't get me telling Dorothy anything, not her, especially something like this. I expect Dorothy disapproves of abortion. I don't expect she's ever been faced with the problem of an unwanted pregnancy.

Marsha Yeah, I wouldn't have told her either. I think it's a real shame she left it so late and then to find out it was twins. That's really hard you know.

Jenny Yes, that's what I think. It's a very hard thing to do and she must feel pretty bad about it. People should support her. It's not easy to make a decision like that. She has to live with it, other people are too quick to give an opinion.

As we returned to work, Frankie concluded the discussion by saying: 'The trouble is, people think it's easy to have an abortion, but it isn't. And so many are against it – that Glenda, what does she know about it?'

Glenda was given the space to present views now familiar from the anti-abortion lobby. Her statements, though, were a poor match for the power of Frankie and Jenny, who consistently held the position that a woman must have ultimate control over her own body. Jenny also pointed to the unhelpful nature of most of the gossip in the department at a time which was so painful for Ros. She wanted the other women to understand just how difficult it was to take control of one's body, and make decisions in a context where morality and emotions were used to confuse the central issue. Marsha suffered these confusions even though she tried to remain supportive to Ros. None of them could quite understand why Ros should confide in Dorothy, one of the production managers. For them, it was a measure of the distress that Ros was experiencing that she should have done this. For everyone else, Dorothy remained on the other side – a woman, but not one who was 'down among the women' and capable of sympathising with Ros's pain.

Ros returned to work, looking pale and sad. She and I talked about her experience:

> It was all right. The clinic was nice. It's just that after they told me it was twins, and I've always wanted twins, I felt really sad about that. But what could I do? My Dad was so upset with my sister and how she's left her husband, I couldn't hurt him any more. He's really in a state, Sal, going deaf and his eyes are bad. In the end me Mum said it was for the best, so I did it. Andy already has two kids and his wife is suing for more maintenance – he didn't really want a baby. I would be all right if people here didn't upset me. Norah really had a go at me because she said she was knitting for me, but I'd spoiled it all. I roared and went in to see Dorothy and Norah said she shouldn't have said that. It's all right for them, but what about me? It's not an easy thing to do, you know. It was really hard, and now I've just got to live with it.

Ros was close to tears as she spoke, reliving the pain and sadness of the event; she remained hurt and saddened. These feelings were coupled with a deep sense of loss, which she expressed on the day that Indira was leaving to have her baby, some weeks after Ros's abortion:

Ros I wish I hadn't had the abortion now. I wish I had kept mine. I haven't really got over it and I still owe me mum £100, which I'm trying to pay off.

Sallie Didn't Andy help you pay for the abortion?

Ros He paid towards it, but I borrowed the rest. He's short of money, anyway.

Sallie How do you feel about him now?

Ros I still see him, but I don't want to marry him any more. I thought I did until the abortion. But I don't trust him any more – or any other man for that matter. I don't see him very much these days, at the weekend, on Saturday night, or if he comes over on Sunday morning, and then maybe once in the week. I don't mind. I'd rather stay in and do my ironing and washing, clean up my room, things like that.

Ros was quieter and more pensive in the wake of the abortion. Knowing that she had been the subject of gossip she shyed away from many of the other women and stayed close to Marsha, Frankie and Jenny. Amid the growing number of pregnancies and the celebration of motherhood that this entailed, even with the support of her friends, she still felt very isolated and alone, she said. It was Frankie – who had herself been through hard times, and who was to experience them again in the ensuing months – who best understood Ros's suffering, and Jenny who gently and quietly supported her through her first month back at work.

The issue confronted and resolved by Ros demonstrated both the power of patriarchal ideologies in relation to women's fertility and sexuality and the ability of some women to 'read' their situation and the situation of women in general with analytically sharp eyes, providing an alternative analysis located, fundamentally, in the insistence on the power of women to decide for themselves.

Frankie was the most articulate of the women and she presented an analysis born out of her own experiences which came together with the politics of the women's movement. She insisted that in her own life she had chosen when and with whom to have her children. But neither her courage in carrying this through, nor her perceptiveness, stopped her being badly beaten up by the man she lived with. How tragic, and how contradictory, that it should be Frankie who, as already described, lay in hospital some months later, a bloody wreck, victim of male violence.

All day, every day

Ros's abortion became part of the history of the department. Wise women recognised it as one part of the drama of a woman's life, because they also knew the hardships associated with being a working-class mother. Like other women, they were forced to seek paid work as a means of raising the living standard of their immediate families – or simply because they were the sole wage earners. In addition, as the last chapter illustrated, they carried the burden of domestic work and organisation as they, themselves, acknowledged: 'Working is really hard for a woman because she's still got to cook and clean and look after the kids: it's two jobs, that's what it is.' Given their understanding of this, it is hardly surprising that some women wanted to do just one job and stay at home with their children. Indeed, there were powerful ideological pressures to encourage them to believe that this was the correct thing to do. They also knew that they would pay a price in terms of isolation and economic dependence, and very few women welcomed either.

Although young women like Tessa and Julie envisaged a prolonged period away from the factory, very few of them would be able to afford this. Like the working mothers in the factory, they, too, would have to seek work and childcare facilities in the city. All the women knew how difficult it was to find good childcare. One answer might well have been crèche facilities at the factory. There is always a danger that such facilities will tie a woman to an employer, thereby making her more vulnerable, but even that could be preferable to homeworking which is common in the hosiery industry. Women like Frankie were adamant that crèche facilities should have been provided by StitchCo and other factories where there were large numbers of working mothers. In fact, as Clare made clear, the company had considered the idea, hoping that it would be an incentive for women with children to return to work:

We were thinking of having a crèche here. We were very short of labour and we were hoping to encourage more women with children. But when we looked into the regulations we needed so much space and special facilities that the company decided against it. You could only have 12 children to one nursery nurse and the main problem was space. The company intended to put in a subsidy and the women would have paid a small amount themselves.

Management's interest in crèche facilities was not shared by the union representatives in the department, nor in the factory overall. When I asked Eve if the union had ever called for nursery provision at the factory, she said: 'No, not that I know of. I'm not keen on the idea. I know some women have to work with a baby, but it's much better if they can look after them themselves.'

Eve had herself been forced to work with a small child and she had arranged a job-share with her sister-in-law, informally, when they both worked in the mills:

We went to see the chap together and she worked mornings and I worked afternoons one week, and then we swapped. We looked after the kids between us. It was a good system while it lasted. After a bit, the orders fell off so we were out of work after a couple of months. It's a good idea, that, more employers should try to help women with children.

Eve knew the difficulties associated with being a working mother and seemed to support the idea of job-sharing – yet still maintained that the best situation was for a mother to be at home with her baby. This view was echoed by the other women. Pauline spoke for many when she said:

> I don't want to work with a family. It's not right, letting your baby go to someone else. I want to be at home with the baby until it goes to school. I don't believe it's good for them to be with a childminder, or in a nursery, they need to be with their own mother.

It was also a position upheld by husbands, who insisted that their wives – as mothers of their children – should be at home. Consequently, Amita reported that her husband now expected her to be at home. 'He says I am a wife and a mother now, and I should be in the house,' but this was not possible because Amita was the only wage earner in the family: after six months, she had to return to work, leaving her baby with a childminder.

Amita was not alone. When Gina was leaving and talking about her plans, they showed that her husband held views similar to those of Amita's husband.

Sallie Will you come back to work?
Gina One day, I expect. But he says I must be at home with the baby, a baby needs its mother until it's really going to school. But I may try to find some part-time work when it's a year or so. He's not keen for me to work at all now. Well, I don't mind if he wants to keep me. But it could get boring. I don't think I'll come back here, though. I think I've had enough of StitchCo and, the way the work is, it's not likely there would be a job for me to come back to.
Sallie Do you believe a baby needs it's mother until it goes to school?
Gina Well, at first, yes. But I think if you've got family, someone could look after it when it gets a bit bigger.

Tessa, on the other hand, like Julie and other women, had no qualms about leaving work. For them, the world of domesticity was associated with freedom:

> Soon I won't have to worry about any of this. I'll be able to do what I like and when I leave this dump I'm not coming back –

they can stuff it. I won't work for five or six years until the kid goes to school. It's better for them, isn't it?

In fact, Tessa's unemployed husband had different plans for her; he envisaged a situation where she would have to go back to work because he was without a job. Tessa just ignored him and, once she had left the factory, she settled into home life. Like Gina, she supported the idea that a relative could look after her child. The emphasis upon relatives as providers of childcare was a measure of the uncertainty which surrounded childminders. Most women preferred to rely upon assistance from the family, like the Indian women who had mothers and mothers-in-law who cared for their children while they were at work. Many women, though, did not have this option and had to rely upon childminders, registered and unregistered. They spent their days at work feeling guilty and anxious about their children.

Many women felt that, though the childminders were good-natured women, they had to take too many children to make the enterprise pay – hence, the children suffered. Children were with minders for most of the day because work started at 8am and finished at 4.45pm four days a week, and 3.30pm on Fridays. Most women tried to use minders close to their homes and, although the cost varied, most women paid £2–£3 a day. Both the cost and the quality of the care deterred women, but very few had a choice as nursery places were so limited. Frankie, in fact, was one of the few women who had any access to nursery provision for her daughter. Nevertheless, getting her child to the nursery was so time-consuming that Frankie always ate breakfast at the first break.

I never get time to have it because I have to take Vicky to the nursery on three buses and then get here. It's a real problem. I've been trying to work out if there are any childminders locally. I am going to need someone for her when she starts school. Once you have a kiddy, everything gets so complicated.

Marsha sympathised with Frankie. As a young black mother without any support from the father of her child, she relied upon her mother to help care for her daughter while she went out to work. She would have preferred a nursery place because she felt that the child was a growing burden to her mother:

My Mum looks after her, but she's very forward and I would like her to go to nursery. My Mum would like her to, but I applied and they are not sure if she can go. They say it would cost £8 a week and I ain't paying that. I can't afford it. For now, she'll have to be with my Mum. But she's very strong-willed and she tires my Mum out.

Marsha did not see the father of the child very often – partly because her mother disapproved. She says, 'He's a Rasta and he's no good,' mimicked Marsha. Even so, Marsha was loath to antagonise her. They lived as three generations of black women, coping as best they could on low wages and other benefits.

Mothers were more usually the people who tried to help out, but in Carey's case it was her father. As she told Julie and Tessa when they insisted they were leaving work for good: 'I said that. But it's no good if they haven't got anything to eat, is it? I said just what you're sayin' – but here I am back at work and glad of a job.' Carey was back at work because her father had stepped in (her mum had left home some time before) and she was both very proud of her dad and grateful to him because she knew that her child was well cared for:

He does everything for him, feeds him, changes him, washes the nappies. He's retired now and he says he wouldn't know what to do if I sent the littl'un out to a minder, and the littl'un really loves him. He watches him wherever he goes, my problem is him getting to know me.

Carey's case showed the strength and flexibility of working-class family life and the way that necessity can generate alternatives at a personal level. Carey received some financial assistance from her boyfriend, but he was unemployed and it was unreliable and their relations were fraught – although Carey was very keen on him. Her dad coped cheerfully with his grandson, enjoying his new role enormously, he told me. Financially, they were poor because Carey did not earn enough to keep them and her father's pension was minimal; they tried to ensure that the child's needs were met first, even if the bills were left unpaid.

The economic difficulties of being a single parent were upper-most in the minds of the women who had to bring up children on their own. They were women who had been strengthened by their struggles and who were very clear about the problems they faced. Jean, for example, had this to say:

My lot [three children] haven't had a father for years and they've done all right. All this stuff about one-parent families is rubbish, I think. It's not that the kids lose out emotionally. Very often they don't because they are not stuck in the middle and they can get closer to one parent. You miss the money, that's the problem – not the quarrels and squabbles and being shouted at by your father. I should know, my Mum brought us up then remarried and had two more kids. But we were 12 by the time the other two arrived and my step-dad was installed. They were tough women, that generation.

The problems were not the emotional deficiencies so beloved of advocates of the nuclear family, but poverty, deprivation and the difficulties of combining work and motherhood. The problems of poverty seemed to be never-ending for Jean. No sooner had two of her children started working and making contributions to the family budget than they were both laid off within months of each other. Jean again found herself in the role of sole breadwinner at a time when all costs were rising and her children's needs had become adult needs. She was philosophical about it; 'We'll manage, we'll have to – though I'm not quite sure how at the moment, the council just put the rent up.'

Women struggled to be good mothers despite the difficulties of poverty and lack of time to spend with their children. They made every effort to provide mothering that was as close to the ideal of the full-time mother at home with her children as possible. The power of this ideal generated feelings of both guilt and deprivation for women because they felt that they did not see enough of their children. Nevertheless, they fiercely denied any suggestion that their children were emotionally deprived or insecure through their absence at work. Wages meant a better standard of living for their children and mothers who were more alive to a world beyond the home. They contested the view that working mothers had a negative effect on children's performance and development, just as the women of Bermondsey had done in Pearl Jephcott's study 20 years earlier, and emphasised the necessity of their wages and their own needs for the company and friendship of the workplace.[16] None of this, as the discussion that follows shows, detracted from their deep commitment to motherhood and their children.

And the future is ours

Despite the difficulties associated with being a working mother and, perhaps, also a single parent, all the women spoke with great warmth and affection about their children. They would defend them fiercely, spoil them if they could, and they developed with them strong and long-lasting bonds as earlier parts of this chapter have shown. It was not only Indian women who gained prestige and power through their children; all women shared in this sense that ultimately family life and loyalty were centred on 'our Mam', or Mum.

During my time at StitchCo the women often talked to each other and to me about their children, and about the experiences they were having at school. They knew I was involved in education and they felt that I might be able to help them unravel the process of schooling which was becoming more and more mystifying, they said. Many felt that schools were now much more human and exciting places than they had been; they were also faced with media versions of schools which highlighted all the sensational and negative aspects, such as indiscipline and illiteracy. The local newspaper was a prime mover in this. It was confusing and difficult to see what was happening and, despite their visits to their children's schools, they could not really put a picture together. They wanted their children to stay on at school and were willing and prepared to finance this, even if it meant hardship (which demonstrates quite clearly that the idea that the middle classes have a monopoly on deferred gratification is wrong).

One of the reasons they wanted their children to stay on at school was so that they would avoid the factory. As Cherry put it: 'There's no future in it, it doesn't get you anywhere. I wanted mine to stay on at college, but they didn't want to – still, they've got good jobs and are training to get a skill. You have more chance that way.' This view was also supported by Jenny. Like many of the women, though, Jenny felt that she could not help her children at school because she was out of touch, and because she was herself a school failure:

> You know, I never did well at school, although the teachers tried. I always tell my kids to ask the teachers if they don't understand things. But the trouble is the teachers don't take enough notice of the kids. It's only after you leave school that

you realise you could have done better. I don't want my kids to be stuck in a factory. All these jobs are the same. I tell my girls to work hard, but I can't help them much. The younger one is stage mad and wants to go on the stage, but that's not going to make a living, she needs to get some qualifications as well.

Jenny had, in fact, taught her daughters to read before they went to school and she was teaching 'littl'un', a boy, while I was in the department. She, like many of the women, did not differentiate between the needs of boys and girls for qualifications. They were needed in both cases, although trades were still considered the preserve of boys and men. It was also common for the women to ask that teachers should be sensitive to children and should listen to them, ask them how they felt and how they were getting on. Another woman, Greta, who also talked to me at length about her son's education, was worried because he was a truant. She felt that the school blamed this on her because she was divorced. She challenged this view and supported her son, maintaining that something at the school must be wrong, and that the school should consult her lad about his reasons for truanting. When she asked him why, it transpired that he had been moved to the bottom stream and nobody in the class bothered to work when, in fact, he wanted some qualifications so that he could pursue a catering course at the local further education college. Finally, he went back to school and worked hard for his exams. Even truancy can be a way of trying to articulate some demands for a better or more relevant education! Greta's approach to her son showed one of the great strengths that many of the women I knew had in relation to their children. Once they were a little older, they were seen as young people with lives of their own to lead, decisions to make. The women granted their children a credibility which was sadly lacking in schools, and the factories and offices, shops and training schemes they joined.

The interest in keeping their children away from the factory was shared by all the women. They also recognised that some of their children did not do well at school, for a variety of reasons; in these cases, they used whatever pull they had to try to secure jobs for them in firms that had a good reputation. Of the trainees who came into the department during the year, none of them had received any careers advice which had made any impact on them.

Instead, they had listened to their mum and their female relatives, most of whom worked in the hosiery industry, and through this network they had been guided towards StitchCo. Just as young men were taken to their father's friends and relatives to be 'set on' as apprentices, so the familial basis of job recruitment continues and, in fact, is emphasised by the current recession. It is another example of the way that family and work come together and one which I mentioned at the beginning of this book.

There were no Indian girls recruited to training lines during my year at StitchCo. This was a measure of their desire to work in shops or offices, rather than in factories, and the support that their parents gave to this. It was a major source of compensation to some of the Indian women that, despite the hardships and suffering they endured, their children were receiving a British education. The Asian communities are well known for the importance that they attach to education and qualifications. It is their hope that, with this cultural capital, the next generation will be able to compete equally with white British. But the younger generation knows the virulence and depths of racism in Britain and how this can override paper qualifications. This has generated a new militancy which co-exists uneasily with the hopes of the older generation.

The older generation saw in England the promise of education and qualifications that would enable their children to earn a living in Britain, or, if necessary, elsewhere. Usha voiced the hopes and feelings of many of her generation when she told me:

> I would like to go to India, people say it is really nice. Maybe when all my children have finished their studies I will go. One is waiting for 'A' levels now, one is at the polytechnic studying biochemistry and one is training for accountancy. You know, they can't find holiday jobs this year. Ah, that reminds me, I need to take this form to Clare, it's the form for grants. We have to put down what we earn and then they assess the grant for my daughters. They don't get much because we are both earning and sometimes one book costs £10 and I have to find the money for that. But I don't mind. England is hard for us, but it is good for our children because they can get educated here and they won't come to the factory.

Usha was comforted by the knowledge that her children were reaping the benefits of life in England. Younger women, like Suraya, were helping to support their brothers and sisters who were still at school. It was hoped they would be successful and gain qualifications which would bring them jobs in technical work (if they were boys) or in offices (if they were girls).

If more members of the Asian communities are beginning to articulate a protest against the racism of British schools and teachers, they are joining the ongoing struggle waged by black teachers, parents and students against a schooling system which labels too many black children disruptive, delinquent and educationally subnormal.[17] Marsha's experience was fairly typical. She told me that she lost interest in school because 'The school and the teachers never showed any interest in us, they never talked to us, they didn't care.' For Marsha, schooling had been a situation in which she had been ignored, or in trouble; because she fought against being ignored, she spent most of her school life in trouble and left school without any qualifications and as soon as she could. Marsha was an intelligent, lively woman and schooling had failed her hopelessly. Nevertheless, she, too, held out the hope that it would be different for her daughter, and was determined to have close links with the schools her daughter would be attending. It was a point that the other black women also emphasised and they took it upon themselves to be the link. Apart from Tula's husband, the men remained at some distance from the schools.

Tula and her husband had come to Britain over 20 years earlier and had lived in Needletown for quite a while. Their three children had done well at school and Tula was very pleased with their achievements. She did not, however, talk about them publicly in the lunch canteen because she was anxious not to appear 'proud' and also because she did not want to antagonise anyone. Those who were close to her – Carol, Rhoda and others – would share the latest information on her family at her machine, or in a quiet corner – just as I did. Though Tula had a special affection for all her children, her daughter's potential especially excited her:

> The eldest did well in his 'A' levels, but he didn't want to go on. The girl is the really clever one, she's doing her 'A' levels now, but she's very quiet about it. She came top in the English mock exam and her teachers are really pleased with her. But she doesn't fuss, she doesn't push herself forward. She wants to go into teaching and to go to university, but some people said to her there's no future for teachers. They try to discourage her, but I've told her if she wants to go, she should

go. I try to encourage them all to stay on at school and to go to university. They are clever, must be from their father – he has the brains.

Later, Tula continued:

I encourage her to go into teaching because if she gets all her qualifications she can go somewhere else from here. England is falling apart and all they can do is blame us, the immigrants, they blame the immigrants. Well, it's not got anything to do with that, it's the Tories attacking working-class people. They voted for her, though. I hate her, this Mrs Thatcher, she's one of the worst things to happen since I came here. I don't know what's going to happen, especially to the young people, and the teachers can't do anything if there are no jobs for them. It can only get worse. It's happening to everyone. We're all suffering because of the Tories and our union is no help.

Tula frowned and looked angry when she contemplated the Tories and their attacks on the working class. She and her husband identified themselves strongly as members of the working class, although they were both aware of the racist elements within that class. Tula's kids had done well in school, and yet this did not mean that Tula and her family closed their eyes to racism and its impact upon themselves, as black people, and for Tula on herself and her daughter, as black women. Indeed, Tula understood very clearly the struggles that the next generation of black people would have in Britain if trends continued. Yet she was also aware of the contradictions in British society. This was expressed in relation to her mates at work and in relation to the school experiences that her own children had had. She was part of a section of Caribbean life in Britain that tried to promote more self-help among Caribbean people and a pride in their own culture. The traits she wanted to promote, through the associations and clubs with which she was involved, were very similar to those supported by white working-class culture. Yet she also understood that racism was something that white working-class women and their kids did not have to live with. Her daughter was exceptional, yet she suffered terrible moments of self-doubt and lack of confidence. She did not believe she would make it to university or that she had the ability to cope once there. Her mother encouraged her and sought ways to explain her self-doubts to her without turning her in on herself. When Tula and I talked about her self-doubts and lack of confidence we agreed that being a black girl was not easy in a white world:

> Yes, I realise that, but you know the schools our kids have been to have always encouraged them. Sonia was headgirl and still she felt she wasn't up to it. I know it's not easy for a black girl and lots of parents are right to complain about what happens to black kids in school. They do get a very bad deal, but you know, Sallie, the parents are at fault as well. When we used to go to parents' evenings and to the school, there weren't any other black parents. They don't go to the school and get to know the teachers. They don't have enough interest in their kids' education. They leave it to the school, then they don't like what the school is doing. I know they say that the teachers don't like black kids because they are difficult and because the teachers are prejudiced, but if the children have support from their parents it helps them.

Tula sought consistently to expand the vision of the future for her children beyond manual work, perhaps, beyond the UK because, having moved once, she knew that mobility and migration might be necessary again. She also knew that their options were decreasing as job opportunities diminished and British racism became more entrenched. Tula knew just how difficult it was going to be for the next generation who would have to wage a struggle against racism and unemployment as Black Britons, divorced from their Caribbean roots in a way that she was not:

> It's not easy for Sonia or the boys. They will all have to fight to be accepted, and I hope we have taught them enough self-respect to do that. Britain is so hard for young blacks, but nobody wants to recognise it, and Thatcher's made it worse. The people who have really helped our kids have been teachers who have shown them they are as clever as anyone else. We try to encourage them and we are involved in a community group which does all kinds of community things, like telling people what their rights are and informing them about schools, trade unions, the elections. It's not to be separate, but to help people livin' here to have a better life. We look after things in the community, but it's even more difficult now because unemployment is so bad and the youngsters have so few

prospects. Thatcher is the worse thing yet to happen to Britain and it's makin' the situation worse for blacks every week. But, it's no good moanin' about it. We have to get organised and West Indian people don't always want to do that, you know.

Tula's concern for her children was never, in all my talks with her, reduced to an individual issue divorced from the fate of young blacks locally and on the national scene. Her pride in her children did not generate a division between them and the struggles of black people. Indeed, Tula saw the latter as essential to the promotion of black self-respect and self-reliance. She was not unaware of the problems associated with organising in the black communities and she did not close her eyes to the divisions between the islanders. Whatever those problems and divisions, there was a clear issue on which they could come together, and that was the struggle against racism. Only in struggle could they promote their talents and potential in a world which was an increasingly racist one. Like many women and men of her generation, she did not support the Rastafarian version of struggle. Although she sympathised with it as a response to the despair generated by urban Britain, she saw a need for a politics which would engage with the white world, force it to sit up and take note. In order to do this, the black communities needed educated and articulate members who remained rooted in their communities and who were prepared to use their skills for the benefit of others. After all, they met in common cause against a racist world.

Despite its length, this chapter has only begun to touch upon many of the crucial issues which surround the fertility and sexuality of women in a patriarchal society. I have tried, in particular, to explore the coincidence between the world of women and the factory as they came together in that awesome adventure, motherhood.

Motherhood was celebrated on the shopfloor as the universal and identifying feature of womanhood. In this, it cut across racial and ethnic divisions, encouraging all women to share in the unity expressed by the mother while, just like the bride, the mother has a historically and culturally specific context. Shopfloor culture celebrated motherhood as the final stage in the process of becoming a woman, a gendered subject who is called forth, not by a woman's work in production, but by the female life-style and a woman's role in reproduction. This emphasis, of course, colludes in the ideology of femininity and a social construction of woman that is tied to domesticity and dependence in the home. It is this version of woman that is crucially a part of the individual subjectivities of the women on the shopfloor and which goes beyond collusion in the way that women embrace motherhood and remain firmly committed to it. But this does not blind women to the context in which they mother and the issues surrounding women's fertility and sexuality. There are women who present a clear feminist critique of the control that men exercise of women's bodies.

The attachment that women have to the friendships of work and the support they gain from one another in the workplace is an important part of what they miss when they walk out through the factory gate. They know that domesticity is not bliss: many women do not want to be at home, although they maintain a commitment to the ideal of the mother in the home. They want, instead, higher wages which will provide them with a better standard of living and which will buy better childcare facilities. They want more and better childcare facilities not necessarily in nurseries, but perhaps under a scheme such as the one available in Sweden, where childminders receive training and a state subsidy. The factory is a vital arena for discussing the issue of childcare and more should be done through trade unions to initiate and support these debates.

The fact that women articulate demands of this nature shows, importantly, that while they are committed to the continuity between generations, they are not interested in simply reproducing the same privations and limitations on their lives and handing these on to the next generation. To do so would be to accept defeat. Instead, they work creatively with the contradictions as part of the struggle for an enlarged definition of their lives: one that includes vital issues on the quality of life which are intricately connected with the politics of class, race and gender. In the conclusion, I want to consider how the complexities of this politics is linked to the actual experiences of women's lives.

10
Conclusion: race and class are feminist issues, too

I have emphasised throughout this book that, in looking at the texture of women's lives across racial and cultural boundaries, it is important to hold both similarity and difference in one's mind's eye. Only in this way can we hope to grasp the contradictions which mark women's lives, giving rise to strength and sisterhood alongside weakness and division. I want to try to hold on to this mosaic of understanding and to relate this to a feminist politics which, as I write, is still in the making. There are no prescriptions for action here and no single, clear route through the complexities. Instead, there are cross-cutting layers, sometimes in coalescence and sometimes in contradiction with one another, shifting and forming in struggle not unlike patterns in a kaleidoscope.

The preceding chapters have shown the interaction of patriarchy and capitalism in the factory and the home, and the response the women make to this by generating and sustaining a shopfloor culture which structures the way that becoming a worker, through a woman's role in production, and becoming a woman, through her role in reproduction, are brought together and reinforced. It is an oppositional culture, providing a focus for resistance to managerial authority and demands, while forging solidarity and sisterhood. It is also an ambiguous resistance because it so clearly colludes in promoting a specific version of womanhood. That version of womanhood is tied to Western, romantic idealisations of love, marriage and motherhood, which promote a subordinate definition of woman founded upon weakness and division. The celebrations surrounding the bride and the mother on the shop-floor offer these as universal representations to all women in the department, but they are located in a culture which has been historically generated and sustained by white working-class women. Yet it is possible for the symbols of the bride and the mother to have a resonance beyond race and class – but only when the symbols are rooted in an essentialist understanding of woman that concentrates on the biological capacity to reproduce that all women share. Is this the crucial issue?

Feminists have long debated the inadequacies of a politics founded upon biology and the universal 'woman' who automatically has common cause with all woman. It is, in effect, a romantic fiction to treat 'woman' as an *a priori*, or natural, category which does not need to be theorised. On the contrary, the task is to theorise difference *and* unity and it is not surprising if, despite our best efforts, we have stumbled in relation to this knotty problem. But it has now been given a new impetus by black women who have attacked the racist assumptions of feminist discourses and demanded that the experiences of black women inform a reconstructed feminism.[1] Hazel Carby reminds us that the absence of black women and their experiences in feminist discourses is not solved by simply adding these on to the already existing corpus of knowledge and ideas.[2] Instead, feminism has to engage in a work of excavation and reconstruction which integrates the insights provided by black women like Pratibha Parmar, who points us towards an understanding of 'racially constructed gender roles'.[3] It is the case, of course, that feminism is not a simple unified whole. Nevertheless, feminisms do coalesce around a fundamental concern with explaining and overcoming the oppression of women and we cannot have an adequate account of either unless we have an understanding of racism and a commitment to fight it.

Most black women, I have suggested, are part of a stratified working class and many of the issues raised by Hazel Carby in relation to black women could be repeated in relation to the lives of working-class women and their representation in feminist discourses. Feminist socialists have consistently tried to bring gender and class together in an effort to hold on to the complexities of both. But rather than adding race on as a further complication and considering the triple oppressions that exist through class relations, patriarchal structures and racism, it is more illuminating, if more complicated, to try to see contradictory and complementary relationships between these areas as they relate to ongoing struggles. The issues cannot be simply theoretical ones because, as Jenny Bourne has reminded us, 'Working against racism means tackling political issues,' and Anna Coote and Beatrix Campbell have emphasised the need for feminists to take issues into the arena of conventional politics and power struggles.[4] However, we must not lose sight of the important focus given to us by both black struggles and women's politics. These have centred upon areas outside the institutional realm, outside the factory gate and, in so doing, have generated a cultural and political creativity and dynamism which was missing from party politics and the politics of production. I want to try to locate my discussion of the politics of gender, race and class in the lives of the women in the factory as a way of grounding the complexities.

In so far as this book has provided an analysis of women's lives within patriarchal capitalism, it has shown that women do two jobs, but still do not earn living wages. The nature of this 'rip off' cannot be explained simply by the mechanisms of class oppression located in the economics of capitalism. Jean Gardiner has pointed to the duality of women's relationship to class.[5] Women are class members because, as workers, they have a relationship to the means of production which, on the whole, gives them non-living wages and makes them an impoverished section of the working class; it is because of this that they look to marriage as a means to higher wages and access to resources controlled by men. This means that women have a second relationship to class through their relationship to the male wage which reinforces their dependence and subordination in relation to men. Although the relevance of this can be seen in this book, it is not the whole story.

First of all, it is important to ask why there is this duality. Second, black workers and immigrant workers are also impoverished; and, third, women may not have access to the male wage because its place may have been taken by state benefits. Consequently, in seeking answers to the question of why women have a dual relationship to class, the reasons must be sought outside the crude economism of 'cheap labour' arguments. Rather, they must be found in the power of sexist and racist ideologies to affect employers and unions and the way that people are positioned in labour markets.

This means that the issues surrounding women's wages and the struggles that have to be fought to secure living wages for women cannot be encompassed in a call for 'equal pay now' because this leaves out the vital question: equal to whom? Attempts to promote equal pay have been tried and they have foundered. Instead, we have to work on a number of fronts: against the ghettoisation of low-paid work in general and white male privileges in highly paid skilled work and, at the same time, against low pay and for living wages sufficient to the needs of women.[6] Such a strategy presents black and white women with a powerful common cause. Although low pay affects men as well (black men and other immigrants, predominantly) women, too, have to fight to raise their own wages because raising male wages has shown itself to be a false strategy for women and no guarantee against female impoverishment.

The women in the department came together to fight targets and rates they considered unfair and it was often Indian women who were in the forefront of these struggles. Similarly, in the discussions surrounding the recession and lay-offs the women emphasised that 'an injury to one was an injury to all' and they insisted that whatever work was available should be shared among all the women. Solidarity and sisterhood marked the struggles around economic issues on the shopfloor. Away from the department, however, wages were negotiated by the recognised organs of the labour movement – the trade unions – and, in this case, the union supported large differentials between male and female wage rates, defending their decision on the basis that men's work was skilled work while women's work was not. This illustrates that the fight against low pay is crucially bound up with a struggle against sexist ideologies in the trade union movement. This book has shown that this is one battle that black and white women fight already. This common struggle does not mean that black women are not also a part of an autonomous black struggle against racism in the trade union movement, or an autonomous black women's struggle against sexism and racism. The struggles overlap because racism is not confined to the trade unions, but extends to the whole British working class.

Black women like Tula and Taruna were aware of the complexities and contradictions in the situation. Tula's angry indictment of Thatcher's attacks on working people were matched by Taruna whenever she talked about Thatcherism – both of them recognised that they had much in common with white working-class women. When I talked to them about racism in the factory, they responded characteristically. Tula took it for granted that the department and the women who were working there were riddled with racism. Taruna was more circumspect, recognising the kindness that women showed to one another and the joint struggles they pursued, and then she said, 'ah, but you do not know what people feel in their hearts.' It was a gentle admission that behind the kindness and the accommodation between the women, lurked the issue of racism which was built into the taken-for-granted world of the department.

This is the contradiction: black and white women workers share in the experience of exploitation under patriarchal capitalism, yet racism cuts through and across a potential unity. It does so not simply because management use racism as a strategy to divide the working class as a whole (such conspiratorial simplicities do not advance our understanding of racism among the working class). Management can only use racism effectively if workers are racist. While both Tula and Taruna recognised this they also showed an awareness of the contradictions that are built into the situation whereby racism does not capture the hearts and minds of everyone and that individuals, although steeped in a racist culture, can often act in ways that belie this. They both knew that there was an anti-racist lobby in Britain despite the growing force of racism and the publicity surrounding the British Movement. They also knew that awareness was growing in their own communities of the common-alities between Asians, Afro-Caribbean peoples and black people born in Britain and that this awareness and the desire to fight back has often brought unity – but also division, especially on an inter-generational level.

The women at StitchCo worked with and against racism at the same time, reproducing it and undermining it through their lives on the shopfloor and beyond, in the city. These dualities were part of the contradictory and complex whole which made up their lives and which were marked, for me, by the extraordinarily powerful creativity that they possessed and the determination they showed in making out of necessity a work of art – a huge landscape into which they insisted they would paint some of the landmarks. This meant that their lives were committed to struggle and the insistence upon a different and better world, predicated not simply upon higher wages or more consumption and, therefore, not located within capitalist imperatives. The complexities of women's lives and the struggles they waged encouraged them to take on a wider vision which was, nevertheless, located in their experiences as black and white working-class women. The view the women expressed incorporated an understanding that the quality of life was badly in need of revision and that this should form an essential part of any programme to change the lives of working people. Much of what the women wanted to promote was connected to the creative and collective response they made to women's issues. They shared with the women's movement an insistence upon a larger set of options for women, and better and more resources for health care, childcare and education; in addition, the issue of control was central. Women wanted more control over their own fertility and sexuality, and they fiercely defended their rights to have children. Their sense of control was vitally important in a situation where they feared ideological and medical attacks on their reproductive rights. Their fears are well grounded as the use of the contraceptive Depo-Provera on black women in Britain and elsewhere demonstrates. These attacks are rooted deep in the Eugenics Movement and bring together the issues of race and class as Angela Davis's writing has shown in relation to the USA.[7] The Eugenics Movement in Britain also had a part to play in locking Empire and Motherhood into an embrace which made 'motherhood' the prerogative of white middle-class women.[8] The issue of sexuality raises further complexities which also need to be uncovered to show the ways in which it became enmeshed with racial stereotypes and a key plank in racist discourses. Again, the work produced by Angela Davis is illuminating, but we are, I think, just at the beginning of the analysis.[9]

Women celebrated babies and part of their vision of the future was bound up with their commitment to their children. Black and white women wanted their daughters to have the opportunity to pursue education and training as a means to a life which would be more autonomous. There was a strong sense from the women that they did not want their daughters to be undervalued or wasted in the way that they had been. Women struggled to make sense of their lives and to invent a future for their children while, at the same time, they looked at the lives they led and analysed marriage and the family in ways that enabled them to see the oppressive elements. Yet, to ask that working-class women on non-living wages should break out of family life and opt for alternatives is to misunderstand the very real constraints that economics places on women and to overlook the meaning of family life for both black and white women. They can see the alternatives, because circumstances often force them into situations where they are single parents trying to provide a home for children without adequate material support. It is hardly surprising (given their relative economic positions) that some working-class women try to insist upon a male commitment to mothers and children which allows them to stay at home. Apart from the ideological push they receive in this direction, it is quite clear that working-class women are committed to the family because it is an experience and a space which offers them some degree of autonomy over their lives and the warmth, support and affection from a group of people who matter and who in turn make a woman feel that she is important and valued. It is not that they do not know about the underside of family life or the way that unemployment affects the contributions that members of families can make. Young men, black and white, can no longer hold out the hope of a family wage or of being a breadwinner. Instead, household resources are more strongly bound to the state and to fertility patterns, potentially generating a situation that Maria Macciocchi found in Naples where children were essential to survival and they became not a burden but, in poverty, an asset because they generated state benefits.[10]

Commitment to family does not mean that friends, 'mates' or sisters are ignored. For many women, the nexus of relationships that makes up family life offers them sisters and friends who provide the essential support for their lives. Women give their energies and their creativity to their families, especially their children, because this is one area where they feel that their strength and competence counts and is exercised to satisfy real needs. Many of the women I knew, despite an already overworked life, wanted to contribute to other aspects of community or cultural life, become involved with campaigns or local issues. However, there never seemed to be a way into these activities for the women, which meant that their abilities and ideas were locked up, and away from society.

It is also quite clear, from the earlier chapters, that the trade union made no effort to connect with or use the women's power and skills. The world of the trade union presented itself, instead, as a frustrating irrelevance which seemed, from the women's point of view, to promote ignorance and powerlessness rather than knowledge and control. What the relations between the women, their culture and the union show with abundant clarity is the way in which current union practices reproduce the subordination of women by ignoring them and their expertise, and by writing out issues that are crucial to women's lives. And this will continue until the trade unions dump their identikit picture of the worker as white, male and skilled. It is simply not enough to produce glossy booklets on women workers or to order leaflets on sexual harassment. Women and black people are waiting to see changes made in the ideologies and practices that make up the trade union movement so that unions can be effective campaigning organisations committed to the anti-racist, anti-sexist struggle. Thus far, it is fairly clear that in relation to both feminist and black struggles the union movement, with all its potential power, has shown itself to be not a champion, but a quaint, outmoded movement that has ossified around issues that are located in the past. Can it change? We have to believe so and work for change because the collective strength of the trade union movement could be *for* us, rather than *against* us. First of all the movement has to engage seriously with feminism, the world of women and black people and take upon itself a future which gives a central role to these struggles. Without this kind of vision, the trade unions seem destined to go on fighting defensive struggles around workplace issues connected to craft privilege. While such action relates to one part of the working class, it cannot pretend to speak for the working class as a whole – let alone the struggles of women and black people.

The women also stayed away from party politics because it looked, and sounded, dreary and alien just like the union – a world of ageing grey men, despite Margaret Thatcher's powerful presence. They were impressed neither by Thatcherism or the calls from the new right, nor by the Labour Party. The Labour Party has neglected both women and the black communities at its peril. It now finds that black people and women do not owe any simple party loyalty to Labour; instead, the black communities are using their energies and skills to forge a black politics outside the Labour Party, and have given notice to the Labour Party that black people now come from a position of strength, not weakness.

The yawning gaps in our cultural life are being made over by black people because they understand that politics is not simply about production, the factory, the union, the party and parliament; it is also about theatre and poetry, the streets and protest. The early black struggle in the United States showed that an autonomous movement could be generated with its roots in the experience of racial exploitation. The women's movement has used this insight and its success has been to establish the terrain of politics as part of everyday life. But if it is to grow and develop, it has to connect with the struggles of working-class women around material issues. Working-class women are proud of their tradition of self-help and this has an important connection with the autonomous politics of the women's movement. We cannot allow self-help to be hijacked by the right and given back to us in ways that deride the power and pride associated with this.

Currently, the women in the factory use their expertise to help one another through pregnancy, death, illness, marriage break-down and sadness. There was no doubt that the women were engrossed in a personal and practical world which they claimed as their own; it was a sisterhood and a culture which had clear parallels with the women's movement's calls for sisterhood and to make the personal political. Black and white women inhabit largely separate worlds outside the factory; both sets of women, however, inhabit their own women's culture because of the divisions between the world of men and the space that is the women's world. The sense the women have that they control their own part of this world sits uneasily with an analysis from feminism that tells them they are powerless, subordinate and dependent. The call for women to develop their sisterhood also seems strange to women who spend most of their lives with other women, who depend on each other, and whose kinship relations are mediated by mothers and sisters, daughters and aunts. Nevertheless, the language of the women's movement has had an impact on women beyond it and, consequently, women have new ways of thinking about their relations with men and work.

The commitment that women have towards their children means that childcare facilities are a major issue in their lives. Women are both forced to work and work because they want to do so; too many of them spent their days worrying about their children. Lack of facilities are, as Prathibha Parmar has pointed out, a major impediment to Asian women joining waged work outside the home and this contributes towards many of them being confined to the super-exploitation of homeworking.[11] But childcare is an immensely complex issue. When I talked to the women about it, many were wary of a suggestion that there should be 24-hour nurseries, or even 10-hour nurseries. The reason for their lack of enthusiasm was that nurseries conjured up pictures of other state institutions – such as schools and hospitals – which were beyond their control and which were marked, in their eyes, by repression and sterility. Consequently, to hand a child into a nursery was to relinquish control over her, just as schools took over from parents and hospitals undermined the power of mothers. Far from regarding the state as a societal benefactor, the women saw the state much more starkly in predatory terms, as powerful and authoritarian. The women who did support nurseries, like Frankie and Marsha, already had contacts with local facilities and the women who ran them and this mediation altered their view. Nurseries did not seem to them like places outside their control and influence; on the contrary, they found that the women who ran them became their friends. It is clear from this that the discussion of nurseries cannot confine itself to provision of childcare in a society where people have so few opportunities to exercise control over the institutions and organisations which provide a major part of the material base of their lives.

There was also another aspect to the response that the women made to nurseries. Both black and white women saw the state as anti-family, not as a set of practices and ideologies which constructed the family, but as one which controlled it. Black women saw in the immigration laws, perpetrated and managed by the state, a set of regulations which destroyed families by separating parents and children, brothers and sisters, and which they regarded as far more pernicious and repressive than the calls to stop new immigrants. And white women saw in the agencies of schooling, health, social work and the police sets of practices designed to deny them control over their own bodies, their own lives, houses or their children. Black women saw this, too, and added the institutional racism of these agencies to their disaffection and their conception of the state. It is important that we try to understand the politics of this situation because the interaction between gender, race and class in relation to the state is a very complex one.

Black people are in the front line in relation to the power of the state, facing racist immigration laws which have culminated in the physical abuse of black women – and that is just the beginning. They face the police, in what is coming to be an almost daily harassment, in their streets and in their homes, and their racial and cultural differences are defined negatively in relation to schools, hospitals, and state benefits. In addition, many black people are employed by the state, in health or transport, and they face the state as an employer. They are both inside and outside the state, producers and consumers of services.[12] As producers they constitute many of the low paid and as consumers they are harassed by the control agents that surround state benefits. However, black people are not simply the victims of this iron mountain; they have fought back and have organised both independently and as members of the working class in common struggle with others who are also 'up against the state'. The struggle around the health services demonstrates a coalescence of issues which simultaneously involve race, class and gender.

The patriarchal assumptions of the British state mean that both black and white women face harassment from social security agents if they are single parents or the heads of households. State benefits in relation to women and children are a crucial factor in promoting the feminisation of poverty in Britain. It is also the case that both black and white working-class women often encounter white middle-class women as teachers, social workers, health visitors and doctors or as state officials, and their relations with them can often be fraught, as this book showed. Feminism has been quick to spot that while the state offers careers and salaries to some women (which provide a material base unknown to most working-class women, black or white), the patriarchal relations of state power have not been changed by the arrival of numbers of women in the so-called 'people-working professions'. Usually, women in these professions are placed in the situation of gate-keepers to state resources and many of those who want access to these resources are women. Or they are placed in a situation where they have power over working-class women through their certificated knowledge as teachers, doctors and paramedics or social workers. Yet, as Tula made clear, there are contradictions in this situation: all teachers are not racists and women in education have played a major part in the struggle against sexism in schools and education generally, insisting upon more opportunities for girls and promoting new practices and new knowledge. It is not surprising, therefore, that feminists working in the state sector should call not simply for more resources, but for a change in working practices and power relations which will not simply give the poor, women and black people, more access to state resources, but will do this in ways which do not deny their own competences and their ability to take hold of their own lives.

As we saw, health issues and childcare are a high priority for all women. Many do not support state nurseries because they see in these another attempt to wrest control from them, and to diminish their power in an area which they insist is theirs. Instead, they were sympathetic to a system of state-subsidised childminders who would be properly trained and paid according to a new status associated with the care of children. It was also clear that education mattered enormously to all the women; even though they knew its limitations and failings, they still felt that it held out a real possibility of something better for their children. And both black and white women were prepared to fight for the kind of education they saw as relevant for their children. It was, in fact, the struggle for women's education in America that prompted Angela Davis to write: 'Sisterhood between black and white women was indeed possible, and as long as it stood on a firm foundation it could give birth to earthshaking accomplishments.'[13]

Perhaps, more now than at any other time, we need 'earthshaking accomplishments'. Despite the ideological and economic climate which seeks to marginalise black struggles, women's issues and socialist alternatives, there are indeed powerful contradictory forces at work. The complexities surrounding the issues of gender, race and class remain, not surprisingly, unresolved. Nonetheless, what is clear is that both the black struggle and feminism have given a new impetus to politics in Britain, which has meant that now at least race and gender issues are on the agenda – for some of us. We must support and protect the efforts being made by those working at the local level, in the unions and left Labour councils, who are trying to forge meaningful alternatives. Generally, though, we are still waiting to see how far our 'brothers' in the trade union movement and our 'comrades' in the Labour Party and on the left can actually move in the direction of a new politics.

I am conscious that in concluding I have concentrated upon strength and struggle. I make no apology for this; I have taken my cue from the lives of the women at StitchCo. We have to believe that we can change the world we live in, in small and large ways that have real effects. This does not mean that I am any less conscious of the deprivation, pain and waste that black and white working-class women live with on a daily basis. For many of them, though, this was a spur to action rather than defeat. The lives of the women at StitchCo were a powerful indictment of the type of society of which we are a part. Their celebration and sisterhood was a vindication of their creativity and resourcefulness in an increasingly bleak world.

Notes

1. Introduction

1. Cynthia Cockburn, *Brothers: Male Dominance and Technological Change* (Pluto Press: 1983), pp. 191–209.
2. Lucy Bland, Charlotte Brunsdon, Dorothy Hobson, Janice Winship, 'Women inside and outside the relations of production', in Women's Studies Group, Centre for Contemporary Cultural Studies (eds), *Women Take Issue: Aspects of Women's Subordination* (Hutchinson: 1978), p. 48.
3. Carol Smart, 'Law and the control of women's sexuality', in Bridget Hutter and Gillian Williams (eds), *Controlling Women* (Croom Helm: 1981), p. 41.
4. Veronica Beechey, 'On patriarchy', *Feminist Review*, no. 3, 1979, pp. 66–82.
5. Heidi Hartmann, 'The unhappy marriage of marxism and feminism', in Lydia Sargent (ed.), *Women and Revolution: A Discussion of the Unhappy Marriage of Marxism and Feminism* (Pluto Press: 1981), pp. 1–42.
6. Sheila Rowbotham, 'The trouble with "patriarchy",' and Sally Alexander and Barbara Taylor, 'In defence of "patriarchy"' were first published in the *New Statesman* as a debate and are now reprinted in Mary Evans (ed.), *The Woman Question* (Fontana: 1982), pp. 73–83.
7. Roisin McDonough and Rachel Harrison, 'Patriarchy and relations of production', in Annette Kuhn and AnnMarie Wolpe (eds), *Feminism and Materialism* (Routledge: 1978), pp. 11–41.
8. Heidi Hartmann, 'The unhappy marriage of marxism and feminism', pp. 14–15.
9. *Ibid.*, p. 33.
10. Brian Easlea, *Science and Sexual Oppression: Patriarchy's Confrontation with Woman and Nature* (Weidenfeld & Nicholson: 1981), chapter 7, 'Socialist feminism and marxist viriculture'.
11. *Ibid.*, p. 221.

12. Paul Willis, *Learning to Labour: How Working-Class Kids Get Working-Class Jobs* (Saxon House: 1977).

13. Amrit Wilson, *Finding A Voice: Asian Women in Britain* (Virago: 1978), p. 15.

14. Annie Phizacklea and Robert Miles, *Labour and Racism* (Routledge: 1980), p. 6.

15. For a much more extended discussion see, Robert Miles, *Racism and Migrant Labour* (Routledge: 1982) and Erroll Lawrence, 'Just plain common sense: the "roots" of racism', in Centre for Contemporary Cultural Studies, *The Empire Strikes Back: Race and racism in 1970s Britain* (Hutchinson: 1982), pp. 47–94.

16. Annie Phizacklea and Robert Miles, *Labour and Racism*, p. 22.

17. Valerie Amos and Pratibha Parmar, 'Resistances and responses: the experiences of black girls in Britain', in Angela McRobbie and Trisha McCabe (eds), *Feminism For Girls: An Adventure Story* (Routledge: 1981), p. 130.

18. *Ibid.*, pp. 146–7.

19. Anna Coote and Beatrix Campbell, *Sweet Freedom: The Struggle for Women's Liberation* (Picador: 1982), p. 51. The rest of this chapter provides a discussion of both waged work and unemployment among women.

20. *Ibid.*, pp. 49–52.

21. D.J.Smith, *Racial Disadvantage in Britain: The PEP Report* (Penguin: 1977), p. 77, showed that in the 1970s 29 per cent of all working women were involved in semi- and unskilled manual work; the figures for black women were much higher – 47 per cent of West Indian women, 48 per cent of Asian women from East Africa and 58 per cent of Indian women.

22. Tom Lupton, *On The Shopfloor: Two Studies of Workshop Organisation and Output* (Pergamon: 1963); Huw Benyon, *Working For Ford* (Penguin: 1973); Theo Nichols and Huw Benyon, *Living with Capitalism: Class Relations and the Modern Factory*, (Routledge: 1977); Theo Nichols and Peter Armstrong, *Workers Divided: A Study of Shopfloor Politics* (Fontana: 1976).

23. Anna Pollert, *Girls, Wives, Factory Lives* (Macmillan: 1981).

2. The domestication of work

1. See Friedman's discussion of the development of the hosiery industry in A.L.Friedman, *Industry and Labour: Class Struggle at Work and Monopoly Capitalism* (Macmillan: 1977), pp. 159–79.

2. F.A.Wells, *The British Hosiery and Knitwear Industry: Its History and Organisation* (Allen & Unwin: 1972), p. 112.

3. See Heidi Hartmann, 'The unhappy marriage of marxism and feminism', in Lydia Sargent (ed.), *Women and Revolution: A*

Discussion of the Unhappy Marriage of Marxism and Feminism (Pluto Press: 1981), pp. 1–42.

4. The issue of women's work as an extension of natural 'feminine' attributes is discussed by D.Elson and R.Pearson in their paper, 'The subordination of women and the internationalisation of factory production', in Kate Young and others (eds), *Of Marriage and The Market: Women's Subordination in International Perspective* (CSE: 1981), pp. 144–66.

5. See Catherine Hakim, 'Job segregation: trends in the 1970s', *Employment Gazette*, December 1981 (HMSO); Anne Phillips and Barbara Taylor, 'Sex and skill: notes towards a feminist economics', *Feminist Review*, no. 6, 1980, pp. 79–88.

6. See in particular Ruth Cavendish, *Women On The Line* (Routledge: 1981).

7. Marianne Herzog, *From Hand to Mouth: Women and Piecework* (Penguin: 1980).

8. Paul Willis, *Learning to Labour: How Working-Class Kids Get Working-Class Jobs* (Saxon House: 1977).

9. This insertion of the culture of femininity into the workplace is comparable with the way in which girls attempt to gain some control over school environment through the use of their femininity. See Angela McRobbie, 'Working-class girls and the culture of femininity', in Women's Studies Group, Centre for Contemporary Cultural Studies (eds) *Women Take Issue: Aspects of Women's Subordination* (Hutchinson: 1978), pp. 96–108.

10. Anna Pollert, *Girls, Wives, Factory Lives* (Macmillan: 1981), pp. 131–6.

11. Heidi Hartmann, 'The unhappy marriage of marxism and feminism', pp. 11–14.

12. P.Armstrong and others, *Ideology and Shopfloor Industrial Relations* (Croom Helm: 1981).

13. I am grateful to Graham Murdock for sharing his knowledge of music hall culture with me.

14. For a discussion of the internal labour market see M.Burawoy, *Manufacturing Consent: Changes in the Labour Process Under Monopoly Capitalism* (University of Chicago Press: 1979), pp. 95–108.

15. Anna Pollert, *Girls, Wives, Factory Lives*, pp. 117–120.

3. Up against the minutes

1. For a demystification see J.Powell, *Work Study* (Arrow Books: 1976). He subtitles his book 'How to beat the con'. For a recent discussion see the handbook by Alan Grant, *Against the Clock* (Pluto: 1983).

2. B.Conboy, *Pay at Work* (Arrow Books: 1976), p. 32.
3. See Andrew Glyn and John Harrison, *The British Economic Disaster* (Pluto Press: 1980) for a discussion of the mid-1970s recession and capital's response to it.
4. Tony Cliff, *The Employers' Offensive: Productivity Deals and How to Fight Them* (Pluto Press: 1970), pp. 50–7.
5. Harry Braverman, *Labour and Monopoly Capital: The Degradation of Work in the Twentieth Century* (Monthly Review Press: 1974). F.W.Taylor pioneered time-and-motion studies in the USA.
6. See, for example, Burawoy, *Manufacturing Consent: Changes in the Labour Process Under Monopoly Capitalism* (University of Chicago Press: 1979); R.Edwards, *Contested Terrain* (Heinemann: 1979); and the recent collection of essays by S.Wood (ed.), *The Degradation of Work? Skill, Deskilling and the Labour Process* (Macmillan: 1982).
7. Harry Braverman, *Labour and Monopoly Capital*, p. 151.
8. A.Friedman, *Industry and Labour: Class Struggle at Work and Monopoly Capitalism* (Macmillan: 1977), p. 78.
9. See S.Wood, *The Degradation of Work?*, pp. 82–3.
10. Anna Pollert, *Girls, Wives, Factory Lives* (Macmillan: 1981), pp. 48–9.
11. J. Powell, *Work Study*, p. 11.
12. Angela Coyle, 'Sex and skill in the organisation of the clothing industry', in J.West (ed.), *Women, Work and the Labour Market* (Routledge: 1982), pp. 10–25, p. 25.
13. Harry Braverman, *Labour and Monopoly Capital*, pp. 424–49.
14. See Angela Coyle's discussion in *Women, Work and the Labour Market*, pp. 13–18.
15. Louise Lamphere, 'Fighting the piece-rate system: new dimensions of an old struggle in the apparel industry', in A.Zimbalist (ed.), *Case Studies in the Labour Process* (Monthly Review Press: 1979), pp. 257–76, p. 271.
16. As Sue Himmelweit has pointed out (using the *Department of Employment Gazette*, 1981), 'Between 1974 and 1981, registered male unemployment increased by approximately 300 per cent, while in the same period, registered female unemployment increased by more than 800 per cent.' See L.Segal (ed.), *What is To Be Done About the Family* (Penguin: 1983), p. 126. For an overview of the effects of Tory policies see, *Thatcher's Britain: A Guide to the Ruins* (Pluto Press and New Socialist: 1983).
17. The subject of the family wage has generated a lively debate since Jane Humphries's article, 'Class struggle and the persistence of the working-class family', *Cambridge Journal of Economics*, vol. 1, no. 3, 1977, was published. Humphries suggests that the family wage was a strategy which benefited the whole of the working class, but later writers have taken issue with this. For example, see, M.Barrett and M.McIntosh, 'The family wage: some problems for socialists and

feminists', *Capital and Class*, no. 11, 1980). Barrett and McIntosh make the point that the family wage was more myth than reality, a view supported by the women on the shopfloor. But it is also the case that some women would like to support the idea of a family wage as a way of wresting more resources from men. Whatever else it may be, there is no doubt that 'the family wage' divides men and women against each other and it is difficult to see how this supports the interests of the working class as a whole.

4. Big brothers and little sisters

1. The National Economic Development Council, Report 1980–1, p. 22 states: '1980 has been a year of unparalleled recession in the textile, clothing and footwear industries . . . Hundreds of factories have closed, over 120,000 jobs have been lost during 1980 and there is extensive short-time working in all sectors.'
2. Anna Coote, in A.Coote and P.Kellner, *Hear This Brother* (New Statesman: 1980), p. 12.
3. For an extended discussion of this point in relation to the printing industry see Cynthia Cockburn, *Brothers: Male Dominance and Technological Change* (Pluto Press: 1983).
4. Sarah Boston, *Women Workers and the Trade Union Movement* (Davis Poynter: 1980).
5. R.Gurnham, *Two Hundred Years: The Hosiery Unions, 1776–1976* (National Union of Hosiery and Knitwear Workers: 1976).
6. National Union of Hosiery and Knitwear Workers, NEC Report 1981, p. 5.
7. *Ibid.*
8. For a discussion of the problems encountered by women in the unions and the way they struggle to overcome these and thereby enrich the trade union movement, see J.Beale, *Getting It Together: Women as Trade Unionists* (Pluto Press: 1982).
9. There have been attempts to promote positive action for women in the unions but the hosiery unions have not, so far, been involved. See Anna Coote and Beatrix Campbell, *Sweet Freedom: The Struggle for Women's Liberation* (Picador: 1982), pp. 160–7.
10. Kate Purcell provides a discussion of 'the myth of the passive woman worker' in her article, 'Militancy and acquiescence amongst women workers', in Sandra Burman (ed.), *Fit Work For Women* (Croom Helm: 1979), pp. 112–33.

5. Shopfloor culture: resistance and celebration

1. S.Hall and T.Jefferson (eds), *Resistance Through Ritual: Youth Subcultures in Post-War Britain* (Hutchinson: 1976), p. 10, offer the

following definition of culture: 'The peculiar and distinctive "way of life" of the group or class, the meanings, values and ideas embedded in institutions, in social relations, in systems of beliefs, in modes and customs, in the uses of objects and material life'.

2. The term 'practical ideologies' comes from Louis Althusser and emphasises the concrete, lived experience of ideologies rather than the abstract theoretical level. See L.Althusser, 'Ideology and ideological state apparatuses: notes towards an investigation', in his *Lenin and Philosophy and Other Essays* (New Left Books: 1971), pp. 123–73.

3. Our understanding of the nature of common sense has been greatly enhanced by the work of Antonio Gramsci who has provided us with an analysis of the processes of ideological hegemony. The hegemony of the ruling class is maintained not by a simple process of domination, but through the ruling-class worldview becoming part of the common-sense world of ordinary people which generates consensus. Common sense is a complex totality in which knowledge born out of the experience of working-class lives becomes enmeshed with ruling-class ideas which support the status quo. Hegemonic control is never fixed, it is constantly contested and fought over by counter-hegemonic ideas and understandings rooted in lived experience. See Q.Hoare and G.Nowell-Smith (eds), *Selections from the Prison Notebooks of Antonio Gramsci* (Lawrence & Wishart: 1971). There is also a large and growing secondary literature on Gramsci. See, for example, Chantal Mouffe, 'Hegemony and ideology in Gramsci', in Chantal Mouffe (ed.), *Gramsci and Marxist Theory* (Routledge: 1979), pp. 168–204.

4. Anna Pollert, *Girls, Wives, Factory Lives* (Macmillan: 1981), pp. 129–58.

5. *Ibid.*, p. 157.

6. Ruth Cavendish reports a similar reality in *Women On the Line* (Routledge: 1982).

7. Kate Purcell, 'Female manual workers: fatalism and the reinforcement of inequalities', paper presented to the British Sociological Association Conference 1981, and published in the BSA volume, edited by D.Robbins and others, *Rethinking Social Inequality* (Gower: 1982). I am very grateful to Kate Purcell for supplying me with a copy of her paper before publication.

6. You sink into his arms

1. See Paul Willis, *Learning to Labour: How Working-Class Kids Get Working-Class Jobs* (Saxon House: 1977).

2. This suggests that, like their male counterparts, young working-class women also compensate for the tedium of work through their

weekend activities. The literature on youth sub-cultures has been dominated by accounts of boys and young men, but there is a growing recognition of the specificity of sub-cultural styles among girls at school and young women at work. The elements of these cultures, with their emphasis upon romance and domesticity, show a marked continuity with shopfloor culture among women which also emphasises the culture of femininity.

For an overview see, M.Brake, *The Sociology of Youth Culture and Youth Subcultures* (Routledge: 1980); Angela McRobbie and Jenny Garber, 'Girls and subcultures', in S.Hall and T.Jefferson (eds), *Resistance Through Rituals: Youth Subcultures in Post-War Britain* (Hutchinson: 1976), pp. 209–22; Angela McRobbie, 'Working-class girls and the culture of femininity', in Women's Studies Group, Centre for Contemporary Cultural Studies (eds), *Women Take Issue; Aspects of Women's Subordination* (Hutchinson: 1978), pp. 96–108. Earlier studies also suggest a historical continuity in the lives of young working-class women, both Pearl Jephcott and F.Zweig, writing in the late 1940s and early 1950s emphasised romance in the lives of young working-class women and the way in which dancing, films and boyfriends compensate for the monotony of factory life. See Pearl Jephcott, *Rising Twenty: Notes on some Ordinary Girls* (Faber & Faber: n.d. but it appears to be 1947), and F.Zweig, *Women's Life and Labour* (Gollancz: 1952), pp. 57–62.

3. As the General Household Survey Statistics (1979) show, only 5 per cent of households are based on a male breadwinner who supports a woman and two children.

4. Diana Leonard's study of courtship and weddings did mention jokes played on the bride which included confetti stuffed into clothes and bags and carrots given to young women, but this is at some distance from the elaborate ritual played out at StitchCo. See Diana Leonard, *Sex and Generation: A Study of Courtship and Weddings* (Tavistock: 1980), pp. 145–7.

5. Marriage was discussed as *the* trade for women in Cicely Hamilton's famous book, *Marriage as a Trade*, first published in 1909 and reprinted by the Women's Press in 1981.

6. Diana Leonard's study, *Sex and Generation*, pp. 147–52, also includes an account of a hen party and it is interesting to note that it is less commercialised and less bawdy than those I attended.

7. See, Rosalind Coward's recent discussion 'Sexual violence and sexuality', *Feminist Review*, no. 11, 1982, pp. 9, 22, for an elaboration.

8. Michèle Barrett and Mary McIntosh, *The Anti-Social Family*, (Verso: 1982), p. 55.

9. Diana Leonard, *Sex and Generation*, chapter 6. This chapter provides details of the wedding ceremony which, in this study, is

more formal than the weddings I attended and the one described here.

7. You sink into his arms . . . by arrangement

1. M.N.Srinivas, 'The caste system in India' in A.Beteille (ed.), *Social Inequality* (Penguin: 1969), p. 265. For a more extended discussion see Richard Lannoy, *The Speaking Tree: A Study of Indian Culture and Society* (Oxford University Press: 1971), pp. 135–67.
2. H.S.Morris, *The Indians of Uganda* (Wiedenfeld & Nicholson: 1968), p. 45.
3. Amrit Wilson, *Finding A Voice: Asian Women in Britain* (Virago: 1978), pp. 11–12.
4. D.F.Pocock, *Kanbi and Patidar: A Study of the Patidar Community of Gujarat* (Oxford, Clarendon Press: 1972).
5. R.Lannoy, *The Speaking Tree*, p. 106.
6. These observations, based upon my own knowledge, have received statistical support in a recent study: A.Sills, Maryrose Tarpey and P.Golding, *Asians in The Inner City* (Inner Area Research Project Social Survey, Second Report, University of Leicester, Centre for Mass Communications Research: 1982).
7. Deaths among Indian women whose inflated dowries have not been paid are a major cause for concern among feminists in India. See, for example, The *Guardian* (28 May 1983) report which details the death of a young bride who was eight and a half months pregnant. Her husband, brother-in-law and mother-in-law were initially sentenced to death for her murder, but the conviction was overturned on appeal. The feminist journal *Manushi* has done much to publicise the fate of young brides in India.
8. Ros Morpeth's work also emphasises this. See A.Penelope Brown, Martha MacIntyre, Ros Morpeth and Shirley Prendergast, 'A daughter: a thing to be given away', in Cambridge Women's Studies Group (eds), *Women in Society: Interdisciplinary Essays* (Virago, 1981), pp. 127–45.
9. R.Lannoy, *The Speaking Tree*, p. 106.
10. Although Manisha Roy's study of Bengali women suggests that the flower-bed night can be a great disappointment. See Manisha Roy, *Bengali Women* (University of Chicago Press: 1975), pp. 92–3.
11. Some of the earlier reformers may be found in Tara Ali Baig (ed.), *Women of India* (Ministry of Information, Delhi: 1958), and later struggles have been described by Gail Omvedt, *We Will Smash This Prison: Indian Women in Struggle* (Zed Press: 1980), and in the pages of *Manushi*. The British situation has been documented by Amrit Wilson in *Finding a Voice*, which is a moving and powerful account of the lives of Asian women in Britain, and in the literature

surrounding the most well-known of the industrial struggles –
Imperial Typewriters and Grunwick. These struggles were part of
the wider anti-racist struggle which continues and which has made
women like Anwar Ditta unwilling celebrities. See *Race Today* and
articles in the *New Statesman*, for example, the 25 February 1983
issue on racism in the East End of London by Amrit Wilson. A new
impetus to the struggle has also been added by *Mukti*, an Asian
woman's magazine produced in six languages by a collective.

8. And end up with your arms in the sink

1. These issues have been discussed a great deal in the women's
   movement and two recent books bring together current debates and
   add to them, see, Michèle Barrett and Mary McIntosh, *The Anti-
   Social Family* (Verso: 1982) and Lynne Segal (ed.), *What Is To Be
   Done About The Family* (Penguin: 1983).
2. Rayna Rapp, 'Family and class in contemporary America: notes
   toward an understanding of ideology', in B.Thorne and M.Yalom
   (eds), *Rethinking the Family: Some Feminist Questions* (Longman:
   1982), pp. 168–87.
3. *Ibid.*, p. 169. See Jack Goody, 'The evolution of the family', in
   P.Laslett and R.Wall (eds), *Household and Family in Past Time*
   (Cambridge University Press: 1972).
4. *Ibid.*, p. 170.
5. Attempts to assess the contribution that domestic labour makes to
   capitalism generated a very lively debate which can be followed via
   Eva Kaluzynska's article, 'Wiping the floor with theory – a survey of
   writings on housework', in *Feminist Review*, no. 6. 1980, pp. 27–54.
   For more detail of some of the contributions, see Ellen Malos (ed.),
   The Politics of Housework (Allison & Busby: 1980).
6. Christine Delphy, *The Main Enemy: A Materialist Analysis of
   Women's Oppression* (Women's Research and Resources Centre:
   1977). (Translated by Lucy ap Roberts and Diana Leonard Barker.)
7. See, for example, Richard Hoggart, *The Uses of Literacy* (Penguin:
   1957).
8. See, for example, Jill Liddington and Jill Norris, *One Hand Tied
   Behind Us: The Rise of the Women's Suffrage Movement* (Virago:
   1978).
9. The point was also made by the women in Pearl Jephcott's study of
   Bermondsey 20 years earlier (see Pearl Jephcott, *Married Women
   Working* (Allen & Unwin: 1962), p. 110) and by women on Anna
   Pollert's study, *Girls, Wives, Factory Lives* (Macmillan: 1981), p.
   121.
10. In the emphasis upon routine the StitchCo women also echoed the
    Peak Frean's workers of Bermondsey, Pearl Jephcott, *Married*

Women Working, p. 125. See also Anna Pollert, *Girls, Wives, Factory Lives*, pp. 109–26.

11. Indian women do, of course, work outside the home, often doing the most menial, insecure and poorly paid work. Women in this situation are not counted as 'ladies'.

12. Rayna Rapp, 'Family and class in contemporary America', p. 169.

13. Maud Pember Reeves, *Round About A Pound A Week* (Virago: 1979), first published in 1913 by Bell & Co.

14. Amrit Wilson, discussing the fate of the Gujarati joint family, writes: 'it looks as though nothing can save it now. When nuclear family segments break off from the joint family for one reason or another, the values of the joint family nevertheless continue to plague them. The maintaining of the male ego in perfect condition remains an essential activity of the nuclear family' (Amrit Wilson, *Finding A Voice*, p. 46).

15. For a much more extended discussion, see Elizabeth Wilson, *What Is To Be Done about Violence against Women?* (Penguin: 1983). This book deals only with white British society when it discusses British society. As the last chapter pointed out, *Manushi*, the Indian feminist journal, has done much to highlight the problem of violence against women in India. See also Penelope Brown, Marthe Macintyre, Ros Morpeth, Shirley Prendergast, 'A daughter: a thing to be given away', in Cambridge Women's Studies Group (eds), *Women in Society: Interdisciplinary Essays* (Virago: 1981), pp. 127–146. Amrit Wilson's book, *Finding A Voice*, pp. 19–20, alongside newspaper accounts, provides examples of the kind of racist attacks that Asian women have been subjected to in Britain. These are part of a wider pattern of racist attacks on all black people in Britain, but these attacks have been consistently fought by young black women and men, and there is now a new urgency to this fight. A compelling account of these struggles may be found in the recent novel *Hand on the Sun* by Tariq Mehmood (Penguin: 1983).

16. Michèle Barrett and Mary McIntosh, *The Anti-Social Family*, p. 21.

17. *Ibid.*, p. 145.

18. *Ibid.*, p. 144.

19. The lives of the women showed a marked continuity with the lives of the women described in Michael Young and Peter Willmott's study of Bethnal Green where men and women operated in separate spheres of activities, friendships and assistance. M.Young and P.Willmott *Family and Kinship in East London* (Routledge: 1957). In a more recent study by the same authors, *The Symmetrical Family* (Routledge: 1973), relationships between husbands and wives were reported to be more egalitarian because they spent more time together, made joint financial decisions and pooled their earnings. However, the authors fail to consider carefully enough whether joint

financial arrangements necessarily mean a substantial shift in the
power relations between men and women.

20. Amrit Wilson, *Finding A Voice*, pp. 30-42.
21. See, for example, Carol B. Stack, *All Our Kin: Strategies for Survival in a Black Community* (Harper & Row: 1974).

9. Women's business: the politics of reproduction

1. Margery Spring Rice, *Working-Class Wives* (Virago: 1981; first published by Penguin: 1939), p. 14.
2. Adrienne Rich, 'Anger and tenderness: the experience of motherhood', in Elizabeth Whitelegg and others (eds), *The Changing Experience of Women* (Open University/Martin Robertson: 1982), p. 242.
3. Elisabeth Badinter, *The Myth of Motherhood: An Historical View of the Maternal Instinct*, translated by Roger de Garis (Souvenir Press: 1981); Barbie Antonis, 'Motherhood and mothering', in Cambridge Women's Studies Group (eds), *Women in Society: Interdisciplinary Essays* (Virago: 1981), pp. 55-75.
4. Adrienne Rich, 'Anger and tenderness', p. 247.
5. *Ibid.*, p. 242.
6. The Women's Co-operative Guild, *Maternity: Letters from Working Women* (Virago: 1976); Margery Spring Rice, *Working-Class Wives*.
7. Ann Oakley's study, *From Here to Maternity: Becoming a Mother* (Penguin: 1981), pp. 125-31, showed that post-natal depression was felt by nearly all the women she interviewed.
8. *Ibid.*, pp. 4-5.
9. *Ibid.*, p. 15.
10. *Ibid.*, p. 22.
11. *Ibid.*, p. 23.
12. Maggie Pearson, 'A brief review of research and publications on ante-natal care for ethnic minorities' (Centre for Ethnic Minority Health Studies, Bradford: 1983). I am indebted to Maggie Pearson for providing me with a copy of the above paper and for sharing her insights on this subject with me. See also C.Ronalds, J.P.Vaughan, and P.Sprackling, '"Asian mothers": use of general practitioner and maternal/child welfare services', *Journal of the Royal College of General Practitioners*, vol. 27, May 1977, pp. 281-4; P.B.Terry, R.G.Coudie and R.S.Settatree, 'Analysis of ethnic differences in perinatal statistics', *British Medical Journal*, vol. 281, 1981, pp. 1307-8; M.Clarke and D.G.Clayton, 'Quality of obstetric care provided for Asian immigrants in Leicestershire', *British Medical Journal*, vol. 286, 1983, pp. 621-3.
13. It is this type of assistance that is being promoted in Tower

Hamlets, for example, as an aid to demystifying the medicalisation of pregnancy and childbirth.

14. I am very grateful to Ros Morpeth for letting me have a copy of her paper, 'Maternal and female infant mortality in the Indian Punjab: a paradox in a patriarchal society'. This paper has been translated by Vanessa Maher and published in Italy, but, so far, it has not been published here.

15. For a more developed discussion, see Manisha Roy, *Bengali Women* (University of Chicago Press: 1975), and Richard Lannoy, *The Speaking Tree: A Study of Indian Culture and Society* (Oxford University Press: 1971), pp. 102–12. For the ceremonies and ritual surrounding pregnancy and birth among the Patidar, see P.G.Pocock, *Kanbi and Patidar: A Study of the Patidar Community of Gujarat* (Oxford University Press: 1972), pp. 113–19.

16. Pearl Jephcott, *Married Women Working* (Allen & Unwin: 1962), p. 136.

17. For a powerful indictment of British schooling and its consequences for black children and young people, see B.Coard, *How the West Indian Child is made Educationally Subnormal in the British School System* (New Beacon Books: 1971); R.Giles, *The West Indian Experience in British Schools: Multi-Racial Education and Social Disadvantage in London* (Heinemann: 1977); and Hazel Carby 'Schooling in Babylon', in Centre for Contemporary Cultural Studies (eds), *The Empire Strikes Back: Race and Racism in 1970s Britain* (Hutchinson: 1982), pp. 183–211.

10. Conclusion: race and class are feminist issues, too

1. See the full discussion by Gloria Joseph, 'The incompatible menage a trois: marxism, feminism and racism', in Lydia Sargent (ed.), *Women and Revolution: The Unhappy Marriage of Marxism and Feminism* (Pluto Press: 1981), pp. 91–107; Cherríe Moraga and Gloria Anzaldúa (eds), *This Bridge Called My Back: Writings By Radical Women of Colour* (Watertown Mass., Persephone Press: 1981); Angela Davis, *Women, Race and Class* (The Women's Press: 1982); *Spare Rib*, no. 132, July 1983.

2. Hazel V. Carby, 'White woman listen! Black feminism and the boundaries of sisterhood', in Centre for Contemporary Cultural Studies (eds), *The Empire Strikes Back: Race and racism in 1970s Britain* (Hutchinson: 1982), pp. 212–35.

3. Pratibha Parmar, 'Gender, race and class: Asian women in resistance', in *The Empire Strikes Back*, p. 237.

4. Jenny Bourne, 'Towards an anti-racist feminism', *Race and Class*, vol. 25, summer 1983, pp. 16; Anna Coote and Beatrix Campbell,

Sweet Freedom: The Struggle For Women's Liberation (Picador: 1982), p. 238.

5. Jean Gardiner, 'Women in the labour process and class structure', in Alan Hunt (ed.), *Class and Class Structure* (Lawrence & Wishart: 1977), pp. 155–63.

6. For the feminist case on women's wages, cogently argued, see, Anne Phillips, *Hidden Hands: Women and Economic Politics* (Pluto: 1983), pp. 102–6.

7. Angela Davis, *Women, Race and Class*, chapter 12.

8. For a more extended discussion of the Eugenics Movement in Britain, see Lorna Duffin, 'Prisoners of progress: women and evolution', in Sara Delamont and Lorna Duffin (eds) *The Nineteenth-Century Woman: Her Cultural and Physical World* (Croom Helm: 1978), pp. 57–91, and Brian Easlea, *Science and Sexual Oppression: Patriarchy's Confrontation with Woman and Nature* (Weidenfeld & Nicholson: 1981), pp. 157–69. The continuity of Eugenicist views is shown in the 1942 *Beveridge Report*, p. 52, where it notes: 'In the next thirty years housewives as mothers have vital work to do in ensuring the adequate continuance of the British race and British ideals.'

9. Angela Davis, *Women, Race and Class*, especially chapters 11 and 12.

10. Maria Antonietta Macciocchi, *Letters from inside the Italian Communist Party to Louis Althusser* translated by Stephen M. Hellman (New Left Books: 1973).

11. Pratibha Parmar, 'Gender, race and class: Asian women in resistance', *The Empire Strikes Back*, p. 253.

12. See the London Weekend Return Group, A Working Group of the CSE, *In and Against the State* (Pluto: 1980).

13. Angela Davis, *Women, Race and Class*, p. 104.

Index

Glossary

English and American usage

Andy Pandy: a puppet from children's television, who always wore striped overalls; equivalent to Raggedy Ann and Andy

Asians: a British colonial term used for the variety of Indian communities settled in East Africa from the Indian subcontinent; term now widely used in the U.K. for Indians generally

Babygro: infant sleeper

braces: suspenders

the budget: annual financial agenda from the government

budgie: parakeet (budgerigar)

chapatis: Indian flat bread made from wheat, like a tortilla

charabanc: bus for sightseeing and outings

chips: french fries

cider: fizzy alcoholic drink made from apples

compere: master of ceremonies

crisps: potato chips

dal: spicy lentils

diddy men: munchkins

dole: unemployment benefit

dual carriageway: two-lane highway

fag: cigarette

gaffers: bosses

ghee: clarified butter used in Indian cookery

Gujarati: language of Gujarat, an area North of Bombay in Western India

gymslip: pinafore worn by girls as school uniform

holiday: vacation

HP: credit (hire-purchase agreement)

knickers: women's underpants

'L' plate: Learner sign attached to cars for novice drivers

'Mild' and 'Bitter': two forms of beer

Mills and Boon: publishing company specializing in romantic fiction *mobcap*: women's cap with high crown and floppy brim, decorated with lace and ribbon

New Commonwealth: official language for black Africa, India, distinguishing these Commonwealth countries from the "old" (white) countries of Australia, Canada, etc.

redundant: laid off

Right to Work campaign: broad left campaign initiated by the Socialist Workers Party (U.S. equivalent, International Socialists U.S.) to protest the level of unemployment in the U.K.; now used more generally as a form of protest by working class organizations in Britain and, therefore, the opposite of the U.S. "Right to Work" movement

sack: to fire

scrubber: floozy, tramp

'semi': a house connected to another by a common wall

set to: argument

Skeggie: slang for Skegness, a holiday resort favored by working class people, close enough to Needletown for day trips

stick: aggravation, hassle

stone: unit of measure, fourteen pounds

St. Trinians: fictional girls school where the girls devoted their energies to pranks rather than study

sweets: candy

Tories: colloquial form for Conservatives

quid: slang for £1

vest: undershirt

Vesta curry: a packaged instant dinner

yobs: loud, potentially aggressive young men

A Note on the Author

Sallie Westwood is a lecturer in the Department of Adult Education, Leicester University, Leicester, England. She is active in teaching and promoting women's studies and in the women's movement. She received her bachelor's degree from the University of London and a Ph.D. from the University of Cambridge. Her previously published work includes articles on Asian women and on adult education.